Mometrix
TEST PREPARATION

I0883890

TerraNova® NEXT Grade 7 Reading and Language Test Prep Guide

Written and edited by the Mometrix Test Preparation Team
Printed in the United States of America

TABLE OF CONTENTS

Introduction

Thank you for purchasing this resource! You have made the choice to prepare yourself for a test that could have a huge impact on your future, and this guide is designed to help you be fully ready for test day. Obviously, it's important to have a solid understanding of the test material, but you also need to be prepared for the unique environment and stressors of the test, so that you can perform to the best of your abilities.

For this purpose, the first section that appears in this guide is the **Success Strategies**. We've devoted countless hours to meticulously researching what works and what doesn't, and we've boiled down our findings to the most impactful steps you can take to improve your performance on the test. We start at the beginning with study planning and move through the preparation process, all the way to the testing strategies that will help you get the most out of what you know when you're finally sitting in front of the test.

We recommend that you start preparing for your test as far in advance as possible. However, if you've bought this guide as a last-minute study resource and only have a few days before your test, we recommend that you skip over the first two Success Strategies since they address a long-term study plan.

If you struggle with **test anxiety**, we strongly encourage you to check out our recommendations for how you can overcome it. Test anxiety is a formidable foe, but it can be beaten, and we want to make sure you have the tools you need to defeat it.

Strategy #1 – Plan Big, Study Small

There's a lot riding on your performance. If you want to ace this test, you're going to need to keep your skills sharp and the material fresh in your mind. You need a plan that lets you review everything you need to know while still fitting in your schedule. We'll break this strategy down into three categories.

Information Organization

Start with the information you already have: the official test outline. From this, you can make a complete list of all the concepts you need to cover before the test. Organize these concepts into groups that can be studied together, and create a list of any related vocabulary you need to learn so you can brush up on any difficult terms. You'll want to keep this vocabulary list handy once you actually start studying since you may need to add to it along the way.

Time Management

Once you have your set of study concepts, decide how to spread them out over the time you have left before the test. Break your study plan into small, clear goals so you have a manageable task for each day and know exactly what you're doing. Then just focus on one small step at a time. When you manage your time this way, you don't need to spend hours at a time studying. Studying a small block of content for a short period each day helps you retain information better and avoid stressing over how much you have left to do. You can relax knowing that you have a plan to cover everything in time. In order for this strategy to be effective though, you have to start studying early and stick to your schedule. Avoid the exhaustion and futility that comes from last-minute cramming!

Study Environment

The environment you study in has a big impact on your learning. Studying in a coffee shop, while probably more enjoyable, is not likely to be as fruitful as studying in a quiet room. It's important to keep distractions to a minimum. You're only planning to study for a short block of time, so make the most of it. Don't pause to check your phone or get up to find a snack. It's also important to **avoid multitasking**. Research has consistently shown that multitasking will make your studying dramatically less effective. Your study area should also be comfortable and well-lit so you don't have the distraction of straining your eyes or sitting on an uncomfortable chair.

The time of day you study is also important. You want to be rested and alert. Don't wait until just before bedtime. Study when you'll be most likely to comprehend and remember. Even better, if you know what time of day your test will be, set that time aside for study. That way your brain will be used to working on that subject at that specific time and you'll have a better chance of recalling information.

Finally, it can be helpful to team up with others who are studying for the same test. Your actual studying should be done in as isolated an environment as possible, but the work of organizing the information and setting up the study plan can be divided up. In between study sessions, you can discuss with your teammates the concepts that you're all studying and quiz each other on the details. Just be sure that your teammates are as serious about the test as you are. If you find that your study time is being replaced with social time, you might need to find a new team.

Strategy #2 – Make Your Studying Count

You're devoting a lot of time and effort to preparing for this test, so you want to be absolutely certain it will pay off. This means doing more than just reading the content and hoping you can remember it on test day. It's important to make every minute of study count. There are two main areas you can focus on to make your studying count.

Retention

It doesn't matter how much time you study if you can't remember the material. You need to make sure you are retaining the concepts. To check your retention of the information you're learning, try recalling it at later times with minimal prompting. Try carrying around flashcards and glance at one or two from time to time or ask a friend who's also studying for the test to quiz you.

To enhance your retention, look for ways to put the information into practice so that you can apply it rather than simply recalling it. If you're using the information in practical ways, it will be much easier to remember. Similarly, it helps to solidify a concept in your mind if you're not only reading it to yourself but also explaining it to someone else. Ask a friend to let you teach them about a concept you're a little shaky on (or speak aloud to an imaginary audience if necessary). As you try to summarize, define, give examples, and answer your friend's questions, you'll understand the concepts better and they will stay with you longer. Finally, step back for a big picture view and ask yourself how each piece of information fits with the whole subject. When you link the different concepts together and see them working together as a whole, it's easier to remember the individual components.

Finally, practice showing your work on any multi-step problems, even if you're just studying. Writing out each step you take to solve a problem will help solidify the process in your mind, and you'll be more likely to remember it during the test.

Modality

Modality simply refers to the means or method by which you study. Choosing a study modality that fits your own individual learning style is crucial. No two people learn best in exactly the same way, so it's important to know your strengths and use them to your advantage.

For example, if you learn best by visualization, focus on visualizing a concept in your mind and draw an image or a diagram. Try color-coding your notes, illustrating them, or creating symbols that will trigger your mind to recall a learned concept. If you learn best by hearing or discussing information, find a study partner who learns the same way or read aloud to yourself. Think about how to put the information in your own words. Imagine that you are giving a lecture on the topic and record yourself so you can listen to it later.

For any learning style, flashcards can be helpful. Organize the information so you can take advantage of spare moments to review. Underline key words or phrases. Use different colors for different categories. Mnemonic devices (such as creating a short list in which every item starts with the same letter) can also help with retention. Find what works best for you and use it to store the information in your mind most effectively and easily.

Strategy #3 – Practice the Right Way

Your success on test day depends not only on how many hours you put into preparing, but also on whether you prepared the right way. It's good to check along the way to see if your studying is paying off. One of the most effective ways to do this is by taking practice tests to evaluate your progress. Practice tests are useful because they show exactly where you need to improve. Every time you take a practice test, pay special attention to these three groups of questions:

- The questions you got wrong
- The questions you had to guess on, even if you guessed right
- The questions you found difficult or slow to work through

This will show you exactly what your weak areas are, and where you need to devote more study time. Ask yourself why each of these questions gave you trouble. Was it because you didn't understand the material? Was it because you didn't remember the vocabulary? Do you need more repetitions on this type of question to build speed and confidence? Dig into those questions and figure out how you can strengthen your weak areas as you go back to review the material.

Additionally, many practice tests have a section explaining the answer choices. It can be tempting to read the explanation and think that you now have a good understanding of the concept. However, an explanation likely only covers part of the question's broader context. Even if the explanation makes perfect sense, **go back and investigate** every concept related to the question until you're positive you have a thorough understanding.

As you go along, keep in mind that the practice test is just that: practice. Memorizing these questions and answers will not be very helpful on the actual test because it is unlikely to have any of the same exact questions. If you only know the right answers to the sample questions, you won't be prepared for the real thing. **Study the concepts** until you understand them fully, and then you'll be able to answer any question that shows up on the test.

It's important to wait on the practice tests until you're ready. If you take a test on your first day of study, you may be overwhelmed by the amount of material covered and how much you need to learn. Work up to it gradually.

On test day, you'll need to be prepared for answering questions, managing your time, and using the test-taking strategies you've learned. It's a lot to balance, like a mental marathon that will have a big impact on your future. Like training for a marathon, you'll need to start slowly and work your way up. When test day arrives, you'll be ready.

Start with the strategies you've read in the first two Success Strategies—plan your course and study in the way that works best for you. If you have time, consider using multiple study resources to get different approaches to the same concepts. It can be helpful to see difficult concepts from more than one angle. Then find a good source for practice tests. Many times, the test website will suggest potential study resources or provide sample tests.

Practice Test Strategy

If you're able to find at least three practice tests, we recommend this strategy:

Untimed and Open-Book Practice

Take the first test with no time constraints and with your notes and study guide handy. Take your time and focus on applying the strategies you've learned.

Timed and Open-Book Practice

Take the second practice test open-book as well, but set a timer and practice pacing yourself to finish in time.

Timed and Closed-Book Practice

Take any other practice tests as if it were test day. Set a timer and put away your study materials. Sit at a table or desk in a quiet room, imagine yourself at the testing center, and answer questions as quickly and accurately as possible.

Keep repeating timed and closed-book tests on a regular basis until you run out of practice tests or it's time for the actual test. Your mind will be ready for the schedule and stress of test day, and you'll be able to focus on recalling the material you've learned.

Strategy #4 – Pace Yourself

Once you're fully prepared for the material on the test, your biggest challenge on test day will be managing your time. Just knowing that the clock is ticking can make you panic even if you have plenty of time left. Work on pacing yourself so you can build confidence against the time constraints of the exam. Pacing is a difficult skill to master, especially in a high-pressure environment, so **practice is vital**.

Set time expectations for your pace based on how much time is available. For example, if a section has 60 questions and the time limit is 30 minutes, you know you have to average 30 seconds or less per question in order to answer them all. Although 30 seconds is the hard limit, set 25 seconds per question as your goal, so you reserve extra time to spend on harder questions. When you budget extra time for the harder questions, you no longer have any reason to stress when those questions take longer to answer.

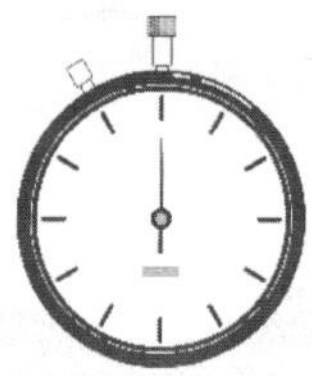

Don't let this time expectation distract you from working through the test at a calm, steady pace, but keep it in mind so you don't spend too much time on any one question. Recognize that taking extra time on one question you don't understand may keep you from answering two that you do understand later in the test. If your time limit for a question is up and you're still not sure of the answer, mark it and move on, and come back to it later if the time and the test format allow. If the testing format doesn't allow you to return to earlier questions, just make an educated guess; then put it out of your mind and move on.

On the easier questions, be careful not to rush. It may seem wise to hurry through them so you have more time for the challenging ones, but it's not worth missing one if you know the concept and just didn't take the time to read the question fully. Work efficiently but make sure you understand the question and have looked at all of the answer choices, since more than one may seem right at first.

Even if you're paying attention to the time, you may find yourself a little behind at some point. You should speed up to get back on track, but do so wisely. Don't panic; just take a few seconds less on each question until you're caught up. Don't guess without thinking, but do look through the answer choices and eliminate any you know are wrong. If you can get down to two choices, it is often worthwhile to guess from those. Once you've chosen an answer, move on and don't dwell on any that you skipped or had to hurry through. If a question was taking too long, chances are it was one of the harder ones, so you weren't as likely to get it right anyway.

On the other hand, if you find yourself getting ahead of schedule, it may be beneficial to slow down a little. The more quickly you work, the more likely you are to make a careless mistake that will affect your score. You've budgeted time for each question, so don't be afraid to spend that time. Practice an efficient but careful pace to get the most out of the time you have.

Test-Taking Strategies

This section contains a list of test-taking strategies that you may find helpful as you work through the test. By taking what you know and applying logical thought, you can maximize your chances of answering any question correctly!

It is very important to realize that every question is different and every person is different: no single strategy will work on every question, and no single strategy will work for every person. That's why we've included all of them here, so you can try them out and determine which ones work best for different types of questions and which ones work best for you.

Question Strategies

☑ Read Carefully

Read the question and the answer choices carefully. Don't miss the question because you misread the terms. You have plenty of time to read each question thoroughly and make sure you understand what is being asked. Yet a happy medium must be attained, so don't waste too much time. You must read carefully and efficiently.

☑ Contextual Clues

Look for contextual clues. If the question includes a word you are not familiar with, look at the immediate context for some indication of what the word might mean. Contextual clues can often give you all the information you need to decipher the meaning of an unfamiliar word. Even if you can't determine the meaning, you may be able to narrow down the possibilities enough to make a solid guess at the answer to the question.

☑ Prefixes

If you're having trouble with a word in the question or answer choices, try dissecting it. Take advantage of every clue that the word might include. Prefixes can be a huge help. Usually, they allow you to determine a basic meaning. *Pre-* means before, *post-* means after, *pro-* is positive, *de-* is negative. From prefixes, you can get an idea of the general meaning of the word and try to put it into context.

☑ Hedge Words

Watch out for critical hedge words, such as *likely, may, can, often, almost, mostly, usually, generally, rarely*, and *sometimes*. Question writers insert these hedge phrases to cover every possibility. Often an answer choice will be wrong simply because it leaves no room for exception. Be on guard for answer choices that have definitive words such as *exactly* and *always*.

☑ Switchback Words

Stay alert for *switchbacks*. These are the words and phrases frequently used to alert you to shifts in thought. The most common switchback words are *but, although*, and *however*. Others include *nevertheless, on the other hand, even though, while, in spite of, despite*, and *regardless of*. Switchback words are important to catch because they can change the direction of the question or an answer choice.

☑ Face Value

When in doubt, use common sense. Accept the situation in the problem at face value. Don't read too much into it. These problems will not require you to make wild assumptions. If you have to go beyond creativity and warp time or space in order to have an answer choice fit the question, then you should move on and consider the other answer choices. These are normal problems rooted in reality. The applicable relationship or explanation may not be readily apparent, but it is there for you to figure out. Use your common sense to interpret anything that isn't clear.

Answer Choice Strategies

ANSWER SELECTION

The most thorough way to pick an answer choice is to identify and eliminate wrong answers until only one is left, then confirm it is the correct answer. Sometimes an answer choice may immediately seem right, but be careful. The test writers will usually put more than one reasonable answer choice on each question, so take a second to read all of them and make sure that the other choices are not equally obvious. As long as you have time left, it is better to read every answer choice than to pick the first one that looks right without checking the others.

ANSWER CHOICE FAMILIES

An answer choice family consists of two (in rare cases, three) answer choices that are very similar in construction and cannot all be true at the same time. If you see two answer choices that are direct opposites or parallels, one of them is usually the correct answer. For instance, if one answer choice says that quantity x increases and another either says that quantity x decreases (opposite) or says that quantity y increases (parallel), then those answer choices would fall into the same family. An answer choice that doesn't match the construction of the answer choice family is more likely to be incorrect. Most questions will not have answer choice families, but when they do appear, you should be prepared to recognize them.

ELIMINATE ANSWERS

Eliminate answer choices as soon as you realize they are wrong, but make sure you consider all possibilities. If you are eliminating answer choices and realize that the last one you are left with is also wrong, don't panic. Start over and consider each choice again. There may be something you missed the first time that you will realize on the second pass.

AVOID FACT TRAPS

Don't be distracted by an answer choice that is factually true but doesn't answer the question. You are looking for the choice that answers the question. Stay focused on what the question is asking for so you don't accidentally pick an answer that is true but incorrect. Always go back to the question and make sure the answer choice you've selected actually answers the question and is not merely a true statement.

EXTREME STATEMENTS

In general, you should avoid answers that put forth extreme actions as standard practice or proclaim controversial ideas as established fact. An answer choice that states the "process should be used in certain situations, if..." is much more likely to be correct than one that states the "process should be discontinued completely." The first is a calm rational statement and doesn't even make a definitive, uncompromising stance, using a hedge word *if* to provide wiggle room, whereas the second choice is far more extreme.

BENCHMARK

As you read through the answer choices and you come across one that seems to answer the question well, mentally select that answer choice. This is not your final answer, but it's the one that will help you evaluate the other answer choices. The one that you selected is your benchmark or standard for judging each of the other answer choices. Every other answer choice must be compared to your benchmark. That choice is correct until proven otherwise by another answer choice beating it. If you find a better answer, then that one becomes your new benchmark. Once you've decided that no other choice answers the question as well as your benchmark, you have your final answer.

⊘ Predict the Answer

Before you even start looking at the answer choices, it is often best to try to predict the answer. When you come up with the answer on your own, it is easier to avoid distractions and traps because you will know exactly what to look for. The right answer choice is unlikely to be word-for-word what you came up with, but it should be a close match. Even if you are confident that you have the right answer, you should still take the time to read each option before moving on.

General Strategies

⊘ Tough Questions

If you are stumped on a problem or it appears too hard or too difficult, don't waste time. Move on! Remember though, if you can quickly check for obviously incorrect answer choices, your chances of guessing correctly are greatly improved. Before you completely give up, at least try to knock out a couple of possible answers. Eliminate what you can and then guess at the remaining answer choices before moving on.

⊘ Check Your Work

Since you will probably not know every term listed and the answer to every question, it is important that you get credit for the ones that you do know. Don't miss any questions through careless mistakes. If at all possible, try to take a second to look back over your answer selection and make sure you've selected the correct answer choice and haven't made a costly careless mistake (such as marking an answer choice that you didn't mean to mark). This quick double check should more than pay for itself in caught mistakes for the time it costs.

⊘ Pace Yourself

It's easy to be overwhelmed when you're looking at a page full of questions; your mind is confused and full of random thoughts, and the clock is ticking down faster than you would like. Calm down and maintain the pace that you have set for yourself. Especially as you get down to the last few minutes of the test, don't let the small numbers on the clock make you panic. As long as you are on track by monitoring your pace, you are guaranteed to have time for each question.

⊘ Don't Rush

It is very easy to make errors when you are in a hurry. Maintaining a fast pace in answering questions is pointless if it makes you miss questions that you would have gotten right otherwise. Test writers like to include distracting information and wrong answers that seem right. Taking a little extra time to avoid careless mistakes can make all the difference in your test score. Find a pace that allows you to be confident in the answers that you select.

⊘ Keep Moving

Panicking will not help you pass the test, so do your best to stay calm and keep moving. Taking deep breaths and going through the answer elimination steps you practiced can help to break through a stress barrier and keep your pace.

Final Notes

The combination of a solid foundation of content knowledge and the confidence that comes from practicing your plan for applying that knowledge is the key to maximizing your performance on test day. As your foundation of content knowledge is built up and strengthened, you'll find that the strategies included in this chapter become more and more effective in helping you quickly sift through the distractions and traps of the test to isolate the correct answer.

Now that you're preparing to move forward into the test content chapters of this book, be sure to keep your goal in mind. As you read, think about how you will be able to apply this information on the test. If you've already seen sample questions for the test and you have an idea of the question format and style, try to come up with questions of your own that you can answer based on what you're reading. This will give you valuable practice applying your knowledge in the same ways you can expect to on test day.

Good luck and good studying!

Reading Language Arts

Main Ideas and Supporting Details

Identifying Topics and Main Ideas

One of the most important skills in reading comprehension is the identification of **topics** and **main ideas**. There is a subtle difference between these two features. The topic is the subject of a text (i.e., what the text is all about). The main idea, on the other hand, is the most important point being made by the author. The topic is usually expressed in a few words at the most while the main idea often needs a full sentence to be completely defined. As an example, a short passage might be written on the topic of penguins, and the main idea could be written as *Penguins are different from other birds in many ways*. In most nonfiction writing, the topic and the main idea will be **stated directly** and often appear in a sentence at the very beginning or end of the text. When being tested on an understanding of the author's topic, you may be able to skim the passage for the general idea by reading only the first sentence of each paragraph. A body paragraph's first sentence is often—but not always—the main **topic sentence** which gives you a summary of the content in the paragraph.

However, there are cases in which the reader must figure out an **unstated** topic or main idea. In these instances, you must read every sentence of the text and try to come up with an overarching idea that is supported by each of those sentences.

Note: The main idea should not be confused with the thesis statement. While the main idea gives a brief, general summary of a text, the thesis statement provides a **specific perspective** on an issue that the author supports with evidence.

Review Video: Topics and Main Ideas
Visit mometrix.com/academy and enter code: 407801

Supporting Details

Supporting details are smaller pieces of evidence that provide backing for the main point. In order to show that a main idea is correct or valid, an author must add details that prove their point. All texts contain details, but they are only classified as supporting details when they serve to reinforce some larger point. Supporting details are most commonly found in informative and persuasive texts. In some cases, they will be clearly indicated with terms like *for example* or *for instance*, or they will be enumerated with terms like *first, second*, and *last*. However, you need to be prepared for texts that do not contain those indicators. As a reader, you should consider whether the author's supporting details really back up his or her main point. Details can be factual and correct, yet they may not be **relevant** to the author's point. Conversely, details can be relevant, but be ineffective because they are based on opinion or assertions that cannot be proven.

Review Video: Supporting Details
Visit mometrix.com/academy and enter code: 396297

Author's Purpose

Author's Purpose

Usually, identifying the author's **purpose** is easier than identifying his or her **position**. In most cases, the author has no interest in hiding his or her purpose. A text that is meant to entertain, for instance, should be written to please the reader. Most narratives, or stories, are written to entertain, though they may also inform or persuade. Informative texts are easy to identify, while the most difficult purpose of a text to identify is persuasion because the author has an interest in making this purpose hard to detect. When a reader discovers that the author is trying to persuade, he or she should be skeptical of the argument. For this reason, persuasive texts often try to establish an entertaining tone and hope to amuse the reader into agreement. On the other hand, an informative tone may be implemented to create an appearance of authority and objectivity.

An author's purpose is evident often in the **organization** of the text (e.g., section headings in bold font points to an informative text). However, you may not have such organization available to you in your exam. Instead, if the author makes his or her main idea clear from the beginning, then the likely purpose of the text is to **inform**. If the author begins by making a claim and provides various arguments to support that claim, then the purpose is probably to **persuade**. If the author tells a story or wants to gain the reader's attention more than to push a particular point or deliver information, then his or her purpose is most likely to **entertain**. As a reader, you must judge authors on how well they accomplish their purpose. In other words, you need to consider the type of passage (e.g., technical, persuasive, etc.) that the author has written and if the author has followed the requirements of the passage type.

Review Video: Understanding the Author's Intent
Visit mometrix.com/academy and enter code: 511819

Informational Texts

An **informational text** is written to educate and enlighten readers. Informational texts are almost always nonfiction and are rarely structured as a story. The intention of an informational text is to deliver information in the most comprehensible way. So, look for the structure of the text to be very clear. In an informational text, the thesis statement is one or two sentences that normally appears at the end of the first paragraph. The author may use some colorful language, but he or she is likely to put more emphasis on clarity and precision. Informational essays do not typically appeal to the emotions. They often contain facts and figures and rarely include the opinion of the author; however, readers should remain aware of the possibility for bias as those facts are presented. Sometimes a persuasive essay can resemble an informative essay, especially if the author maintains an even tone and presents his or her views as if they were established fact.

Review Video: Informational Text
Visit mometrix.com/academy and enter code: 924964

Persuasive Writing

In a persuasive essay, the author is attempting to change the reader's mind or **convince** him or her of something that he or she did not believe previously. There are several identifying characteristics of **persuasive writing**. One is **opinion presented as fact**. When authors attempt to persuade readers, they often present their opinions as if they were fact. Readers must be on guard for statements that sound factual but which cannot be subjected to research, observation, or experiment. Another characteristic of persuasive writing is **emotional language**. An author will often try to play on the emotions of readers by appealing to their sympathy or sense of morality. When an author uses colorful or evocative language with the intent of arousing the reader's passions, then the author may be attempting to persuade. Finally, in many cases, a persuasive text will give an **unfair explanation of opposing positions**, if these positions are mentioned at all.

Entertaining Texts

The success or failure of an author's intent to **entertain** is determined by those who read the author's work. Entertaining texts may be either fiction or nonfiction, and they may describe real or imagined people, places, and events. Entertaining texts are often narratives or poems. A text that is written to entertain is likely to contain **colorful language** that engages the imagination and the emotions. Such writing often features a great deal of figurative language, which typically enlivens the subject matter with images and analogies.

Though an entertaining text is not usually written to persuade or inform, authors may accomplish both of these tasks in their work. An entertaining text may *appeal to the reader's emotions* and cause him or her to think differently about a particular subject. In any case, entertaining texts tend to showcase the personality of the author more than other types of writing.

Descriptive Text

In a sense, almost all writing is descriptive, insofar as an author seeks to describe events, ideas, or people to the reader. Some texts, however, are primarily concerned with **description**. A descriptive text focuses on a particular subject and attempts to depict the subject in a way that will be clear to readers. Descriptive texts contain many adjectives and adverbs (i.e., words that give shades of meaning and create a more detailed mental picture for the reader). A descriptive text fails when it is unclear to the reader. A descriptive text will certainly be informative and may be persuasive and entertaining as well.

Review Video: Descriptive Texts
Visit mometrix.com/academy and enter code: 174903

Expression of Feelings

When an author intends to **express feelings**, he or she may use **expressive and bold language**. An author may write with emotion for any number of reasons. Sometimes, authors will express feelings because they are describing a personal situation of great pain or happiness. In other situations, authors will attempt to persuade the reader and will use emotion to stir up the passions. This kind of expression is easy to identify when the writer uses phrases like *I felt* and *I sense*. However, readers may find that the author will simply describe feelings without introducing them. As a reader, you must know the importance of recognizing when an author is expressing emotion and not to become overwhelmed by sympathy or passion. Readers should maintain some **detachment** so that they can still evaluate the strength of the author's argument or the quality of the writing.

Review Video: Emotional Language in Literature
Visit mometrix.com/academy and enter code: 759390

Expository Passage

An **expository** passage aims to **inform** and enlighten readers. Expository passages are nonfiction and usually center around a simple, easily defined topic. Since the goal of exposition is to teach, such a passage should be as clear as possible. Often, an expository passage contains helpful organizing words, like *first*, *next*, *for example*, and *therefore*. These words keep the reader **oriented** in the text. Although expository passages do not need to feature colorful language and artful writing, they are often more effective with these features. For a reader, the challenge of expository passages is to maintain steady attention. Expository passages are not always about subjects that will naturally interest a reader, so the writer is often more concerned with **clarity** and **comprehensibility** than with engaging the reader. By reading actively, you can ensure a good habit of focus when reading an expository passage.

Review Video: Expository Passages
Visit mometrix.com/academy and enter code: 256515

Narrative Passage

A **narrative** passage is a story that can be fiction or nonfiction. However, there are a few elements that a text must have in order to be classified as a narrative. First, the text must have a **plot** (i.e., a series of events). Narratives often proceed in a clear sequence, but this is not a requirement. If the narrative is good, then these events will be interesting to readers. Second, a narrative has **characters**. These characters could be people, animals, or even inanimate objects—so long as they participate in the plot. Third, a narrative passage often contains **figurative language** which is meant to stimulate the imagination of readers by making comparisons and observations. For instance, a *metaphor*, a common piece of figurative language, is a description of one thing in terms of another. *The moon was a frosty snowball* is an example of a metaphor. In the literal sense this is obviously untrue, but the comparison suggests a certain mood for the reader.

Technical Passage

A **technical** passage is written to *describe* a complex object or process. Technical writing is common in medical and technological fields, in which complex ideas of mathematics, science, and engineering need to be explained *simply* and *clearly*. To ease comprehension, a technical passage usually proceeds in a very logical order. Technical passages often have clear headings and subheadings, which are used to keep the reader oriented in the text. Additionally, you will find that these passages divide sections up with numbers or letters. Many technical passages look more like an outline than a piece of prose. The amount of **jargon** or difficult vocabulary will vary in a technical passage depending on the intended audience. As much as possible, technical passages try to avoid language that the reader will have to research in order to understand the message, yet readers will find that jargon cannot always be avoided.

Review Video: Technical Passages
Visit mometrix.com/academy and enter code: 478923

Common Organizations of Texts

Organization of the Text

The way a text is organized can help readers understand the author's intent and his or her conclusions. There are various ways to organize a text, and each one has a purpose and use. Usually, authors will organize information logically in a passage so the reader can follow and locate the information within the text. However, since not all passages are written with the same logical structure, you need to be familiar with several different types of passage structure.

Review Video: Sequence of Events in a Story
Visit mometrix.com/academy and enter code: 807512

Chronological

When using **chronological** order, the author presents information in the order that it happened. For example, biographies are typically written in chronological order. The subject's birth and childhood are presented first, followed by their adult life, and lastly the events leading up to the person's death.

Cause and Effect

One of the most common text structures is **cause and effect**. A **cause** is an act or event that makes something happen, and an **effect** is the thing that happens as a result of the cause. A cause-and-effect relationship is not always explicit, but there are some terms in English that signal causes, such as *since*, *because*, and *due to*. Furthermore, terms that signal effects include *consequently, therefore, this leads to*. As an example, consider the sentence *Because the sky was clear, Ron did not bring an umbrella*. The cause is the clear sky, and the effect is that Ron did not bring an umbrella. However, readers may find that sometimes the cause-and-effect relationship will not be clearly noted. For instance, the sentence *He was* *late and missed the meeting* does not contain any signaling words, but the sentence still contains a cause (he was late) and an effect (he missed the meeting).

Review Video: Cause and Effect
Visit mometrix.com/academy and enter code: 868099

Review Video: Rhetorical Strategy of Cause and Effect Analysis
Visit mometrix.com/academy and enter code: 725944

Multiple Effects

Be aware of the possibility for a single cause to have **multiple effects.** (e.g., *Single cause*: Because you left your homework on the table, your dog engulfed the assignment. *Multiple effects*: As a result, you receive a failing grade, your parents do not allow you to go out with your friends, you miss out on the new movie, and one of your classmates spoils it for you before you have another chance to watch it).

Multiple Causes

Also, there is the possibility for a single effect to have **multiple causes.** (e.g., *Single effect*: Alan has a fever. *Multiple causes*: An unexpected cold front came through the area, and Alan forgot to take his multi-vitamin to avoid getting sick.) Additionally, an effect can in turn be the cause of another effect, in what is known as a cause-and-effect chain. (e.g., As a result of her disdain for procrastination, Lynn prepared for her exam. This led to her passing her test with high marks. Hence, her resume was accepted and her application was approved.)

Cause and Effect in Persuasive Essays

Persuasive essays, in which an author tries to make a convincing argument and change the minds of readers, usually include cause-and-effect relationships. However, these relationships should not always be taken at face value. Frequently, an author will assume a cause or take an effect for granted. To read a persuasive essay effectively, readers need to judge the cause-and-effect relationships that the author is presenting. For instance, imagine an author wrote the following: *The parking deck has been unprofitable because people would prefer to ride their bikes.* The relationship is clear: the cause is that people prefer to ride their bikes, and the effect is that the parking deck has been unprofitable. However, readers should consider whether this argument is conclusive. Perhaps there are other reasons for the failure of the parking deck: a down economy, excessive fees, etc. Too often, authors present causal relationships as if they are fact rather than opinion. Readers should be on the alert for these dubious claims.

Problem-Solution

Some nonfiction texts are organized to **present a problem** followed by a solution. For this type of text, the problem is often explained before the solution is offered. In some cases, as when the problem is well known, the solution may be introduced briefly at the beginning. Other passages may focus on the solution, and the problem will be referenced only occasionally. Some texts will outline multiple solutions to a problem, leaving readers to choose among them. If the author has an interest or an allegiance to one solution, he or she may fail to mention or describe accurately some of the other solutions. Readers should be careful of the author's agenda when reading a problem-solution text. Only by understanding the author's perspective and interests can one develop a proper judgment of the proposed solution.

Compare and Contrast

Many texts follow the **compare-and-contrast** model in which the similarities and differences between two ideas or things are explored. Analysis of the similarities between ideas is called **comparison.** In an ideal comparison, the author places ideas or things in an equivalent structure, i.e., the author presents the ideas in the same way. If an author wants to show the similarities between cricket and baseball, then he or she may do so by summarizing the equipment and rules for each game. Be mindful of the similarities as they appear in the passage and take note of any differences that are mentioned. Often, these small differences will only reinforce the more general similarity.

Review Video: Compare and Contrast
Visit mometrix.com/academy and enter code: 798319

Thinking critically about ideas and conclusions can seem like a daunting task. One way to ease this task is to understand the basic elements of ideas and writing techniques. Looking at the ways different ideas relate to each other can be a good way for readers to begin their analysis. For instance, sometimes authors will write about two ideas that are in opposition to each other. Or, one author will provide his or her ideas on a topic, and another author may respond in opposition. The analysis of these opposing ideas is known as **contrast**. Contrast is often marred by the author's obvious partiality to one of the ideas. A discerning reader will be put off by an author who does not engage in a fair fight. In an analysis of opposing ideas, both ideas should be presented in clear and reasonable terms. If the author does prefer a side, you need to read carefully to determine the areas where the author shows or avoids this preference. In an analysis of opposing ideas, you should proceed through the passage by marking the major differences point by point with an eye that is looking for an explanation of each side's view. For instance, in an analysis of capitalism and communism, there is an importance in outlining each side's view on labor, markets, prices, personal responsibility, etc. Additionally, as you read through the passages, you should note whether the opposing views present each side in a similar manner.

SEQUENCE

Readers must be able to identify a text's **sequence**, or the order in which things happen. Often, when the sequence is very important to the author, the text is indicated with signal words like *first*, *then*, *next*, and *last*. However, a sequence can be merely implied and must be noted by the reader. Consider the sentence *He walked through the garden and gave water and fertilizer to the plants.* Clearly, the man did not walk through the garden before he collected water and fertilizer for the plants. So, the implied sequence is that he first collected water, then he collected fertilizer, next he walked through the garden, and last he gave water or fertilizer as necessary to the plants. Texts do not always proceed in an orderly sequence from first to last. Sometimes they begin at the end and start over at the beginning. As a reader, you can enhance your understanding of the passage by taking brief notes to clarify the sequence.

Review Video: Sequence
Visit mometrix.com/academy and enter code: 489027

Making and Evaluating Predictions

MAKING PREDICTIONS

When we read literature, **making predictions** about what will happen in the writing reinforces our purpose for reading and prepares us mentally. A **prediction** is a guess about what will happen next. Readers constantly make predictions based on what they have read and what they already know. We can make predictions before we begin reading and during our reading. Consider the following sentence: *Staring at the computer screen in shock, Kim blindly reached over for the brimming glass of water on the shelf to her side.* The sentence suggests that Kim is distracted, and that she is not looking at the glass that she is going to pick up. So, a reader might predict that Kim is going to knock over the glass. Of course, not every prediction will be accurate: perhaps Kim will pick the glass up cleanly. Nevertheless, the author has certainly created the expectation that the water might be spilled.

As we read on, we can test the accuracy of our predictions, revise them in light of additional reading, and confirm or refute our predictions. Predictions are always subject to revision as the reader acquires more information. A reader can make predictions by observing the title and illustrations; noting the structure, characters, and subject; drawing on existing knowledge relative to the subject; and asking "why" and "who" questions. Connecting reading to what we already know enables us to learn new information and construct meaning. For example, before third-graders read a book about Johnny Appleseed, they may start a KWL chart—a list of what they *Know*, what they *Want* to know or learn, and what they have *Learned* after reading. Activating existing background knowledge and thinking about the text before reading improves comprehension.

Review Video: Predictive Reading
Visit mometrix.com/academy and enter code: 437248

Test-taking tip: To respond to questions requiring future predictions, your answers should be based on evidence of past or present behavior and events.

Evaluating Predictions

When making predictions, readers should be able to explain how they developed their prediction. One way readers can defend their thought process is by citing textual evidence. Textual evidence to evaluate reader predictions about literature includes specific synopses of the work, paraphrases of the work or parts of it, and direct quotations from the work. These references to the text must support the prediction by indicating, clearly or unclearly, what will happen later in the story. A text may provide these indications through literary devices such as foreshadowing. Foreshadowing is anything in a text that gives the reader a hint about what is to come by emphasizing the likelihood of an event or development. Foreshadowing can occur through descriptions, exposition, and dialogue. Foreshadowing in dialogue usually occurs when a character gives a warning or expresses a strong feeling that a certain event will occur. Foreshadowing can also occur through irony. However, unlike other forms of foreshadowing, the events that seem the most likely are the opposite of what actually happens. Instances of foreshadowing and irony can be summarized, paraphrased, or quoted to defend a reader's prediction.

Review Video: Textual Evidence for Predictions
Visit mometrix.com/academy and enter code: 261070

Making Inferences and Drawing Conclusions

Inferences are logical conclusions that readers make based on their observations and previous knowledge. An inference is based on both what is found in a passage or a story and what is known from personal experience. For instance, a story may say that a character is frightened and can hear howling in the distance. Based on both what is in the text and personal knowledge, it is a logical conclusion that the character is frightened because he hears the sound of wolves. A good inference is supported by the information in a passage.

Implicit and Explicit Information

By inferring, readers construct meanings from text that are personally relevant. By combining their own schemas or concepts and their background information pertinent to the text with what they read, readers interpret it according to both what the author has conveyed and their own unique perspectives. Inferences are different from **explicit information**, which is clearly stated in a passage. Authors do not always explicitly spell out every meaning in what they write; many meanings are implicit. Through inference, readers can comprehend implied meanings in the text, and also derive personal significance from it, making the text meaningful and memorable to them. Inference is a natural process in everyday life. When readers infer, they can draw conclusions about what the author is saying, predict what may reasonably follow, amend these predictions as they continue to read, interpret the import of themes, and analyze the characters' feelings and motivations through their actions.

EXAMPLE OF DRAWING CONCLUSIONS FROM INFERENCES

Read the excerpt and decide why Jana finally relaxed.

> Jana loved her job, but the work was very demanding. She had trouble relaxing. She called a friend, but she still thought about work. She ordered a pizza, but eating it did not help. Then, her kitten jumped on her lap and began to purr. Jana leaned back and began to hum a little tune. She felt better.

You can draw the conclusion that Jana relaxed because her kitten jumped on her lap. The kitten purred, and Jana leaned back and hummed a tune. Then she felt better. The excerpt does not explicitly say that this is the reason why she was able to relax. The text leaves the matter unclear, but the reader can infer or make a "best guess" that this is the reason she is relaxing. This is a logical conclusion based on the information in the passage. It is the best conclusion a reader can make based on the information he or she has read. Inferences are based on the information in a passage, but they are not directly stated in the passage.

Test-taking tip: While being tested on your ability to make correct inferences, you must look for **contextual clues**. An answer can be true, but not the best or most correct answer. The contextual clues will help you find the answer that is the **best answer** out of the given choices. Be careful in your reading to understand the context in which a phrase is stated. When asked for the implied meaning of a statement made in the passage, you should immediately locate the statement and read the **context** in which the statement was made. Also, look for an answer choice that has a similar phrase to the statement in question.

Review Video: Inference
Visit mometrix.com/academy and enter code: 379203

Review Video: How to Support a Conclusion
Visit mometrix.com/academy and enter code: 281653

Critical Reading Skills

OPINIONS, FACTS, AND FALLACIES

Critical thinking skills are mastered through understanding various types of writing and the different purposes authors can have for writing different passages. Every author writes for a purpose. When you understand their purpose and how they accomplish their goal, you will be able to analyze their writing and determine whether or not you agree with their conclusions.

Readers must always be aware of the difference between fact and opinion. A **fact** can be subjected to analysis and proven to be true. An **opinion**, on the other hand, is the author's personal thoughts or feelings and may not be altered by research or evidence. If the author writes that the distance from New York City to Boston is about two hundred miles, then he or she is stating a fact. If the author writes that New York City is too crowded, then he or she is giving an opinion because there is no objective standard for overpopulation. Opinions are often supported by facts. For instance, an author might use a comparison between the population density of New York City and that of other major American cities as evidence of an overcrowded population. An opinion supported by facts tends to be more convincing. On the other hand, when authors support their opinions with other opinions, readers should employ critical thinking and approach the argument with skepticism.

Review Video: Distinguishing Fact and Opinion
Visit mometrix.com/academy and enter code: 870899

RELIABLE SOURCES

When you read an argumentative passage, you need to be sure that facts are presented to the reader from **reliable sources**. An opinion is what the author thinks about a given topic. An opinion is not common knowledge or proven by expert sources, instead the information is the personal beliefs and thoughts of the author. To distinguish between fact and opinion, a reader needs to consider the type of source that is presenting information, the information that backs-up a claim, and the author's motivation to have a certain point-of-view on a given topic. For example, if a panel of scientists has conducted multiple studies on the effectiveness of taking a certain vitamin, then the results are more likely to be factual than those of a company that is selling a vitamin and simply claims that taking the vitamin can produce positive effects. The company is motivated to sell their product, and the scientists are using the scientific method to prove a theory. Remember, if you find sentences that contain phrases such as "I think...", then the statement is an opinion.

BIASES

In their attempts to persuade, writers often make mistakes in their thought processes and writing choices. These processes and choices are important to understand so you can make an informed decision about the author's credibility. Every author has a point of view, but authors demonstrate a **bias** when they ignore reasonable counterarguments or distort opposing viewpoints. A bias is evident whenever the author's claims are presented in a way that is unfair or inaccurate. Bias can be intentional or unintentional, but readers should be skeptical of the author's argument in either case. Remember that a biased author may still be correct. However, the author will be correct in spite of, not because of, his or her bias.

A **stereotype** is a bias applied specifically to a group of people or a place. Stereotyping is considered to be particularly abhorrent because it promotes negative, misleading generalizations about people. Readers should be very cautious of authors who use stereotypes in their writing. These faulty assumptions typically reveal the author's ignorance and lack of curiosity.

Review Video: Bias and Stereotype
Visit mometrix.com/academy and enter code: 644829

Persuasion and Rhetoric

PERSUASIVE TECHNIQUES

To **appeal using reason**, writers present logical arguments, such as using "If... then... because" statements. To **appeal to emotions**, authors may ask readers how they would feel about something or to put themselves in another's place, present their argument as one that will make the audience feel good, or tell readers how they should feel. To **appeal to character**, **morality**, or **ethics**, authors present their points to readers as the right or most moral choices. Authors cite expert opinions to show readers that someone very knowledgeable about the subject or viewpoint agrees with the author's claims. **Testimonials**, usually via anecdotes or quotations regarding the author's subject, help build the audience's trust in an author's message through positive support from ordinary people. **Bandwagon appeals** claim that everybody else agrees with the author's argument and persuade readers to conform and agree, also. Authors **appeal to greed** by presenting their choice as cheaper, free, or more valuable for less cost. They **appeal to laziness** by presenting their views as more convenient, easy, or relaxing. Authors also anticipate potential objections and argue against them before audiences think of them, thereby depicting those objections as weak.

Authors can use **comparisons** like analogies, similes, and metaphors to persuade audiences. For example, a writer might represent excessive expenses as "hemorrhaging" money, which the author's recommended solution will stop. Authors can use negative word connotations to make some choices unappealing to readers, and positive word connotations to make others more appealing. Using **humor** can relax readers and garner their agreement. However, writers must take care: ridiculing opponents can be a successful strategy for appealing to readers who already agree with the author, but can backfire by angering other readers. **Rhetorical questions** need no answer, but create effect that can force agreement, such as asking the question, "Wouldn't you rather be paid more than less?" **Generalizations** persuade readers by being impossible to disagree with. Writers can easily make generalizations that appear to support their viewpoints, like saying, "We all want peace, not war" regarding more specific political arguments. **Transfer** and **association** persuade by example: if advertisements show attractive actors enjoying their products, audiences imagine they will experience the same. **Repetition** can also sometimes effectively persuade audiences.

Review Video: Using Rhetorical Strategies for Persuasion
Visit mometrix.com/academy and enter code: 302658

Classical Author Appeals

In his *On Rhetoric,* ancient Greek philosopher Aristotle defined three basic types of appeal used in writing, which he called *pathos*, *ethos*, and *logos*. ***Pathos*** means suffering or experience and refers to appeals to the emotions (the English word *pathetic* comes from this root). Writing that is meant to entertain audiences, by making them either happy, as with comedy, or sad, as with tragedy, uses *pathos*. Aristotle's *Poetics* states that evoking the emotions of terror and pity is one of the criteria for writing tragedy. ***Ethos*** means character and connotes ideology (the English word *ethics* comes from this root). Writing that appeals to credibility, based on academic, professional, or personal merit, uses *ethos*. ***Logos*** means "I say" and refers to a plea, opinion, expectation, word or speech, account, opinion, or reason (the English word *logic* comes from this root.) Aristotle used it to mean persuasion that appeals to the audience through reasoning and logic to influence their opinions.

Rhetorical Devices

- An **anecdote** is a brief story authors may relate to their argument, which can illustrate their points in a more real and relatable way.
- **Aphorisms** concisely state common beliefs and may rhyme. For example, Benjamin Franklin's "Early to bed and early to rise / Makes a man healthy, wealthy, and wise" is an aphorism.
- **Allusions** refer to literary or historical figures to impart symbolism to a thing or person and to create reader resonance. In John Steinbeck's *Of Mice and Men,* protagonist George's last name is Milton. This alludes to John Milton, who wrote *Paradise Lost*, and symbolizes George's eventual loss of his dream.
- **Satire** exaggerates, ridicules, or pokes fun at human flaws or ideas, as in the works of Jonathan Swift and Mark Twain.
- A **parody** is a form of satire that imitates another work to ridicule its topic or style.
- A **paradox** is a statement that is true despite appearing contradictory.
- **Hyperbole** is overstatement using exaggerated language.
- An **oxymoron** combines seeming contradictions, such as "deafening silence."
- **Analogies** compare two things that share common elements.
- **Similes** (stated comparisons using the words *like* or *as*) and **metaphors** (stated comparisons that do not use *like* or *as*) are considered forms of analogy.
- When using logic to reason with audiences, **syllogism** refers either to deductive reasoning or a deceptive, very sophisticated, or subtle argument.
- **Deductive reasoning** moves from general to specific, **inductive reasoning** from specific to general.
- **Diction** is author word choice that establishes tone and effect.
- **Understatement** achieves effects like contrast or irony by downplaying or describing something more subtly than warranted.

- **Chiasmus** uses parallel clauses, the second reversing the order of the first. Examples include T. S. Eliot's "Has the Church failed mankind, or has mankind failed the Church?" and John F. Kennedy's "Ask not what your country can do for you; ask what you can do for your country."
- **Anaphora** regularly repeats a word or phrase at the beginnings of consecutive clauses or phrases to add emphasis to an idea. A classic example of anaphora was Winston Churchill's emphasis of determination: "[W]e shall fight on the beaches, we shall fight on the landing grounds, we shall fight in the fields and in the streets, we shall fight in the hills; we shall never surrender..."

Reading Comprehension and Connecting with Texts

Comparing Two Stories

When presented with two different stories, there will be **similarities** and **differences** between the two. A reader needs to make a list, or other graphic organizer, of the points presented in each story. Once the reader has written down the main point and supporting points for each story, the two sets of ideas can be compared. The reader can then present each idea and show how it is the same or different in the other story. This is called **comparing and contrasting ideas**.

The reader can compare ideas by stating, for example: "In Story 1, the author believes that humankind will one day land on Mars, whereas in Story 2, the author believes that Mars is too far away for humans to ever step foot on." Note that the two viewpoints are different in each story that the reader is comparing. A reader may state that: "Both stories discussed the likelihood of humankind landing on Mars." This statement shows how the viewpoint presented in both stories is based on the same topic, rather than how each viewpoint is different. The reader will complete a comparison of two stories with a conclusion.

Review Video: How to Compare and Contrast
Visit mometrix.com/academy and enter code: 833765

Outlining a Passage

As an aid to drawing conclusions, **outlining** the information contained in the passage should be a familiar skill to readers. An effective outline will reveal the structure of the passage and will lead to solid conclusions. An effective outline will have a title that refers to the basic subject of the text, though the title does not need to restate the main idea. In most outlines, the main idea will be the first major section. Each major idea in the passage will be established as the head of a category. For instance, the most common outline format calls for the main ideas of the passage to be indicated with Roman numerals. In an effective outline of this kind, each of the main ideas will be represented by a Roman numeral and none of the Roman numerals will designate minor details or secondary ideas. Moreover, all supporting ideas and details should be placed in the appropriate place on the outline. An outline does not need to include every detail listed in the text, but it should feature all of those that are central to the argument or message. Each of these details should be listed under the corresponding main idea.

Review Video: Outlining as an Aid to Drawing Conclusions
Visit mometrix.com/academy and enter code: 584445

Using Graphic Organizers

Ideas from a text can also be organized using **graphic organizers**. A graphic organizer is a way to simplify information and take key points from the text. A graphic organizer such as a timeline may have an event listed for a corresponding date on the timeline, while an outline may have an event listed under a key point that occurs in the text. Each reader needs to create the type of graphic organizer that works the best for him or her in terms of being able to recall information from a story. Examples include a spider-map, which takes a main idea from the story and places it in a bubble with supporting points branching off the main idea. An outline is useful for diagramming the main and supporting points of the entire story, and a Venn diagram compares and contrasts characteristics of two or more ideas.

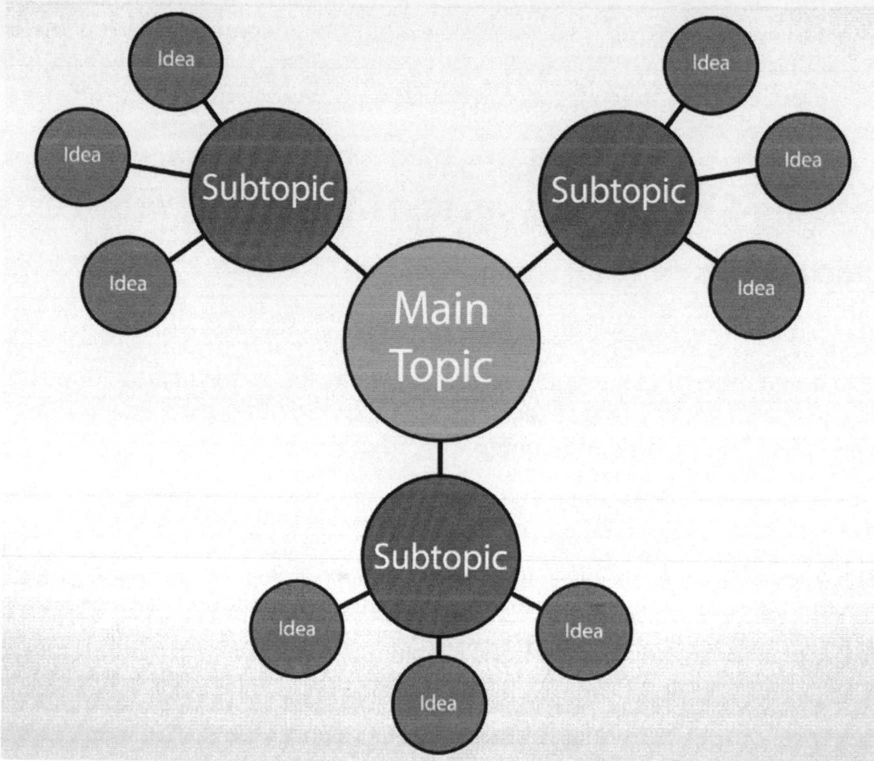

Review Video: Graphic Organizers
Visit mometrix.com/academy and enter code: 665513

Making Logical Conclusions About a Passage

A reader should always be drawing conclusions from the text. Sometimes conclusions are **implied** from written information, and other times the information is **stated directly** within the passage. One should always aim to draw conclusions from information stated within a passage, rather than to draw them from mere implications. At times an author may provide some information and then describe a counterargument. Readers should be alert for direct statements that are subsequently rejected or weakened by the author. Furthermore, you should always read through the entire passage before drawing conclusions. Many readers are trained to expect the author's conclusions at either the beginning or the end of the passage, but many texts do not adhere to this format.

Drawing conclusions from information implied within a passage requires confidence on the part of the reader. **Implications** are things that the author does not state directly, but readers can assume based on what the author does say. Consider the following passage: *I stepped outside and opened my umbrella. By the time I got to work, the cuffs of my pants were soaked.* The author never states that it is raining, but this fact is clearly implied. Conclusions based on implication must be well supported by the text. In order to draw a solid conclusion, readers should have **multiple pieces of evidence**. If readers have only one piece, they must be assured that there is no other possible explanation than their conclusion. A good reader will be able to draw many conclusions from information implied by the text, which will be a great help on the exam.

Drawing Conclusions

A common type of inference that a reader has to make is **drawing a conclusion**. The reader makes this conclusion based on the information provided within a text. Certain facts are included to help a reader come to a specific conclusion. For example, a story may open with a man trudging through the snow on a cold winter day, dragging a sled behind him. The reader can logically **infer** from the setting of the story that the man is wearing heavy winter clothes in order to stay warm. Information is implied based on the setting of a story, which is why **setting** is an important element of the text. If the same man in the example was trudging down a beach on a hot summer day, dragging a surf board behind him, the reader would assume that the man is not wearing heavy clothes. The reader makes inferences based on their own experiences and the information presented to them in the story.

Test-taking tip: When asked to identify a conclusion that may be drawn, look for critical "hedge" phrases, such as *likely*, *may*, *can*, and *will often*, among many others. When you are being tested on this knowledge, remember the question that writers insert into these hedge phrases to cover every possibility. Often an answer will be wrong simply because there is no room for exception. Extreme positive or negative answers (such as always or never) are usually not correct. When answering these questions, the reader **should not** use any outside knowledge that is not gathered directly or reasonably inferred from the passage. Correct answers can be derived straight from the passage.

Example

Read the following sentence from *Little Women* by Louisa May Alcott and draw a conclusion based upon the information presented:

> *You know the reason Mother proposed not having any presents this Christmas was because it is going to be a hard winter for everyone; and she thinks we ought not to spend money for pleasure, when our men are suffering so in the army.*

Based on the information in the sentence, the reader can conclude, or **infer**, that the men are away at war while the women are still at home. The pronoun *our* gives a clue to the reader that the character is speaking about men she knows. In addition, the reader can assume that the character is speaking to a brother or sister, since the term "Mother" is used by the character while speaking to another person. The reader can also come to the conclusion that the characters celebrate Christmas, since it is mentioned in the **context** of the sentence. In the sentence, the mother is presented as an unselfish character who is opinionated and thinks about the wellbeing of other people.

Summarizing

A helpful tool is the ability to **summarize** the information that you have read in a paragraph or passage format. This process is similar to creating an effective outline. First, a summary should accurately define the main idea of the passage, though the summary does not need to explain this main idea in exhaustive detail. The summary should continue by laying out the most important supporting details or arguments from the passage. All of the significant supporting details should be included, and none of the details included should be irrelevant or insignificant. Also, the summary should accurately report all of these details. Too often, the desire for brevity in a summary leads to the sacrifice of clarity or accuracy. Summaries are often difficult to read because they omit all of the graceful language, digressions, and asides that distinguish great writing. However, an effective summary should communicate the same overall message as the original text.

Review Video: Summarizing Text
Visit mometrix.com/academy and enter code: 172903

PARAPHRASING

Paraphrasing is another method that the reader can use to aid in comprehension. When paraphrasing, one puts what they have read into their own words by rephrasing what the author has written, or one "translates" all of what the author shared into their own words by including as many details as they can.

EVALUATING A PASSAGE

It is important to understand the logical conclusion of the ideas presented in an informational text. **Identifying a logical conclusion** can help you determine whether you agree with the writer or not. Coming to this conclusion is much like making an inference: the approach requires you to combine the information given by the text with what you already know and make a logical conclusion. If the author intended for the reader to draw a certain conclusion, then you can expect the author's argumentation and detail to be leading in that direction.

One way to approach the task of drawing conclusions is to make brief **notes** of all the points made by the author. When the notes are arranged on paper, they may clarify the logical conclusion. Another way to approach conclusions is to consider whether the reasoning of the author raises any pertinent questions. Sometimes you will be able to draw several conclusions from a passage. On occasion these will be conclusions that were never imagined by the author. Therefore, be aware that these conclusions must be **supported directly by the text**.

EVALUATION OF SUMMARIES

A summary of a literary passage is a condensation in the reader's own words of the passage's main points. Several guidelines can be used in evaluating a summary. The summary should be complete yet concise. It should be accurate, balanced, fair, neutral, and objective, excluding the reader's own opinions or reactions. It should reflect in similar proportion how much each point summarized was covered in the original passage. Summary writers should include tags of attribution, like "Macaulay argues that" to reference the original author whose ideas are represented in the summary. Summary writers should not overuse quotations; they should only quote central concepts or phrases they cannot precisely convey in words other than those of the original author. Another aspect of evaluating a summary is considering whether it can stand alone as a coherent, unified composition. In addition, evaluation of a summary should include whether its writer has cited the original source of the passage they have summarized so that readers can find it.

MAKING CONNECTIONS TO ENHANCE COMPREHENSION

Reading involves thinking. For good comprehension, readers make **text-to-self**, **text-to-text**, and **text-to-world connections**. Making connections helps readers understand text better and predict what might occur next based on what they already know, such as how characters in the story feel or what happened in another text. Text-to-self connections with the reader's life and experiences make literature more personally relevant and meaningful to readers. Readers can make connections before, during, and after reading—including whenever the text reminds them of something similar they have encountered in life or other texts. The genre, setting, characters, plot elements, literary structure and devices, and themes an author uses allow a reader to make connections to other works of literature or to people and events in their own lives. Venn diagrams and other graphic organizers help visualize connections. Readers can also make double-entry notes: key content, ideas, events, words, and quotations on one side, and the connections with these on the other.

Comparing Two Texts

Synthesis of Multiple Texts

Synthesizing, i.e., understanding and integrating, information from multiple texts can at times be among the most challenging skills for some students to succeed with on tests and in school, and yet it is also among the most important. Students who read at the highest cognitive levels can select related material from different text sources and construct coherent arguments that account for these varied information sources. Synthesizing ideas and information from multiple texts actually combines other reading skills that students should have mastered previously in reading one text at a time, and applies them in the context of reading more than one text. For example, students are required to read texts closely, including identifying explicit and implicit meanings; use critical thinking and reading; draw inferences; assess author reasoning; analyze supporting evidence; and formulate opinions they can justify, based on more passages than one. When two paired texts represent opposing sides of the same argument, students can find analyzing them easier; but this is not always the case.

Similarities in Texts

When students are called upon to compare things two texts share in common, the most obvious commonality might be the same subject matter or specific topic. However, two texts need not be about the same thing to compare them. Some other features texts can share include structural characteristics. For example, they may both be written using a sequential format, such as narrating events or giving instructions in chronological order; listing and/or discussing subtopics by order of importance; or describing a place spatially in sequence from each point to the next. They may both use a comparison-contrast structure, identifying similarities and differences between, among, or within topics. They might both organize information by identifying cause-and-effect relationships. Texts can be similar in type, e.g., description, narration, persuasion, or exposition. They can be similar in using technical vocabulary or using formal or informal language. They may share similar tones and/or styles, e.g., humorous, satirical, serious, etc. They can share similar purposes, e.g., to alarm audiences, incite them to action, reassure them, inspire them, provoke strong emotional responses, etc.

Contrasts in Texts

When analyzing paired or multiple texts, students might observe differences in tone; for example, one text might take a serious approach while another uses a humorous one. Even within approaches or treatments, style can differ: one text may be humorous in a witty, sophisticated, clever way while another may exercise broad, "lowbrow" humor; another may employ mordant sarcasm; another may use satire, couching outrageous suggestions in a "deadpan" logical voice to lampoon social attitudes and behaviors as Jonathan Swift did in *A Modest Proposal*. Serious writing can range from darkly pessimistic to alarmist to objective and unemotional. Texts might have similar information, yet organize it using different structures. One text may support points or ideas using logical arguments, while another may seek to persuade its audience by appealing to their emotions. A very obvious difference in text is genre: for example, the same mythological or traditional stories have been told as oral folk tales, written dramas, written novels, etc.; and/or set in different times and places (e.g., Shakespeare's *Romeo and Juliet* vs. Laurents, Bernstein, and Sondheim's *West Side Story*).

Reading Informational Texts

Language Use

Literal and Figurative Language

As in fictional literature, informational text also uses both **literal language**, which means just what it says, and **figurative language**, which imparts more than literal meaning. For example, an informational text author might use a simile or direct comparison, such as writing that a racehorse "ran like the wind." Informational text authors also use metaphors or implied comparisons, such as "the cloud of the Great Depression." Imagery may also appear in informational texts to increase the reader's understanding of ideas and concepts discussed in the text.

Explicit and Implicit Information

When informational text states something explicitly, the reader is told by the author exactly what is meant, which can include the author's interpretation or perspective of events. For example, a professor writes, "I have seen students go into an absolute panic just because they weren't able to complete the exam in the time they were allotted." This explicitly tells the reader that the students were afraid, and by using the words "just because," the writer indicates their fear was exaggerated out of proportion relative to what happened. However, another professor writes, "I have had students come to me, their faces drained of all color, saying 'We weren't able to finish the exam.'" This is an example of implicit meaning: the second writer did not state explicitly that the students were panicked. Instead, he wrote a description of their faces being "drained of all color." From this description, the reader can infer that the students were so frightened that their faces paled.

Review Video: Explicit and Implicit Information
Visit mometrix.com/academy and enter code: 735771

Making Inferences About Informational Text

With informational text, reader comprehension depends not only on recalling important statements and details, but also on reader inferences based on examples and details. Readers add information from the text to what they already know to draw inferences about the text. These inferences help the readers to fill in the information that the text does not explicitly state, enabling them to understand the text better. When reading a nonfictional autobiography or biography, for example, the most appropriate inferences might concern the events in the book, the actions of the subject of the autobiography or biography, and the message the author means to convey. When reading a nonfictional expository (informational) text, the reader would best draw inferences about problems and their solutions, and causes and their effects. When reading a nonfictional persuasive text, the reader will want to infer ideas supporting the author's message and intent.

Structures or Organizational Patterns in Informational Texts

Informational text can be **descriptive**, appealing to the five senses and answering the questions what, who, when, where, and why. Another method of structuring informational text is sequence and order. **Chronological** texts relate events in the sequence that they occurred, from start to finish, while how-to texts organize information into a series of instructions in the sequence in which the steps should be followed. **Comparison-contrast** structures of informational text describe various ideas to their readers by pointing out how things or ideas are similar and how they are different. **Cause and effect** structures of informational text describe events that occurred and identify the causes or reasons that those events occurred. **Problem and solution** structures of informational texts introduce and describe problems and offer one or more solutions for each problem described.

Determining an Informational Author's Purpose

Informational authors' purposes are why they write texts. Readers must determine authors' motivations and goals. Readers gain greater insight into a text by considering the author's motivation. This develops critical reading skills. Readers perceive writing as a person's voice, not simply printed words. Uncovering author motivations and purposes empowers readers to know what to expect from the text, read for relevant details, evaluate authors and their work critically, and respond effectively to the motivations and persuasions of the text. The main idea of a text is what the reader is supposed to understand from reading it; the purpose of the text is why the author has written it and what the author wants readers to do with its information. Authors state some purposes clearly, while other purposes may be unstated but equally significant. When stated purposes contradict other parts of a text, the author may have a hidden agenda. Readers can better evaluate a text's effectiveness, whether they agree or disagree with it, and why they agree or disagree through identifying unstated author purposes.

Identifying Author's Point of View or Purpose

In some informational texts, readers find it easy to identify the author's point of view and purpose, such as when the author explicitly states his or her position and reason for writing. But other texts are more difficult, either because of the content or because the authors give neutral or balanced viewpoints. This is particularly true in scientific texts, in which authors may state the purpose of their research in the report, but never state their point of view except by interpreting evidence or data.

To analyze text and identify point of view or purpose, readers should ask themselves the following four questions:

1. With what main point or idea does this author want to persuade readers to agree?
2. How does this author's word choice affect the way that readers consider this subject?
3. How do this author's choices of examples and facts affect the way that readers consider this subject?
4. What is it that this author wants to accomplish by writing this text?

Review Video: Understanding the Author's Intent
Visit mometrix.com/academy and enter code: 511819

Review Video: Author's Position
Visit mometrix.com/academy and enter code: 827954

Evaluating Arguments Made by Informational Text Writers

When evaluating an informational text, the first step is to identify the argument's conclusion. Then identify the author's premises that support the conclusion. Try to paraphrase premises for clarification and make the conclusion and premises fit. List all premises first, sequentially numbered, then finish with the conclusion. Identify any premises or assumptions not stated by the author but required for the stated premises to support the conclusion. Read word assumptions sympathetically, as the author might. Evaluate whether premises reasonably support the conclusion. For inductive reasoning, the reader should ask if the premises are true, if they support the conclusion, and if so, how strongly. For deductive reasoning, the reader should ask if the argument is valid or invalid. If all premises are true, then the argument is valid unless the conclusion can be false. If it can, then the argument is invalid. An invalid argument can be made valid through alterations such as the addition of needed premises.

Use of Rhetoric in Informational Texts

There are many ways authors can support their claims, arguments, beliefs, ideas, and reasons for writing in informational texts. For example, authors can appeal to readers' sense of **logic** by communicating their reasoning through a carefully sequenced series of logical steps to help "prove" the points made. Authors can appeal to readers' **emotions** by using descriptions and words that evoke feelings of sympathy, sadness, anger, righteous indignation, hope, happiness, or any other emotion to reinforce what they express and share with their audience. Authors may appeal to the **moral** or **ethical values** of readers by using words and descriptions that can convince readers that something is right or wrong. By relating personal anecdotes, authors can supply readers with more accessible, realistic examples of points they make, as well as appealing to their emotions. They can provide supporting evidence by reporting case studies. They can also illustrate their points by making analogies to which readers can better relate.

Organizational Features in Texts

Text Features in Informational Texts

- The **title of a text** gives readers some idea of its content.
- The **table of contents** is a list near the beginning of a text, showing the book's sections and chapters and their coinciding page numbers. This gives readers an overview of the whole text and helps them find specific chapters easily.
- An **appendix**, at the back of the book or document, includes important information that is not present in the main text.
- Also at the back, an **index** lists the book's important topics alphabetically with their page numbers to help readers find them easily.
- **Glossaries**, usually found at the backs of books, list technical terms alphabetically with their definitions to aid vocabulary learning and comprehension. Boldface print is used to emphasize certain words, often identifying words included in the text's glossary where readers can look up their definitions.
- **Headings** separate sections of text and show the topic of each.
- **Subheadings** divide subject headings into smaller, more specific categories to help readers organize information.
- **Footnotes**, at the bottom of the page, give readers more information, such as citations or links.
- **Bullet points** list items separately, making facts and ideas easier to see and understand.
- A **sidebar** is a box of information to one side of the main text giving additional information, often on a more focused or in-depth example of a topic.

Visual Features in Texts

- **Illustrations** and **photographs** are pictures that visually emphasize important points in text.
- The **captions** below the illustrations explain what those images show.
- **Charts** and **tables** are visual forms of information that make something easier to understand quickly.
- **Diagrams** are drawings that show relationships or explain a process.
- **Graphs** visually show the relationships among multiple sets of information plotted along vertical and horizontal axes.
- **Maps** show geographical information visually to help readers understand the relative locations of places covered in the text.
- **Timelines** are visual graphics that show historical events in chronological order to help readers see their sequence.

Visual Information in Informational Texts

CHARTS, GRAPHS, AND VISUALS

TABLES

Tables are presented in a standard format so they will be easy to read and understand. A title is at the top, a short phrase indicating the information the table or graph intends to convey. The title of a table could be something like "Median Income for Various Education Levels" or "Price of Milk Compared to Demand." A table is composed of information laid out in vertical columns and horizontal rows. Typically, each column will have a label. If "Median Income for Various Education Levels" was placed in a table format, the two columns could be labeled "Education Level" and "Median Annual Salary." Each location on the table is called a cell, which holds a piece of information. Cells are defined by their column and row (e.g., second column, fifth row).

Median Annual Salary for Various Education Levels

Education Level	Median Annual Salary
Associate degree	$52,260
Bachelor's degree	$74,464
Master's degree	$86,372
Professional degree	$108,160
Doctoral degree	$108,316

GRAPHS

Like a table, a graph typically has a title at the top. This title may simply state the identities of the two axes: e.g., "Income vs. Education." However, the title may also be something more descriptive, like "A comparison of average income with level of education." In any case, bar and line graphs are laid out along two perpendicular lines, or axes. The vertical axis is called the *y*-axis, and the horizontal axis is called the *x*-axis. It is typical for the *x*-axis to be the independent variable and the *y*-axis to be the dependent variable. The independent variable is the one manipulated by the researcher or creator of the graph. In the above example, the independent variable would be "education level," since the maker of the graph will define these values (associate degree, bachelor's degree, master's degree, etc.). The dependent value is not controlled by the researcher.

When selecting a graph format, it is important to consider the intention and the structure of the presentation. A bar graph is appropriate for displaying the relations between a series of distinct quantities that are on the same scale. For instance, if one wanted to display the amount of money spent on groceries during the months of a year, a bar graph would be appropriate. The vertical axis would represent values of money, and the horizontal axis would identify each month. A line graph also requires data expressed in common units, but it is better for demonstrating the general trend in that data. If the grocery expenses were plotted on a line graph instead of a bar graph, there would be more emphasis on whether the amount of money spent rose or fell over the course of the year. Whereas a bar graph is good for showing the relationships between the different values plotted, the line graph is good for showing whether the values tended to increase, decrease, or remain stable.

Pie Chart

A pie chart, also known as a circle graph, is useful for depicting how a single unit or category is divided. The standard pie chart is a circle with designated wedges. Each wedge is **proportional** in size to a part of the whole. For instance, consider Shawna, a student at City College, who uses a pie chart to represent her budget. If she spends half of her money on rent, then the pie chart will represent that amount with a line through the center of the pie. If she spends a quarter of her money on food, there will be a line extending from the edge of the circle to the center at a right angle to the line depicting rent. This illustration would make it clear that the student spends twice the amount of money on rent as she does on food.

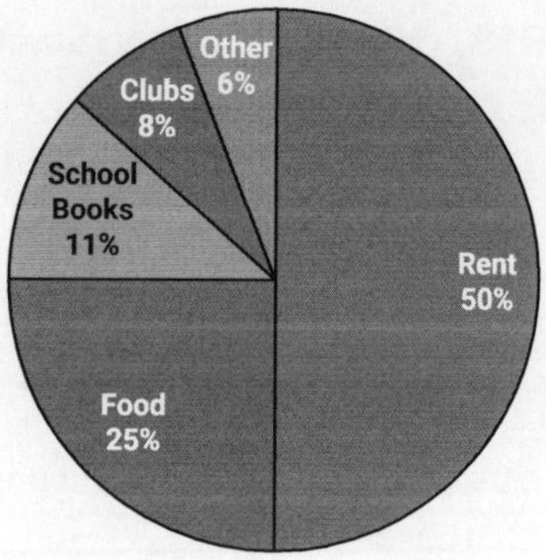

A pie chart is effective at showing how a single entity is divided into parts. They are not effective at demonstrating the relationships between parts of different wholes. For example, an unhelpful use of a pie chart would be to compare the respective amounts of state and federal spending devoted to infrastructure since these values are only meaningful in the context of the entire budget.

Bar Graph

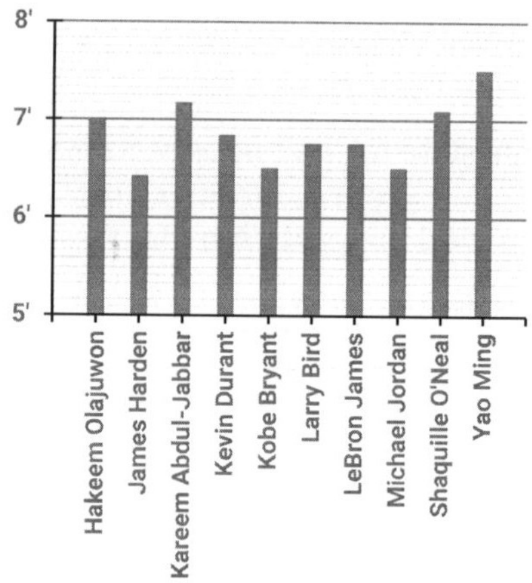

The bar graph is one of the most common visual representations of information. **Bar graphs** are used to illustrate sets of numerical **data**. The graph has a vertical axis (along which numbers are listed) and a horizontal axis (along which categories, words, or some other indicators are placed). One example of a bar graph is a depiction of the respective heights of famous basketball players: the vertical axis would contain numbers ranging from five to eight feet, and the horizontal axis would contain the names of the players. The length of the bar above the player's name would illustrate his height, and the top of the bar would stop perpendicular to the height listed along the left side. In this representation, one would see that Yao Ming is taller than Michael Jordan because Yao's bar would be higher.

Line Graph

A line graph is a type of graph that is typically used for measuring trends over time. The graph is set up along a vertical and a horizontal **axis**. The variables being measured are listed along the left side and the bottom side of the axes. Points are then plotted along the graph as they correspond with their values for each variable. For instance, consider a line graph measuring a person's income for each month of the year. If the person earned $1500 in January, there should be a point directly above January (perpendicular to the horizontal axis) and directly to the right of $1500 (perpendicular to the vertical axis). Once all of the lines are plotted, they are connected with a line from left to right. This line provides a nice visual illustration of the general **trends** of the data, if they exist. For instance, using the earlier example, if the line sloped up, then one would see that the person's income had increased over the course of the year.

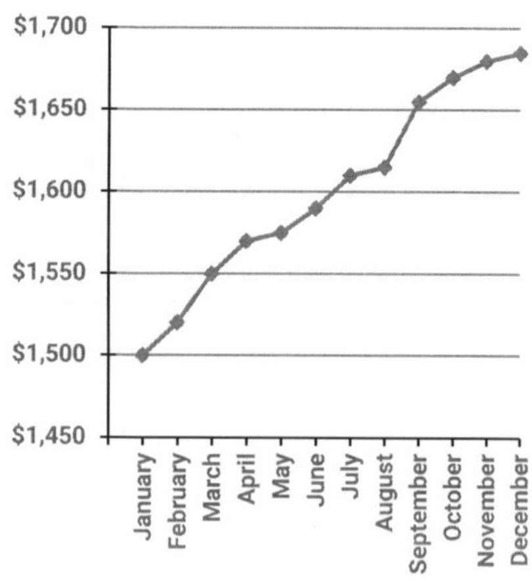

PICTOGRAPHS

A **pictograph** is a graph, generally in the horizontal orientation, that uses pictures or symbols to represent the data. Each pictograph must have a key that defines the picture or symbol and gives the quantity each picture or symbol represents. Pictures or symbols on a pictograph are not always shown as whole elements. In this case, the fraction of the picture or symbol shown represents the same fraction of the quantity a whole picture or symbol stands for.

Review Video: Pictographs
Visit mometrix.com/academy and enter code: 147860

Genres in Fiction

COMMON GENRES IN PROSE FICTION

- The **mystery** genre includes stories with plots that follow a protagonist as they work to solve an unexplained situation, such as a murder, disappearance, or robbery. Protagonists of mysteries may be hired professionals or amateurs who solve the mystery despite their lack of experience and resources. Mysteries allow the reader to solve the case along with the protagonist, and often grant the reader an advantageous perspective, creating dramatic irony. The *Sherlock Holmes* novels by Sir Arthur Conan Doyle are examples of mystery novels.
- **Science fiction** is a genre that is based on the manipulation and exaggeration of real scientific discoveries and processes. These works are speculative and frequently depict a world where scientific discoveries and society have progressed beyond the point reached at the time of the work's creation. Works of science fiction often take place in a distant location or time, allowing for the dramatic advancements and conveniences they often depict. *Dune*, written by Frank Herbert, is an example of a science-fiction novel.
- The **fantasy** genre includes stories that feature imaginary creatures and supernatural abilities, but often take place in settings that resemble real places and cultures in history. Fantasy novels usually follow a gifted protagonist from humble beginnings as they embark on a quest, journey, or adventure and encounter mystical beings and personally challenging obstacles. Common themes in the fantasy genre include personal growth, good versus evil, and the value of the journey. J.R.R. Tolkien's *The Lord of the Rings* trilogy belongs to the fantasy genre.
- **Realistic fiction** describes fictional narratives that include events and characters that do not exist, but could appear in reality. Within the narrative, these characters and events may be depicted in real places. For example, Pip, the protagonist of Charles Dickens's *Great Expectations*, was not a real person, but the novel shows him living in London, England for much of his young adulthood. Realistic fiction contains no far-fetched or impossible elements and presents situations that can or do occur in real life. A contemporary example of realistic fiction is *Wonder* by R.J. Palacio.
- **Historical fiction** includes works that take place in the past and model their setting after real historical cultures, societies, and time periods. These works may include real historical figures and events, but they also may not. Works of historical fiction must be fully informed by the period and location they are set in, meaning both the major and minor details of the work must be historically compatible with the work's setting. Examples of historical fiction include Kathryn Stockett's *The Help* and Markus Zusak's *The Book Thief*.
- The phrase **literary nonfiction** describes nonfiction narratives that present true facts and events in a way that entertains readers and displays creativity. Literary nonfiction, also called creative nonfiction, may resemble fiction in its style and flow, but the truth of the events it describes sets it apart from fictional literature. Different types of books may be considered literary nonfiction, such as biographies, if they appear to employ creativity in their writing. An example of literary nonfiction is *The Immortal Life of Henrietta Lacks* by Rebecca Skloot.

Realism and Satire

Realism

Realism is a literary form with the goal of representing reality as faithfully as possible. Its genesis in Western literature was a reaction against the sentimentality and extreme emotionalism of the works written during the Romantic literary movement, which championed feelings and emotional expression. Realists focused in great detail on immediacy of time and place, on specific actions of their characters, and the justifiable consequences of those actions. Some techniques of **realism** include writing in vernacular (conversational language), using specific dialects, and placing an emphasis on character rather than plot. Realistic literature also often addresses ethical issues. Historically, realistic works have often concentrated on the middle classes of the authors' societies. Realists eschew treatments that are too dramatic or sensationalistic as exaggerations of the reality that they strive to portray as closely as they are able. Influenced by his own bleak past, Fyodor Dostoevsky wrote several novels, such as *Crime and Punishment* (1866) that shunned romantic ideals and sought to portray a stark reality. Henry James was a prominent writer of realism in novels such as *Daisy Miller* (1879). Samuel Clemens (Mark Twain) skillfully represented the language and culture of lower-class Mississippi in his novel *The Adventures of Huckleberry Finn* (1885).

Satire

Satire uses sarcasm, irony, and humor as social criticism to lampoon human folly. Unlike realism, which intends to depict reality as it exists without exaggeration, **satire** often involves creating situations or ideas that deliberately exaggerate reality to appear ridiculous to illuminate flawed behaviors. Ancient Roman satirists included Horace and Juvenal. Alexander Pope's poem "The Rape of the Lock" satirized the values of fashionable members of the 18th-century upper-middle class, which Pope found shallow and trivial. The theft of a lock of hair from a young woman is blown out of proportion: the poem's characters regard it as seriously as they would a rape. Irishman Jonathan Swift satirized British society, politics, and religion in works like "A Modest Proposal" and *Gulliver's Travels.* In "A Modest Proposal," Swift used essay form and mock-serious tone, satirically "proposing" cannibalism of babies and children as a solution to poverty and overpopulation. He satirized petty political disputes in *Gulliver's Travels.*

Types of Stories

Other Common Types of Prose

- A **narrative** is any composition that tells a story. Narratives have characters, settings, and a structure. Narratives may be fiction or nonfiction stories and may follow a linear or nonlinear structure. The purpose of a narrative is generally to entertain, but nonfiction narratives can be informative, as well. Narratives also appear in a variety of structures and formats.
- **Biographies** are books written about another person's life. Biographies can be valuable historical resources. Though they provide a narrow view of the relevant time period and culture, their specificity can also provide a unique context for that period or culture. Biographies, especially those whose subject was a well-known and influential figure, can provide a more complete picture of the figure's life or contributions. Biographies can also serve as a source of inspiration or communicate a moral because of their focus on one person over an extended period of time.

- **Myths** that explain how the world works, its creation, and human behavior exist in most ancient cultures and continue to influence modern cultures. Myths are stories that are part of a certain **mythology**, such as Norse mythology. Myths are so influential that they have even inspired numerous pieces of modern literature and media in popular culture. While popular culture most clearly references myths from the Ancient Greek and Roman cultures, literature has been influenced by mythologies from around the entire world. Since myths are so prevalent in ancient literature, it makes sense that universal themes and morals often appear in mythologies from different cultures. The similarities and parallels in different mythologies (e.g., Greek myths about Zeus are very similar to Roman myths about Jupiter) suggest connections between cultures.
- **Folktales** are stories that have withstood time and are usually popular in a particular region or culture. Folktales often depict the clever success of a common person, though the story may, alternatively, end poorly for the protagonist. A collection of folktales relevant to a particular region or culture is referred to as that culture's **folklore**. There are three common types of folktales: fables, fairy tales, and legends.
    - **Fables** are short, didactic stories that typically feature imaginary creatures or talking animals. The famous story "The Tortoise and the Hare" is a fable. Fables are still told and used today because of their universally understandable morals and characters, which also make them suitable for children's literature and media.
    - **Fairy tales** are stories that involve fictional creatures or realistic characters with fantastical traits and abilities. Fairy tales often end happily and depict the victory of good over evil. The plots and characters in fairy tales are often far-fetched and whimsical.
    - **Legends** are stories that typically focus on one character and highlight their victory over a particular enemy or obstacle. Legends often feature some facts or are inspired by true events, but are generally considered both unproven and unprovable. Heroes are often the protagonists of legends, and they generally save or protect others as they conquer enemies and obstacles.
- A **short story** is a fictional narrative that is shorter than a novel. However, there is not a definite page or word count that defines the short story category. Short stories tend to focus on one or few elements of a story in order to efficiently tell the story. Though they are often brief, short stories may still contain a moral or impact their readers.

Review Video: Myths, Fables, Legends, and Fairy Tales
Visit mometrix.com/academy and enter code: 347199

Poetry

Poetry Terminology

Unlike prose, which traditionally (except in forms like stream of consciousness) consists of complete sentences connected into paragraphs, poetry is written in **verses**. These may form complete sentences, clauses, or phrases. Poetry may be written with or without rhyme. It can be metered, following a particular rhythmic pattern such as iambic, dactylic, spondaic, trochaic, or **anapestic**, or may be without regular meter. The terms **iamb** and **trochee**, among others, identify stressed and unstressed syllables in each verse. Meter is also described by the number of beats or stressed syllables per verse: **dimeter** (2), **trimeter** (3), **tetrameter** (4), **pentameter** (5), and so forth. Using the symbol ᴗ to denote unstressed and / to denote stressed syllables, **iambic** = ᴗ/; **trochaic** = /ᴗ; **spondaic** =//; **dactylic** =/ᴗᴗ; **anapestic** =ᴗᴗ/. **Rhyme schemes** identify which lines rhyme, such as ABAB, ABCA, AABA, and so on. Poetry with neither rhyme nor meter is called **free verse**. Poems may be in free verse, metered but unrhymed, rhymed but without meter, or using both rhyme and meter. In English, the most common meter is iambic pentameter. Unrhymed iambic pentameter is called **blank verse**.

Review Video: Different Types of Rhyme
Visit mometrix.com/academy and enter code: 999342

Review Video: Evocative Words and Rhythm
Visit mometrix.com/academy and enter code: 894610

Major Forms of Poetry

From man's earliest days, he expressed himself with poetry. A large percentage of the surviving literature from ancient times is in **epic poetry**, utilized by Homer and other Greco-Roman poets. Epic poems typically recount heroic deeds and adventures, using stylized language and combining dramatic and lyrical conventions. **Epistolary poems**, poems that are written and read as letters, also developed in ancient times. In the fourteenth and fifteenth centuries, the **ballad** became a popular convention. Ballads often follow a rhyme scheme and meter and focus on subjects such as love, death, and religion. Many ballads tell stories, and several modern ballads are put to music. From these early conventions, numerous other poetic forms developed, such as **elegies**, **odes**, and **pastoral poems**. Elegies are mourning poems written in three parts: lament, praise of the deceased, and solace for loss. Odes evolved from songs to the typical poem of the Romantic time period, expressing strong feelings and contemplative thoughts. Pastoral poems idealize nature and country living. Poetry can also be used to make short, pithy statements. **Epigrams** (memorable rhymes with one or two lines) and **limericks** (two lines of iambic dimeter followed by two lines of iambic dimeter and another of iambic trimeter) are known for humor and wit.

Haiku

Haiku was originally a Japanese poetry form. In the 13th century, haiku was the opening phrase of renga, a 100-stanza oral poem. By the 16th century, haiku diverged into a separate short poem. When Western writers discovered haiku, the form became popular in English, as well as other languages. A haiku has 17 syllables, traditionally distributed across three lines as 5/7/5, with a pause after the first or second line. Haiku are syllabic and unrhymed. Haiku philosophy and technique are that brevity's compression forces writers to express images concisely, depict a moment in time, and evoke illumination and enlightenment. An example is 17th-century haiku master Matsuo Basho's classic: "An old silent pond... / A frog jumps into the pond, / splash! Silence again." Modern American poet Ezra Pound revealed the influence of haiku in his two-line poem "In a Station of the Metro." In this poem, line 1 has 12 syllables (combining the syllable count of the first two lines of a haiku) and line 2 has 7, but it still preserves haiku's philosophy and imagistic technique: "The apparition of these faces in the crowd; / Petals on a wet, black bough."

SONNETS

The sonnet traditionally has 14 lines of iambic pentameter, tightly organized around a theme. The Petrarchan sonnet, named for 14th-century Italian poet Petrarch, has an eight-line stanza, the octave, and a six-line stanza, the sestet. There is a change or turn, known as the volta, between the eighth and ninth verses, setting up the sestet's answer or summary. The rhyme scheme is ABBA/ABBA/CDECDE or CDCDCD. The English or Shakespearean sonnet has three quatrains and one couplet, with the rhyme scheme ABAB/CDCD/EFEF/GG. This format better suits English, which has fewer rhymes than Italian. The final couplet often contrasts sharply with the preceding quatrains, as in Shakespeare's sonnets—for example, Sonnet 130, "My mistress' eyes are nothing like the sun...And yet, by heaven, I think my love as rare / As any she belied with false compare." Variations on the sonnet form include Edmund Spenser's Spenserian sonnet in the 16th century, John Milton's Miltonic sonnet in the 17th century, and sonnet sequences. Sonnet sequences are seen in works such as John Donne's *La Corona* and Elizabeth Barrett Browning's *Sonnets from the Portuguese.*

Review Video: Structural Elements of Poetry
Visit mometrix.com/academy and enter code: 265216

Plot and Story Structure

PLOT AND STORY STRUCTURE

The **plot** includes the events that happen in a story and the order in which they are told to the reader. There are several types of plot structures, as stories can be told in many ways. The most common plot structure is the chronological plot, which presents the events to the reader in the same order they occur for the characters in the story. Chronological plots usually have five main parts, the **exposition**, **rising action**, the **climax**, **falling action**, and the **resolution**. This type of plot structure guides the reader through the story's events as the characters experience them and is the easiest structure to understand and identify. While this is the most common plot structure, many stories are nonlinear, which means the plot does not sequence events in the same order the characters experience them. Such stories might include elements like flashbacks that cause the story to be nonlinear.

Review Video: How to Make a Story Map
Visit mometrix.com/academy and enter code: 261719

EXPOSITION

The **exposition** is at the beginning of the story and generally takes place before the rising action begins. The purpose of the exposition is to give the reader context for the story, which the author may do by introducing one or more characters, describing the setting or world, or explaining the events leading up to the point where the story begins. The exposition may still include events that contribute to the plot, but the **rising action** and main conflict of the story are not part of the exposition. Some narratives skip the exposition and begin the story with the beginning of the rising action, which causes the reader to learn the context as the story intensifies.

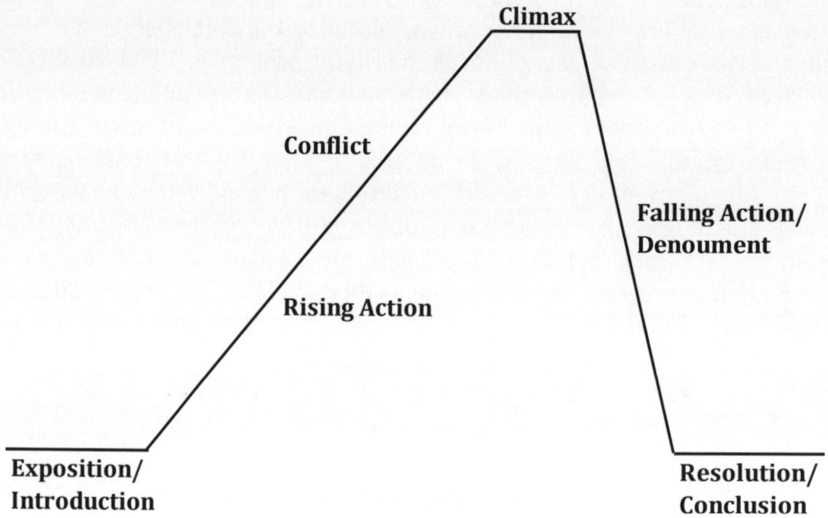

Review Video: Plot Line
Visit mometrix.com/academy and enter code: 944011

CONFLICT

A **conflict** is a problem to be solved. Literary plots typically include one conflict or more. Characters' attempts to resolve conflicts drive the narrative's forward movement. **Conflict resolution** is often the protagonist's primary occupation. Physical conflicts like exploring, wars, and escapes tend to make plots most suspenseful and exciting. Emotional, mental, or moral conflicts tend to make stories more personally gratifying or rewarding for many audiences. Conflicts can be external or internal. A major type of internal conflict is some inner personal battle, or **man versus self**. Major types of external conflicts include **man versus nature**, **man versus man**, and **man versus society**. Readers can identify conflicts in literary plots by identifying the protagonist and antagonist and asking why they conflict, what events develop the conflict, where the climax occurs, and how they identify with the characters.

Read the following paragraph and discuss the type of conflict present:

> Timothy was shocked out of sleep by the appearance of a bear just outside his tent. After panicking for a moment, he remembered some advice he had read in preparation for this trip: he should make noise so the bear would not be startled. As Timothy started to hum and sing, the bear wandered away.

There are three main types of conflict in literature: **man versus man**, **man versus nature**, and **man versus self**. This paragraph is an example of man versus nature. Timothy is in conflict with the bear. Even though no physical conflict like an attack exists, Timothy is pitted against the bear. Timothy uses his knowledge to "defeat" the bear and keep himself safe. The solution to the conflict is that Timothy makes noise, the bear wanders away, and Timothy is safe.

Review Video: Conflict
Visit mometrix.com/academy and enter code: 559550

Review Video: Determining Relationships in a Story
Visit mometrix.com/academy and enter code: 929925

Rising Action

The **rising action** is the part of the story where conflict **intensifies**. The rising action begins with an event that prompts the main conflict of the story. This may also be called the **inciting incident**. The main conflict generally occurs between the protagonist and an antagonist, but this is not the only type of conflict that may occur in a narrative. After this event, the protagonist works to resolve the main conflict by preparing for an altercation, pursuing a goal, fleeing an antagonist, or doing some other action that will end the conflict. The rising action is composed of several additional events that increase the story's tension. Most often, other developments will occur alongside the growth of the main conflict, such as character development or the development of minor conflicts. The rising action ends with the **climax**, which is the point of highest tension in the story.

Climax

The **climax** is the event in the narrative that marks the height of the story's conflict or tension. The event that takes place at the story's climax will end the rising action and bring about the results of the main conflict. If the conflict was between a good protagonist and an evil antagonist, the climax may be a final battle between the two characters. If the conflict is an adventurer looking for heavily guarded treasure, the climax may be the adventurer's encounter with the final obstacle that protects the treasure. The climax may be made of multiple scenes, but can usually be summarized as one event. Once the conflict and climax are complete, the **falling action** begins.

Falling Action

The **falling action** shows what happens in the story between the climax and the resolution. The falling action often composes a much smaller portion of the story than the rising action does. While the climax includes the end of the main conflict, the falling action may show the results of any minor conflicts in the story. For example, if the protagonist encountered a troll on the way to find some treasure, and the troll demanded the protagonist share the treasure after retrieving it, the falling action would include the protagonist returning to share the treasure with the troll. Similarly, any unexplained major events are usually made clear during the falling action. Once all significant elements of the story are resolved or addressed, the story's resolution will occur. The **resolution** is the end of the story, which shows the final result of the plot's events and shows what life is like for the main characters once they are no longer experiencing the story's conflicts.

Resolution

The way the conflict is **resolved** depends on the type of conflict. The plot of any book starts with the lead up to the conflict, then the conflict itself, and finally the solution, or **resolution**, to the conflict. In **man versus man** conflicts, the conflict is often resolved by two parties coming to some sort of agreement or by one party triumphing over the other party. In **man versus nature** conflicts, the conflict is often resolved by man coming to some realization about some aspect of nature. In **man versus self** conflicts, the conflict is often resolved by the character growing or coming to an understanding about part of himself.

Theme

A **theme** is a central idea demonstrated by a passage. Often, a theme is a lesson or moral contained in the text, but it does not have to be. It also is a unifying idea that is used throughout the text; it can take the form of a common setting, idea, symbol, design, or recurring event. A passage can have two or more themes that convey its overall idea. The theme or themes of a passage are often based on **universal themes**. They can frequently be expressed using well-known sayings about life, society, or human nature, such as "Hard work pays off" or "Good triumphs over evil." Themes are not usually stated **explicitly**. The reader must figure them out by carefully reading the passage. Themes are created through descriptive language or events in the plot. The events of a story help shape the themes of a passage.

Example

Explain why "if you care about something, you need to take care of it" accurately describes the theme of the following excerpt.

> Luca collected baseball cards, but he wasn't very careful with them. He left them around the house. His dog liked to chew. One day, Luca and his friend Bart were looking at his collection. Then they went outside. When Luca got home, he saw his dog chewing on his cards. They were ruined.

This excerpt tells the story of a boy who is careless with his baseball cards and leaves them lying around. His dog ends up chewing them and ruining them. The lesson is that if you care about something, you need to take care of it. This is the theme, or point, of the story. Some stories have more than one theme, but this is not really true of this excerpt. The reader needs to figure out the theme based on what happens in the story. Sometimes, as in the case of fables, the theme is stated directly in the text. However, this is not usually the case.

Review Video: Themes in Literature
Visit mometrix.com/academy and enter code: 732074

Narrator's Point of View

Point of View

Another element that impacts a text is the author's point of view. The **point of view** of a text is the perspective from which a passage is told. An author will always have a point of view about a story before he or she draws up a plot line. The author will know what events they want to take place, how they want the characters to interact, and how they want the story to resolve. An author will also have an opinion on the topic or series of events which is presented in the story that is based on their prior experience and beliefs.

The two main points of view that authors use, especially in a work of fiction, are first person and third person. If the narrator of the story is also the main character, or *protagonist*, the text is written in first-person point of view. In first person, the author writes from the perspective of *I*. Third-person point of view is probably the most common that authors use in their passages. Using third person, authors refer to each character by using *he* or *she*. In third-person omniscient, the narrator is not a character in the story and tells the story of all of the characters at the same time.

Review Video: Point of View
Visit mometrix.com/academy and enter code: 383336

First-Person Narration

First-person narratives let narrators express inner feelings and thoughts, especially when the narrator is the protagonist as Lemuel Gulliver is in Jonathan Swift's *Gulliver's Travels.* The narrator may be a close friend of the protagonist, like Dr. Watson in Sir Arthur Conan Doyle's *Sherlock Holmes.* Or, the narrator can be less involved with the main characters and plot, like Nick Carraway in F. Scott Fitzgerald's *The Great Gatsby.* When a narrator reports others' narratives, she or he is a "**frame narrator**," like the nameless narrator of Joseph Conrad's *Heart of Darkness* or Mr. Lockwood in Emily Brontë's *Wuthering Heights.* **First-person plural** is unusual but can be effective. Isaac Asimov's *I, Robot*, William Faulkner's *A Rose for Emily*, Maxim Gorky's *Twenty-Six Men and a Girl*, and Jeffrey Eugenides' *The Virgin Suicides* all use first-person plural narration. Author Kurt Vonnegut is the first-person narrator in his semi-autobiographical novel *Timequake.* Also unusual, but effective, is a **first-person omniscient** (rather than the more common third-person omniscient) narrator, like Death in Markus Zusak's *The Book Thief* and the ghost in Alice Sebold's *The Lovely Bones.*

SECOND-PERSON NARRATION

While **second-person** address is very commonplace in popular song lyrics, it is the least used form of narrative voice in literary works. Popular serial books of the 1980s like *Fighting Fantasy* or *Choose Your Own Adventure* employed second-person narratives. In some cases, a narrative combines both second-person and first-person voices, using the pronouns *you* and *I*. This can draw readers into the story, and it can also enable the authors to compare directly "your" and "my" feelings, thoughts, and actions. When the narrator is also a character in the story, as in Edgar Allan Poe's short story "The Tell-Tale Heart" or Jay McInerney's novel *Bright Lights, Big City,* the narrative is better defined as first-person despite it also addressing "you."

THIRD-PERSON NARRATION

Narration in the third person is the most prevalent type, as it allows authors the most flexibility. It is so common that readers simply assume without needing to be informed that the narrator is not a character in the story, or involved in its events. **Third-person singular** is used more frequently than **third-person plural**, though some authors have also effectively used plural. However, both singular and plural are most often included in stories according to which characters are being described. The third-person narrator may be either objective or subjective, and either omniscient or limited. **Objective third-person** narration does not include what the characters described are thinking or feeling, while **subjective third-person** narration does. The **third-person omniscient** narrator knows everything about all characters, including their thoughts and emotions, and all related places, times, and events. However, the **third-person limited** narrator may know everything about a particular character, but is limited to that character. In other words, the narrator cannot speak about anything that character does not know.

ALTERNATING-PERSON NARRATION

Although authors more commonly write stories from one point of view, there are also instances wherein they alternate the narrative voice within the same book. For example, they may sometimes use an omniscient third-person narrator and a more intimate first-person narrator at other times. In J. K. Rowling's series of *Harry Potter* novels, she often writes in a third-person limited narrative, but sometimes changes to narration by characters other than the protagonist. George R. R. Martin's series *A Song of Ice and Fire* changes the point of view to coincide with divisions between chapters. The same technique is used by Erin Hunter (a pseudonym for several authors of the *Warriors, Seekers,* and *Survivors* book series). Authors using first-person narrative sometimes switch to third-person to describe significant action scenes, especially those where the narrator was absent or uninvolved, as Barbara Kingsolver does in her novel *The Poisonwood Bible.*

Review Video: The Narrator of a Story
Visit mometrix.com/academy and enter code: 742528

Setting, Mood, and Tone

Setting and Time Frame

A literary text has both a setting and time frame. A **setting** is the place in which the story as a whole is set. The **time frame** is the period in which the story is set. This may refer to the historical period the story takes place in or if the story takes place over a single day. Both setting and time frame are relevant to a text's meaning because they help the reader place the story in time and space. An author uses setting and time frame to anchor a text, create a mood, and enhance its meaning. This helps a reader understand why a character acts the way he does, or why certain events in the story are important. The setting impacts the **plot** and character **motivations**, while the time frame helps place the story in **chronological context**.

Example

Read the following excerpt from The Adventures of Huckleberry Finn by Mark Twain and analyze the relevance of setting to the text's meaning:

> We said there warn't no home like a raft, after all. Other places do seem so cramped up and smothery, but a raft don't. You feel mighty free and easy and comfortable on a raft.

This excerpt from *The Adventures of Huckleberry Finn* by Mark Twain reveals information about the **setting** of the book. By understanding that the main character, Huckleberry Finn, lives on a raft, the reader can place the story on a river, in this case, the Mississippi River in the South before the Civil War. The information about the setting also gives the reader clues about the **character** of Huck Finn: he clearly values independence and freedom, and he likes the outdoors. The information about the setting in the quote helps the reader to better understand the rest of the text.

Syntax and Word Choice

Authors use words and **syntax**, or sentence structure, to make their texts unique, convey their own writing style, and sometimes to make a point or emphasis. They know that word choice and syntax contribute to the reader's understanding of the text as well as to the tone and mood of a text.

Review Video: Syntax
Visit mometrix.com/academy and enter code: 242280

Mood and Tone

Mood is a story's atmosphere, or the feelings the reader gets from reading it. The way authors set the mood in writing is comparable to the way filmmakers use music to set the mood in movies. Instead of music, though, writers judiciously select descriptive words to evoke certain **moods**. The mood of a work may convey joy, anger, bitterness, hope, gloom, fear, apprehension, or any other emotion the author wants the reader to feel. In addition to vocabulary choices, authors also use figurative expressions, particular sentence structures, and choices of diction that project and reinforce the moods they want to create. Whereas mood is the reader's emotions evoked by reading what is written, **tone** is the emotions and attitudes of the writer that she or he expresses in the writing. Authors use the same literary techniques to establish tone as they do to establish mood. An author may use a humorous tone, an angry or sad tone, a sentimental or unsentimental tone, or something else entirely.

Mood and Tone in The Great Gatsby

To understand the difference between mood and tone, look at this excerpt from F. Scott Fitzgerald's *The Great Gatsby*. In this passage, Nick Caraway, the novel's narrator, is describing his affordable house, which sits in a neighborhood full of expensive mansions.

> "I lived at West Egg, the—well the less fashionable of the two, though this is a most superficial tag to express the bizarre and not a little sinister contrast between them. My house was at the very tip of the egg, only fifty yard from the Sound, and squeezed between two huge places that rented for twelve or fifteen thousand a season ... My own house was an eyesore, but it was a small eyesore, and it had been overlooked, so I had a view of the water, a partial view of my neighbor's lawn, and the consoling proximity of millionaires—all for eighty dollars a month."

In this description, the mood created for the reader does not match the tone created through the narrator. The mood in this passage is one of dissatisfaction and inferiority. Nick compares his home to his neighbors', saying he lives in the "less fashionable" neighborhood and that his house is "overlooked," an "eyesore," and "squeezed between two huge" mansions. He also adds that his placement allows him the "consoling proximity of millionaires." A literal reading of these details leads the reader to have negative feelings toward Nick's house and his economic inferiority to his neighbors, creating the mood.

However, Fitzgerald also conveys an opposing attitude, or tone, through Nick's description. Nick calls the distinction between the neighborhoods "superficial," showing a suspicion of the value suggested by the neighborhoods' titles, properties, and residents. Nick also undermines his critique of his own home by calling it "a small eyesore" and claiming it has "been overlooked." However, he follows these statements with a description of his surroundings, claiming that he has "a view of the water" and can see some of his wealthy neighbor's property from his home, and a comparison between the properties' rent. While the mental image created for the reader depicts a small house shoved between looming mansions, the tone suggests that Nick enjoys these qualities about his home, or at least finds it charming. He acknowledges its shortcomings, but includes the benefits of his home's unassuming appearance.

Review Video: Style, Tone, and Mood
Visit mometrix.com/academy and enter code: 416961

Historical and Social Context

Fiction that is heavily influenced by a historical or social context cannot be comprehended as the author intended if the reader does not keep this context in mind. Many important elements of the text will be influenced by any context, including symbols, allusions, settings, and plot events. These contexts, as well as the identity of the work's author, can help to inform the reader about the author's concerns and intended meanings. For example, George Orwell published his novel *1984* in the year 1949, soon after the end of World War II. At that time, following the defeat of the Nazis, the Cold War began between the Western Allied nations and the Eastern Soviet Communists. People were therefore concerned about the conflict between the freedoms afforded by Western democracies versus the oppression represented by Communism. Orwell had also previously fought in the Spanish Civil War against a Spanish regime that he and his fellows viewed as oppressive. From this information, readers can infer that Orwell was concerned about oppression by totalitarian governments. This informs *1984*'s story of Winston Smith's rebellion against the oppressive "Big Brother" government, of the fictional dictatorial state of Oceania, and his capture, torture, and ultimate conversion by that government. Some literary theories also seek to use historical and social contexts to reveal deeper meanings and implications in a text.

Character Development and Dialogue

Character Development

When depicting characters or figures in a written text, authors generally use actions, dialogue, and descriptions as characterization techniques. Characterization can occur in both fiction and nonfiction and is used to show a character or figure's personality, demeanor, and thoughts. This helps create a more engaging experience for the reader by providing a more concrete picture of a character or figure's tendencies and features. Characterizations also gives authors the opportunity to integrate elements such as dialects, activities, attire, and attitudes into their writing.

To understand the meaning of a story, it is vital to understand the characters as the author describes them. We can look for contradictions in what a character thinks, says, and does. We can notice whether the author's observations about a character differ from what other characters in the story say about that character. A character may be dynamic, meaning they change significantly during the story, or static, meaning they remain the same from beginning to end. Characters may be two-dimensional, not fully developed, or may be well developed with characteristics that stand out vividly. Characters may also symbolize universal properties. Additionally, readers can compare and contrast characters to analyze how each one developed.

A well-known example of character development can be found in Charles Dickens's *Great Expectations*. The novel's main character, Pip, is introduced as a young boy, and he is depicted as innocent, kind, and humble. However, as Pip grows up and is confronted with the social hierarchy of Victorian England, he becomes arrogant and rejects his loved ones in pursuit of his own social advancement. Once he achieves his social goals, he realizes the merits of his former lifestyle, and lives with the wisdom he gained in both environments and life stages. Dickens shows Pip's ever-changing character through his interactions with others and his inner thoughts, which evolve as his personal values and personality shift.

Dialogue

Effectively written dialogue serves at least one, but usually several, purposes. It advances the story and moves the plot, develops the characters, sheds light on the work's theme or meaning, and can, often subtly, account for the passage of time not otherwise indicated. It can alter the direction that the plot is taking, typically by introducing some new conflict or changing existing ones. **Dialogue** can establish a work's narrative voice and the characters' voices and set the tone of the story or of particular characters. When fictional characters display enlightenment or realization, dialogue can give readers an understanding of what those characters have discovered and how. Dialogue can illuminate the motivations and wishes of the story's characters. By using consistent thoughts and syntax, dialogue can support character development. Skillfully created, it can also represent real-life speech rhythms in written form. Via conflicts and ensuing action, dialogue also provides drama.

Dialogue in Fiction

In fictional works, effectively written dialogue does more than just break up or interrupt sections of narrative. While **dialogue** may supply exposition for readers, it must nonetheless be believable. Dialogue should be dynamic, not static, and it should not resemble regular prose. Authors should not use dialogue to write clever similes or metaphors, or to inject their own opinions. Nor should they use dialogue at all when narrative would be better. Most importantly, dialogue should not slow the plot movement. Dialogue must seem natural, which means careful construction of phrases rather than actually duplicating natural speech, which does not necessarily translate well to the written word. Finally, all dialogue must be pertinent to the story, rather than just added conversation.

Figurative Language

Literal and Figurative Meaning

When language is used **literally**, the words mean exactly what they say and nothing more. When language is used **figuratively**, the words mean something beyond their literal meaning. For example, "The weeping willow tree has long, trailing branches and leaves" is a literal description. But "The weeping willow tree looks as if it is bending over and crying" is a figurative description—specifically, a **simile** or stated comparison. Another figurative language form is **metaphor**, or an implied comparison. A good example is the metaphor of a city, state, or city-state as a ship, and its governance as sailing that ship. Ancient Greek lyrical poet Alcaeus is credited with first using this metaphor, and ancient Greek tragedian Aeschylus then used it in *Seven Against Thebes,* and then Plato used it in the *Republic.*

Figures of Speech

A **figure of speech** is a verbal expression whose meaning is figurative rather than literal. For example, the phrase "butterflies in the stomach" does not refer to actual butterflies in a person's stomach. It is a metaphor representing the fluttery feelings experienced when a person is nervous or excited—or when one "falls in love," which does not mean physically falling. "Hitting a sales target" does not mean physically hitting a target with arrows as in archery; it is a metaphor for meeting a sales quota. "Climbing the ladder of success" metaphorically likens advancing in one's career to ascending ladder rungs. Similes, such as "light as a feather" (meaning very light, not a feather's actual weight), and hyperbole, like "I'm starving/freezing/roasting," are also figures of speech. Figures of speech are often used and crafted for emphasis, freshness of expression, or clarity.

Review Video: Figures of Speech
Visit mometrix.com/academy and enter code: 111295

Figurative Language

Figurative language extends past the literal meanings of words. It offers readers new insight into the people, things, events, and subjects covered in a work of literature. Figurative language also enables readers to feel they are sharing the authors' experiences. It can stimulate the reader's senses, make comparisons that readers find intriguing or even startling, and enable readers to view the world in different ways. When looking for figurative language, it is important to consider the context of the sentence or situation. Phrases that appear out of place or make little sense when read literally are likely instances of figurative language. Once figurative language has been recognized, context is also important to determining the type of figurative language being used and its function. For example, when a comparison is being made, a metaphor or simile is likely being used. This means the comparison may emphasize or create irony through the things being compared. Seven specific types of figurative language include: alliteration, onomatopoeia, personification, imagery, similes, metaphors, and hyperbole.

Review Video: Figurative Language
Visit mometrix.com/academy and enter code: 584902

Alliteration and Onomatopoeia

Alliteration describes a series of words beginning with the same sounds. **Onomatopoeia** uses words imitating the sounds of things they name or describe. For example, in his poem "Come Down, O Maid," Alfred Tennyson writes of "The moan of doves in immemorial elms, / And murmuring of innumerable bees." The word "moan" sounds like some sounds doves make, "murmuring" represents the sounds of bees buzzing. Onomatopoeia also includes words that are simply meant to represent sounds, such as "meow," "kaboom," and "whoosh."

Review Video: Alliteration in Everyday Expressions
Visit mometrix.com/academy and enter code: 462837

Personification

Another type of figurative language is **personification**. This is describing a non-human thing, like an animal or an object, as if it were human. The general intent of personification is to describe things in a manner that will be comprehensible to readers. When an author states that a tree *groans* in the wind, he or she does not mean that the tree is emitting a low, pained sound from a mouth. Instead, the author means that the tree is making a noise similar to a human groan. Of course, this personification establishes a tone of sadness or suffering. A different tone would be established if the author said that the tree was *swaying* or *dancing*. Alfred Tennyson's poem "The Eagle" uses all of these types of figurative language: "He clasps the crag with crooked hands." Tennyson used alliteration, repeating /k/ and /kr/ sounds. These hard-sounding consonants reinforce the imagery, giving visual and tactile impressions of the eagle.

Review Video: Personification
Visit mometrix.com/academy and enter code: 260066

Similes and Metaphors

Similes are stated comparisons using "like" or "as." Similes can be used to stimulate readers' imaginations and appeal to their senses. Because a simile includes *like* or *as,* the device creates more space between the description and the thing being described than a metaphor does. If an author says that *a house was like a shoebox*, then the tone is different than the author saying that the house *was* a shoebox. Authors will choose between a metaphor and a simile depending on their intended tone.

Similes also help compare fictional characters to well-known objects or experiences, so the reader can better relate to them. William Wordsworth's poem about "Daffodils" begins, "I wandered lonely as a cloud." This simile compares his loneliness to that of a cloud. It is also personification, giving a cloud the human quality loneliness. In his novel *Lord Jim* (1900), Joseph Conrad writes in Chapter 33, "I would have given anything for the power to soothe her frail soul, tormenting itself in its invincible ignorance like a small bird beating about the cruel wires of a cage." Conrad uses the word "like" to compare the girl's soul to a small bird. His description of the bird beating at the cage shows the similar helplessness of the girl's soul to gain freedom.

Review Video: Similes
Visit mometrix.com/academy and enter code: 642949

A **metaphor** is a type of figurative language in which the writer equates something with another thing that is not particularly similar, instead of using *like* or *as*. For instance, *the bird was an arrow arcing through the sky*. In this sentence, the arrow is serving as a metaphor for the bird. The point of a metaphor is to encourage the reader to consider the item being described in a *different way*. Let's continue with this metaphor for a flying bird. You are asked to envision the bird's flight as being similar to the arc of an arrow. So, you imagine the flight to be swift and bending. Metaphors are a way for the author to describe an item *without being direct and obvious*. This literary device is a lyrical and suggestive way of providing information. Note that the reference for a metaphor will not always be mentioned explicitly by the author. Consider the following description of a forest in winter: *Swaying skeletons reached for the sky and groaned as the wind blew through them.* In this example, the author is using *skeletons* as a metaphor for leafless trees. This metaphor creates a spooky tone while inspiring the reader's imagination.

Literary Examples of Metaphor

A **metaphor** is an implied comparison, i.e., it compares something to something else without using "like", "as", or other comparative words. For example, in "The Tyger" (1794), William Blake writes, "Tyger Tyger, burning bright, / In the forests of the night." Blake compares the tiger to a flame not by saying it is like a fire, but by simply describing it as "burning." Henry Wadsworth Longfellow's poem "O Ship of State" (1850) uses an extended metaphor by referring consistently throughout the entire poem to the state, union, or republic as a seagoing vessel, referring to its keel, mast, sail, rope, anchors, and to its braving waves, rocks, gale, tempest, and "false lights on the shore." Within the extended metaphor, Longfellow uses a specific metaphor: "the anchors of thy hope!"

Ted Hughes' Animal Metaphors

Ted Hughes frequently used animal metaphors in his poetry. In "The Thought Fox," a model of concise, structured beauty, Hughes characterizes the poet's creative process with succinct, striking imagery of an idea entering his head like a wild fox. Repeating "loneliness" in the first two stanzas emphasizes the poet's lonely work: "Something else is alive / Beside the clock's loneliness." He treats an idea's arrival as separate from himself. Three stanzas detail in vivid images a fox's approach from the outside winter forest at starless midnight—its nose, "Cold, delicately" touching twigs and leaves; "neat" paw prints in snow; "bold" body; brilliant green eyes; and self-contained, focused progress—"Till, with a sudden sharp hot stink of fox," he metaphorically depicts poetic inspiration as the fox's physical entry into "the dark hole of the head." Hughes ends by summarizing his vision of a poet as an interior, passive idea recipient, with the outside world unchanged: "The window is starless still; the clock ticks, / The page is printed."

Review Video: Metaphors in Writing
Visit mometrix.com/academy and enter code: 133295

Metonymy

Metonymy is naming one thing with words or phrases of a closely related thing. This is similar to metaphor. However, the comparison has a close connection, unlike metaphor. An example of metonymy is to call the news media *the press*. Of course, *the press* is the machine that prints newspapers. Metonymy is a way of naming something without using the same name constantly.

Synecdoche

Synecdoche points to the whole by naming one of the parts. An example of synecdoche would be calling a construction worker a *hard hat*. Like metonymy, synecdoche is an easy way of naming something without having to overuse a name. The device allows writers to highlight pieces of the thing being described. For example, referring to businessmen as *suits* suggests professionalism and unity.

Review Video: Metonymy and Synecdoche
Visit mometrix.com/academy and enter code: 900306

Hyperbole

Hyperbole is excessive exaggeration used for humor or emphasis rather than for literal meaning. For example, in *To Kill a Mockingbird*, Harper Lee wrote, "People moved slowly then. There was no hurry, for there was nowhere to go, nothing to buy and no money to buy it with, nothing to see outside the boundaries of Maycomb County." This was not literally true; Lee exaggerates the scarcity of these things for emphasis. In "Old Times on the Mississippi," Mark Twain wrote, "I... could have hung my hat on my eyes, they stuck out so far." This is not literal, but makes his description vivid and funny. In his poem "As I Walked Out One Evening", W. H. Auden wrote, "I'll love you, dear, I'll love you / Till China and Africa meet, / And the river jumps over the mountain / And the salmon sing in the street." He used things not literally possible to emphasize the duration of his love.

Understatement

Understatement is the opposite of hyperbole. This device discounts or downplays something. Think about someone who climbs Mount Everest. Then, they say that the journey was *a little stroll*. As with other types of figurative language, understatement has a range of uses. The device may show self-defeat or modesty as in the Mount Everest example. However, some may think of understatement as false modesty (i.e., an attempt to bring attention to you or a situation). For example, a woman is praised on her diamond engagement ring. The woman says, *Oh, this little thing?* Her understatement might be heard as stuck-up or unfeeling.

Review Video: Hyperbole and Understatement
Visit mometrix.com/academy and enter code: 308470

Literary Devices

Literary Irony

In literature, irony demonstrates the opposite of what is said or done. The three types of irony are **verbal irony**, **situational irony**, and **dramatic irony**. Verbal irony uses words opposite to the meaning. Sarcasm may use verbal irony. One common example is describing something that is confusing as "clear as mud." For example, in his 1986 movie *Hannah and Her Sisters*, author, director, and actor Woody Allen says to his character's date, "I had a great evening; it was like the Nuremburg Trials." Notice these employ similes. In situational irony, what happens contrasts with what was expected. O. Henry's short story *The Gift of the Magi* uses situational irony: a husband and wife each sacrifice their most prized possession to buy each other a Christmas present. The irony is that she sells her long hair to buy him a watch fob, while he sells his heirloom pocket-watch to buy her the jeweled combs for her hair she had long wanted; in the end, neither of them can use their gifts. In dramatic irony, narrative informs audiences of more than its characters know. For example, in *Romeo and Juliet*, the audience is made aware that Juliet is only asleep, while Romeo believes her to be dead, which then leads to Romeo's death.

Review Video: Irony
Visit mometrix.com/academy and enter code: 374204

Idioms

Idioms create comparisons, and often take the form of similes or metaphors. Idioms are always phrases and are understood to have a meaning that is different from its individual words' literal meaning. For example, "break a leg" is a common idiom that is used to wish someone luck or tell them to perform well. Literally, the phrase "break a leg" means to injure a person's leg, but the phrase takes on a different meaning when used as an idiom. Another example is "call it a day," which means to temporarily stop working on a task, or find a stopping point, rather than literally referring to something as "a day." Many idioms are associated with a region or group. For example, an idiom commonly used in the American South is "'til the cows come home." This phrase is often used to indicate that something will take or may last for a very long time, but not that it will literally last until the cows return to where they reside.

Allusion

An allusion is an uncited but recognizable reference to something else. Authors use language to make allusions to places, events, artwork, and other books in order to make their own text richer. For example, an author may allude to a very important text in order to make his own text seem more important. Martin Luther King, Jr. started his "I Have a Dream" speech by saying "Five score years ago…" This is a clear allusion to President Abraham Lincoln's "Gettysburg Address" and served to remind people of the significance of the event. An author may allude to a place to ground his text or make a cultural reference to make readers feel included. There are many reasons that authors make allusions.

Review Video: Allusions
Visit mometrix.com/academy and enter code: 294065

Comic Relief

Comic relief is the use of comedy by an author to break up a dramatic or tragic scene and infuse it with a bit of **lightheartedness**. In William Shakespeare's *Hamlet*, two gravediggers digging the grave for Ophelia share a joke while they work. The death and burial of Ophelia are tragic moments that directly follow each other. Shakespeare uses an instance of comedy to break up the tragedy and give his audience a bit of a break from the tragic drama. Authors sometimes use comic relief so that their work will be less depressing; other times they use it to create irony or contrast between the darkness of the situation and the lightness of the joke. Often, authors will use comedy to parallel what is happening in the tragic scenes.

Review Video: Comic Relief
Visit mometrix.com/academy and enter code: 779604

Foreshadowing

Foreshadowing is a device authors use to give readers **hints** about events that will take place later in a story. Foreshadowing most often takes place through a character's dialogue or actions. Sometimes the character will know what is going to happen and will purposefully allude to future events. For example, consider a protagonist who is about to embark on a journey through the woods. Just before the protagonist begins the trip, another character says, "Be careful, you never know what could be out in those woods!" This alerts the reader that the woods may be dangerous and prompts the reader to expect something to attack the protagonist in the woods. This is an example of foreshadowing through warning. Alternatively, a character may unknowingly foreshadow later events. For example, consider a story where a brother and sister run through their house and knock over a vase and break it. The brother says, "Don't worry, we'll clean it up! Mom will never know!" However, the reader knows that their mother will most likely find out what they have done, so the reader expects the siblings to later get in trouble for running, breaking the vase, and hiding it from their mother.

Symbolism

Symbolism describes an author's use of a **symbol**, an element of the story that **represents** something else. Symbols can impact stories in many ways, including deepening the meaning of a story or its elements, comparing a story to another work, or foreshadowing later events in a story. Symbols can be objects, characters, colors, numbers, or anything else the author establishes as a symbol. Symbols can be clearly established through direct comparison or repetition, but they can also be established subtly or gradually over a large portion of the story. Another form of symbolism is **allusion**, which is when something in a story is used to prompt the reader to think about another work. Many well-known works use **Biblical allusions**, which are allusions to events or details in the Bible that inform a work or an element within it.

Examples of Themes and Plots in Literature

Themes in Literature

When we read parables, their themes are the lessons they aim to teach. When we read fables, the moral of each story is its theme. When we read fictional works, the authors' perspectives regarding life and human behavior are their themes. Unlike in parables and fables, themes in literary fiction are usually not meant to preach or teach the readers a lesson. Hence, themes in fiction are not as explicit as they are in parables or fables. Instead, they are implicit, and the reader only infers them. By analyzing the fictional characters through thinking about their actions and behavior, understanding the setting of the story, and reflecting on how its plot develops, the reader comes to infer the main theme of the work. When writers succeed, they communicate with their readers such that common ground is established between author and audience. While a reader's individual experience may differ in its details from the author's written story, both may share universal underlying truths which allow author and audience to connect.

Determining Theme

In well-crafted literature, theme, structure, and plot are interdependent and inextricable: each element informs and reflects the others. The structure of a work is how it is organized. The theme is the central idea or meaning found in it. The plot is what happens in the story. Titles can also inform us of a work's theme. For instance, the title of Edgar Allan Poe's "The Tell-Tale Heart" informs readers of the story's theme of guilt before they even read about the repeated heartbeat the protagonist hears immediately before and constantly after committing and hiding a murder. Repetitive patterns of events or behaviors also give clues to themes. The same is true of symbols. For example, in F. Scott Fitzgerald's *The Great Gatsby,* for Jay Gatsby the green light at the end of the dock symbolizes Daisy Buchanan and his own dreams for the future. More generally, it is also understood as a symbol of the American Dream, and narrator Nick Carraway explicitly compares it to early settlers' sight of America rising from the ocean.

Thematic Development

Theme in The Great Gatsby

In *The Great Gatsby*, F. Scott Fitzgerald portrayed 1920s America as greedy, cynical, and rife with moral decay. Jay Gatsby's lavish weekly parties symbolize the reckless excesses of the Jazz Age. The growth of bootlegging and organized crime in reaction to Prohibition is symbolized by the character of Meyer Wolfsheim and by Gatsby's own ill-gotten wealth. Fitzgerald symbolized social divisions using geography. The "old money" aristocrats like the Buchanans lived on East Egg, while the "new money" bourgeois like Gatsby lived on West Egg. Fitzgerald also used weather, as many authors have, to reinforce narrative and emotional tones in the novel. Just as in *Romeo and Juliet*, where William Shakespeare set the confrontation of Tybalt and Mercutio and its deadly consequences on the hottest summer day under a burning sun, in *The Great Gatsby*, Fitzgerald did the same with Tom Wilson's deadly confrontation with Gatsby. Both works are ostensible love stories carrying socially critical themes about the destructiveness of pointless and misguided behaviors—family feuds in the former, pursuit of money in the latter.

Review Video: Thematic Development
Visit mometrix.com/academy and enter code: 576507

THEME IN LES MISÉRABLES

In Victor Hugo's novel *Les Misérables*, the overall metamorphosis of protagonist Jean Valjean from a cynical ex-convict into a noble benefactor demonstrates Hugo's theme of the importance of love and compassion for others. Hugo also reflects this in more specific plot events. For example, Valjean's love for Cosette sustains him through many difficult periods and trying events. Hugo illustrates how love and compassion for others beget the same in them: Bishop Myriel's kindness to Valjean eventually inspires him to become honest. Years later, Valjean, as M. Madeleine, has rescued Fauchelevent from under a fallen carriage, Fauchelevent returns the compassionate act by giving Valjean sanctuary in the convent. M. Myriel's kindness also ultimately enables Valjean to rescue Cosette from the Thénardiers. Receiving Valjean's father-like love enables Cosette to fall in love with and marry Marius, and the love between Cosette and Marius enables the couple to forgive Valjean for his past crimes when they are revealed.

THEME IN "THE TELL-TALE HEART"

In one of his shortest stories, "The Tell-Tale Heart," Poe used economy of language to emphasize the murderer-narrator's obsessive focus on bare details like the victim's cataract-milky eye, the sound of a heartbeat, and insistence he is sane. The narrator begins by denying he is crazy, even citing his extreme agitation as proof of sanity. Contradiction is then extended: the narrator loves the old man, yet kills him. His motives are irrational—not greed or revenge, but to relieve the victim of his "evil eye." Because "eye" and "I" are homonyms, readers may infer that eye/I symbolizes the old man's identity, contradicting the killer's delusion that he can separate them. The narrator distances himself from the old man by perceiving his eye as separate, and dismembering his dead body. This backfires when he imagines the victim's heartbeat, which is really his own, just before he kills him and frequently afterward. Guilty and paranoid, he gives himself away. Poe predated Freud in exploring the paradox of killing those we love and the concept of projecting our own processes onto others.

THEME IN THE WORKS OF WILLIAM FAULKNER AND CHARLES DICKENS

William Faulkner contrasts the traditions of the antebellum South with the rapid changes of post-Civil War industrialization in his short story "A Rose for Emily." Living inside the isolated world of her house, Emily Grierson denies the reality of modern progress. Contradictorily, she is both a testament to time-honored history and a mysterious, eccentric, unfathomable burden. Faulkner portrays her with deathlike imagery even in life, comparing her to a drowned woman and referring to her skeleton. Emily symbolizes the Old South; as her social status is degraded, so is the antebellum social order. Like Miss Havisham in Charles Dickens' *Great Expectations,* Emily preserves her bridal bedroom, denying change and time's passage. Emily tries to control death through denial, shown in her necrophilia with her father's corpse and her killing of Homer Barron to stop him from leaving her, then also denying his death. Faulkner uses the motif of dust throughout to represent not only the decay of Emily, her house, and Old Southern traditions, but also how her secrets are obscured from others.

THEME IN MOBY-DICK

The great White Whale in *Moby-Dick* plays various roles to different characters. In Captain Ahab's obsessive, monomaniacal quest to kill it, the whale represents all evil, and Ahab believes it his duty and destiny to rid the world of it. Ishmael attempts through multiple scientific disciplines to understand the whale objectively, but fails—it is hidden underwater and mysterious to humans—reinforcing Melville's theme that humans can never know everything; here the whale represents the unknowable. Melville reverses white's usual connotation of purity in Ishmael's dread of white, associated with crashing waves, polar animals, albinos—all frightening and unnatural. White is often viewed as an absence of color, yet white light is the sum total of all colors in the spectrum. In the same way, white can signify both absence of meaning, and totality of meaning incomprehensible to humans. As a creature of nature, the whale also symbolizes how 19th-century white men's exploitative expansionistic actions were destroying the natural environment.

THEME IN THE OLD MAN AND THE SEA

Because of the old fisherman Santiago's struggle to capture a giant marlin, some people characterize Ernest Hemingway's *The Old Man and the Sea* as telling of man against nature. However, it can more properly be interpreted as telling of man's role as part of nature. Both man and fish are portrayed as brave, proud, and honorable. In Hemingway's world, all creatures, including humans, must either kill or be killed. Santiago reflects, "man can be destroyed but not defeated," following this principle in his life. As heroes are often created through their own deaths, Hemingway seems to believe that while being destroyed is inevitable, destruction enables living beings to transcend it by fighting bravely with honor and dignity. Hemingway echoes Romantic poet John Keats' contention that only immediately before death can we understand beauty as it is about to be destroyed. He also echoes ancient Greek and Roman myths and the Old Testament with the tragic flaw of overweening pride or overreaching. Like Icarus, Prometheus, and Adam and Eve, the old man "went out too far."

UNIVERSAL THEMES

The Old Testament book of Genesis, the Quran, and the Epic of Gilgamesh all contain flood stories. Versions differ somewhat, yet marketed similarities also exist. Genesis describes a worldwide flood, attributing it to God's decision that mankind, his creation, had become incontrovertibly wicked in spirit and must be destroyed for the world to start anew. The Quran describes the flood as regional, caused by Allah after sending Nuh (notice the similarity in name to Noah) as a messenger to his people to cease their evil. The Quran stipulates that Allah only destroys those who deny or ignore messages from his messengers. In the Gilgamesh poems Utnapishtim, like Noah, is instructed to build a ship to survive the flood. Both men also send out birds afterward as tests, using doves and a raven, though with different outcomes. Many historians and archeologists believe a Middle Eastern tidal wave was a real basis for these stories. However, their universal themes remain the same: the flood was seen as God's way of wiping out humans whose behavior had become ungodly.

THEME OF OVERREACHING

A popular theme throughout literature is the human trait of **reaching too far** or **presuming too much**. In Greek mythology, Daedalus constructed wings of feathers and wax that men might fly like birds. He permitted his son Icarus to try them, but cautioned the boy not to fly too close to the sun. The impetuous youth (in what psychologist David Elkind later named adolescence's myth of invincibility) ignored this, flying too close to the sun. The wax melted, the wings disintegrated, and Icarus fell into the sea and perished. In the Old Testament, God warned Adam and Eve not to eat fruit from the tree of knowledge of good and evil. Because they ignored this command, they were banished from Eden's eternal perfection, condemning them to mortality and suffering. The Romans were themselves examples of overreaching in their conquest and assimilation of most of the then-known world and their ultimate demise. In Christopher Marlowe's *Dr. Faustus* and Johann Wolfgang von Goethe's *Faust,* the protagonist sells his soul to the Devil for unlimited knowledge and success, ultimately leading to his own tragic end.

STORY VS. DISCOURSE

In terms of plot, "story" is the characters, places, and events originating in the author's mind, while "discourse" is how the author arranges and sequences events—which may be chronological or not. Story is imaginary; discourse is words on the page. Discourse allows a story to be told in different ways. One element of plot structure is relating events differently from the order in which they occurred. This is easily done with cause-and-effect; for example, in the sentence, "He died following a long illness," we know the illness preceded the death, but the death precedes the illness in words. In Kate Chopin's short story "The Story of an Hour" (1894), she tells some of the events out of chronological order, which has the effect of amplifying the surprise of the ending for the reader. Another element of plot structure is selection. Chopin omits some details, such as Mr. Mallard's trip home; this allows readers to be as surprised at his arrival as Mrs. Mallard is.

Plot and Meaning

Novelist E. M. Forster has made the distinction between story as relating a series of events, such as a king dying and then his queen dying, versus plot as establishing motivations for actions and causes for events, such as a king dying and then his queen dying from grief over his death. Thus, plot fulfills the function of helping readers understand cause-and-effect in events and underlying motivations in characters' actions, which in turn helps them understand life. This affects a work's meaning by supporting its ability to explain why things happen, why people do things, and ultimately the meaning of life. Some authors find that while story events convey meaning, they do not tell readers there is any one meaning in life or way of living, but rather are mental experiments with various meanings, enabling readers to explore. Hence stories may not necessarily be constructed to impose one definitive meaning, but rather to find some shape, direction, and meaning within otherwise random events.

Classic Analysis of Plot Structure

In *Poetics,* Aristotle defined plot as "the arrangement of the incidents." He meant not the story, but how it is structured for presentation. In tragedies, Aristotle found results driven by chains of cause and effect preferable to those driven by the protagonist's personality or character. He identified "unity of action" as necessary for a plot's wholeness, meaning its events must be internally connected, not episodic or relying on *deus ex machina* or other external intervention. A plot must have a beginning, middle, and end. Gustav Freytag adapted Aristotle's ideas into his Pyramid (1863). The beginning, today called the exposition, incentive, or inciting moment, emphasizes causes and de-emphasizes effects. Aristotle called the ensuing cause and effect *desis,* or tying up, today called complications which occur during the rising action. These culminate in a crisis or climax, Aristotle's *peripateia.* This occurs at the plot's middle, where cause and effect are both emphasized. The falling action, which Aristotle called the *lusis* or unraveling, is today called the dénouement. The resolution comes at the catastrophe, outcome, or end, when causes are emphasized and effects de-emphasized.

Review Video: Plot Line
Visit mometrix.com/academy and enter code: 944011

Analysis of Plot Structures Through Recurring Patterns

Authors of fiction select characters, places, and events from their imaginations and arrange them to create a story that will affect their readers. One way to analyze plot structure is to compare and contrast different events in a story. For example, in Kate Chopin's "The Story of an Hour," a very simple but key pattern of repetition is the husband's leaving and then returning. Such patterns fulfill the symmetrical aspect that Aristotle said was required of sound plot structure. In James Baldwin's short story, "Sonny's Blues," the narrator is Sonny's brother. In an encounter with one of Sonny's old friends early in the story, the brother initially disregards his communication. In a subsequent flashback, Baldwin informs us that this was the same way he had treated Sonny. In Nathaniel Hawthorne's "Young Goodman Brown," a pattern is created by the protagonist's recurrent efforts not to go farther into the wood. In Herman Melville's "Bartleby the Scrivener" and in William Faulkner's "Barn Burning," patterns are also created by repetition such as Bartleby's repeated refusals and the history of barn-burning episodes, respectively.

Literary Analysis

Analyzing Literary Texts

The best literary analysis shows special insight into at least one important aspect of a text. When **analyzing literary texts**, it can be difficult to find a starting place. Many texts can be analyzed several different ways, often leaving an overwhelming number of options for writers to consider. However, narrowing the focus to a particular element of literature can be helpful when preparing to analyze a text. Symbolism, themes, and motifs are common starting points for literary analysis. These three methods of analysis can lead to a holistic analysis of a text, since they involve elements that are often distributed throughout the text. However, not all texts feature these elements in a way that facilitates a strong analysis, if they are present at all. It is also common to focus on character or plot development for analysis. These elements are compatible with theme, symbolism, and allusion. Setting and imagery, figurative language, and any external contexts can also contribute to analysis or complement one of these other elements. The application of a critical, or literary, theory to a text can also provide a thorough and strong analysis.

Literary Theories and Criticism and Interpretation

Literary theory includes ideas that guide readers through the process of interpreting literature. Literary theory, as a subject, encompasses several specific, focused theories that lead readers to interpret or analyze literature through the context of the theory using the subjects and elements it involves. Some commonly used and discussed literary theories include **postcolonial theory**, **gender and feminist theory**, **structuralism**, **new historicism**, **reader-response theory**, and **sociological criticism**.

- **Postcolonial theory** involves the historical and geographical context of a work and leads readers to consider how colonization informs the plot, characters, setting, and other elements in the work.
- **Gender and feminist theory** invites readers to interpret a text by looking at its treatment of and suggestions about women and a culture's treatment of women. As with most literary theories, this information can be clearly stated or strongly implied in a work, but it may also be gleaned through looking closely at symbols, characters, and plot elements in a work.
- **Structuralism** uses the structure and organization of a work and the foundations of language to examine how and what a text conveys about the human experience and how those findings connect to common human experiences.
- **New historicism** heavily relies on the cultural and historical context of a work, including when it was written, where the author lives or lived, the culture and history of that location, and other works from the same culture. New historical readings seek to examine these details to expose the ideologies of the location and culture that influenced the work.
- **Reader-response theory** uses the individual reader's response to the text and experience while reading the text to examine the meaning of the reader's relationship with the text and what that relationship suggests about the reader or the factors impacting their experience.
- **Sociological criticism** considers the societies that are relevant to a text. The author's society and any reader's society are important to the text, as sociological criticism seeks to uncover what the text implies or reveals about those societies. This method of criticism can also involve studying the presentation of a society within the text and applying it to the author's society or their other writings.

Language

The Writing Process

Brainstorming

When choosing what to write about, activities like brainstorming can help inspire new ideas or help writers see how their ideas go together. **Brainstorming** means considering a variety of topics or ideas and is mainly used to find a creative approach to a subject or problem. A good first step in brainstorming is simple **free-association** with a topic. One way of doing this is sitting down with paper and pen and writing every thought that comes to mind about the topic in a word or phrase. It does not matter how helpful or good the thought seems at first; the writer should write down everything that comes to mind about the topic. Then, the writer should read the list over a few times. Next, he or she should look for patterns, repetitions, and clusters of ideas. This allows a variety of fresh ideas to come as the writer thinks about the topic.

Free Writing

Free writing is a more organized form of brainstorming. **Free writing** means taking a limited amount of time, like 2 to 3 minutes, to write everything that comes to mind about a topic in complete sentences. When the time is up, the writer should review everything he or she has written down. Many of the sentences may not make sense, but they may contain ideas and details that help the writer organize his or her ideas and prepare to plan the composition. Usually, free writing results in more useful ideas than brainstorming because the writer's thoughts and connections are written in complete sentences. However, both methods can be used together to help the writer prepare to plan and write a composition.

Mapping

One specific way to use graphic organizers is to map an essay. There are many different types of graphic organizers. One easy method to create one is to draw a circle in the middle of the page and write a broad topic in it. Then, draw smaller circles with related topics and ideas, or with topics that fit within the broad topic, written inside and draw line to connect each circle to the main circle. This method can show ideas that fit within the broad topic and will help guide the essay, or it can show which ideas may work better as the main topic of the essay.

Once the main idea and other ideas and details for the essay have been chosen, they can be used to map the essay. Mapping is another word for using a certain type of graphic organizer. These graphic organizers look like a map and organize ideas and details as they will appear in the essay. The essay map can have the main idea at the top or in the center. If the main idea is at the top, the supporting ideas will appear below it in a row, and any additional details will appear under the supporting idea they go with. If the main idea appears in the center, the supporting ideas may appear around it, and the additional details will appear around the supporting ideas they go with.

PLANNING

Planning is the process of organizing a piece of writing before writing a draft. At the beginning of planning, writers should decide **why they are writing** and **who will read what they write**. The writer must also choose a **genre**, which is the **type** of composition he or she will write. There are fiction genres, such as comedy, folklore, action, and mystery. There are also nonfiction genres, such as essays, reports, poems, and journals. To plan his or her composition, a writer may create an outline or a graphic organizer, such as a Venn diagram, a spider-map, or a flowchart. These methods should help the writer choose their topic, main ideas, and how to organize the composition. If the writer needs to do research for the composition, he or she may also do so as they plan. Planning helps writers organize all of their ideas and decide if they have enough information to begin their first draft. However, writers should remember that the decisions they make during planning may change later, so their plan does not have to be perfect.

DRAFTING

Writers may then use their plan, outline, or graphic organizer to compose their first draft. They may write more drafts after the first one to improve their writing. Writing multiple drafts can help writers think of different ways to state their ideas and correct mistakes that may be hard to fix without rewriting a section of the composition, or the whole composition. There is no "right" number of drafts, so different writers may write a different number of drafts. Writing drafts also makes it easier to write freely because a writer can improve his or her composition with each draft they write.

REVISING, EDITING, AND PROOFREADING

Once a writer completes a draft, he or she can move on to revising, editing, and proofreading to improve the draft. **Revising** is making sure that the composition is right for the audience, is not missing important information, is on topic, and is well organized. The writer should also consider the composition's style when revising and ensure that it is appropriately formal or serious. Revising may happen after the first draft so that errors are not repeated in the next draft. Each draft should be revised before the next one is written so that no mistakes are missed. **Editing** comes next. Editing a composition includes steps like improving transitions between paragraphs and making sure each paragraph is on topic. While editing, the writer must pay attention to the words he or she uses and the way the information in each paragraph is organized. Writers may also fix grammar mistakes in the editing phase, since some errors will require a writer to rewrite large parts of their work. **Proofreading** means fixing misspelled words, errors in grammar, and any other small mistakes in the composition.

During the revising, editing, and proofreading steps, it can be helpful for writers to ask a peer to read their work, since he or she may notice mistakes or problems the writer missed before. A writer may also choose to read his or her own work aloud, or listen to someone else read it. Hearing a composition aloud can help writers find mistakes or opportunities for improvement in their work more easily. This happens because when something is read aloud, the person reading the text must pay closer attention to the words on the page. When a writer or a peer reads the composition, they should point out any sentence that confuses them the first time they read it. Most of these sentences can be revised in a way that makes it easier to read and understand.

ADDING AND REMOVING INFORMATION

While both revising and editing may involve changing the words in a composition, they can also involve adding or taking away words. When a writer has completed a draft and reread it, he or she may notice that something, such as a transition, important details, or an explanatory sentence, is missing. Simply changing the words to make the passage sound better will not solve this problem, so the writer must **add** whatever words and information is needed to make the passage make sense and achieve the writer's purpose.

In other cases, a writer may have words, a sentence, or sometimes an entire paragraph that gives unnecessary information or explains the information in a way that is confusing. When this happens, the extra words and information weaken the composition and must be **removed**. Sometimes, this is difficult for writers to do because it may require them to remove writing they are proud of or a fact they find interesting. Despite this, revising and editing are steps meant to improve and strengthen a composition, so the writer should change, add, or remove parts of his or her writing in a way that makes it better and achieves his or her purpose.

Revising Sentences

Sentence variety is important to consider when writing an essay. A variety of sentence lengths and types can make an essay more engaging, and different types of sentences can sometimes help readers better understand information. For example, a sentence containing a list may make more sense when written with a simple sentence structure, since writing a compound sentence containing a list may give the reader too much information at once. On the other hand, information that is closely related and can be connected with a conjunction should be written in a compound sentence, rather than a simple sentence, since a compound sentence helps the reader see that the information goes together.

Using only simple sentences often makes writing boring and bothersome to read. Writing using only compound sentences makes it difficult for writers to explain information well and difficult for readers to understand, since every sentence will include a coordinating conjunction. To check an essay for sentence variety, it is helpful to look at whether the essay contains different sentence structures and lengths. It is also important to pay attention to the way each sentence starts and avoid beginning with the same words or phrases.

Revising Vocabulary

When writing informational or argumentative texts, it is important to use **precise vocabulary**, or **word choice**, to explain your main idea and supporting details. Generalized vocabulary will not help the audience fully understand the points that you are attempting to make because it will not accurately explain your main idea and supporting details. Precise vocabulary is important to use because it will accurately describe the ideas that are central to your text. When you research a subject, make sure to familiarize yourself with any vocabulary that is involved in its explanation. Use context clues, dictionaries, or, if necessary, a technical dictionary to decode any words that you are not familiar with. Precise vocabulary also impacts the effectiveness of narrative text. Carefully choosing vocabulary to describe sensory details, or imagery, helps writers paint the best possible picture of the events they are describing through their writing.

Recursive Writing Process

Brainstorming, planning, drafting, revising, editing, and proofreading are all steps in the **writing process**. This process is helpful to remember when beginning a new composition, but once a writer has practiced these steps in this order, he or she can use the **recursive writing process**. The recursive writing process is the same as the normal writing process, but the steps in the recursive writing process do not have to happen in the same order. For example, one writer may need to repeat steps after completing other steps. A different writer may discover that he or she can practice the planning and revising steps as he or she writes a draft. The recursive writing process involves moving back and forth between planning, drafting, and revising, followed by more planning, more drafting, and more revising until the writer is happy with his or her work. Each writer can use the recursive writing process in their own way, as long as it helps them improve their work and write the best they can.

Review Video: Recursive Writing Process
Visit mometrix.com/academy and enter code: 951611

Essay Structure and Organization

Central Ideas and Supporting Details

In the first paragraph of a composition, writers include a sentence that explains the **central idea.** This sentence is also known as the **thesis**. The rest of the paragraph shows the reader why the topic of the essay is interesting and includes details that support the central idea. One way to understand the relationship between the central idea and supporting information is to think about a table: the tabletop is the central idea, and each of the table's legs is a supporting detail or group of details. All of the legs work together to support the tabletop and create a table, just like the supporting details work together to support the central idea and create a composition.

Introduction

The introduction is used to capture the reader's attention and announce the essay's central idea. Normally, the introduction contains about 3-5 sentences. An introduction can begin with an interesting quote, a question, a strong opinion, or something else that will **interest** the reader's and prompt them to keep reading. If the composition has a prompt, the introduction should **restate** or **summarize** some part of the prompt so that the reader will have an idea of what information will be in the essay. Finally, your introduction should include the **central idea**, the primary thing the essay will tell the reader.

> **Review Video: Introduction**
> Visit mometrix.com/academy and enter code: 961328

Body

In an essay's introduction, the writer states the central idea and prepares the reader for the information in the rest of the composition. In the body of the composition, the writer **explains**, **demonstrates**, and **gives more information about** the **central idea**. This is done using supporting details and examples that are relevant to the central idea of the composition. For example, if the composition's central idea is a vacation the writer took, the body will include descriptions of where the writer went, what they experienced, and what they thought of the trip. If the composition's central idea is the writer's opinion, the body will include examples and facts that show why he or she has formed that opinion. If composition's central idea is a topic and the writer wants to instruct the reader, the body will contain facts, explanations, and examples that help teach the reader about the central idea. A writer will use supporting details to explain the central idea throughout the body.

The body should also contain multiple paragraphs, and the order the writer puts these paragraphs in is important. Each paragraph should include at least one supporting detail, but a paragraph may include more than one if two or more supporting details work together to support the central idea. If the central idea is to describe something that happened, the paragraphs should match the order in which the events occurred. If the central idea is to present an opinion or instruct the reader, the paragraphs should be ordered in the way that would make the most sense to the reader. The order of body paragraphs is important because it can impact how easy a composition is to read.

> **Review Video: Drafting Body Paragraphs**
> Visit mometrix.com/academy and enter code: 724590

Choosing Supporting Details and Examples

When writing an informative or argumentative text, writers must choose supporting details carefully. Including details that are irrelevant, inaccurate, or vague does not strengthen the author's writing, while relevant, accurate, provable, and specific details do strengthen the author's writing. These details can make the writer's meaning clearer or give evidence that the author's points are true or logical. Such details may include examples or facts, such as statistics, statements from others who have authority on the subject, and common events or experiences. Choosing appropriate supporting details can also help the author show that they put effort into forming their ideas. This can also make the composition more intriguing and enjoyable to read, since the writer's own interest and insight will be apparent to the reader.

Paragraphs

After the introduction of a passage, the body paragraphs will explain and elaborate upon the central idea. While each paragraph should relate to the central idea of the composition, each paragraph should focus on one point or supporting detail. Normally, a paragraph has a good topic sentence that summarizes the paragraph's main point. A topic sentence is a sentence that gives an introduction to the paragraph and its contents. Topic sentences should contain information that is more specific than what is in the introduction and may include a supporting detail, but they should not contain explanations or examples.

The next sentences in the paragraph should support the topic sentence. These sentences can contain examples, explanations, or other specific information that supports the topic sentence, which supports the central idea of the composition. While a paragraph may be structured in any way, as long as it logically provides information that supports the central idea, it can be best to use a template or pattern to make sure that each paragraph is complete and well organized. For example, a good template to follow is topic sentence, evidence, explanation, conclusion. This means that after the topic sentence, the next sentence should provide evidence, like a quote or example, that supports the paragraph's main point. Next, the paragraph should include a sentence that explains how that evidence supports the paragraph's main point. If there are multiple examples or quotes, more than one sentence may be used to explain them. Finally, there should be a concluding sentence that helps the reader understand the paragraph and prepares them for the next one.

A paragraph must contain enough information to support its main point and the composition's central idea. A paragraph of two or three sentences will most likely not support the main point or central idea because it is not likely to contain enough information, explanation, or evidence. When a paragraph does not support the main point or central idea, it does not help the writer achieve their purpose or goal for writing the essay. A helpful, informative paragraph will often have somewhere from three to five sentences. Also, it is important that the sentences within the paragraph lead the reader through the information. Each paragraph should flow logically and stay on topic throughout.

Starting a New Paragraph

For most forms of writing, you will need to use multiple paragraphs. This means that deciding when to start a new paragraph is very important. Reasons for starting a new paragraph include:

- To separate the introduction and conclusion from the body paragraphs
- To move from one supporting detail or point to another
- To indicate an important shift in time or place
- To show a comparison, contrast, or cause and effect relationship

TRANSITIONS

Transitions between sentences and paragraphs guide readers from idea to idea and show relationships between sentences and paragraphs. Writers should use transitions carefully and only when they are truly helpful. They should also be selected to fit the author's purpose. Transitions can show relationships such as time, comparison, an order of events, and cause and effect. Transitions are often used at the beginning of a phrase, sentence, or paragraph, since this helps prepare the reader for the next piece of information.

Review Video: Transitions in Writing
Visit mometrix.com/academy and enter code: 233246

TYPES OF TRANSITIONAL WORDS

Time	Afterward, immediately, earlier, meanwhile, recently, lately, now, since, soon, when, then, until, before, etc.
Sequence	too, first, second, further, moreover, also, again, and, next, still, besides, finally
Comparison	similarly, in the same way, likewise, also, again, once more
Contrasting	but, although, despite, however, instead, nevertheless, on the one hand... on the other hand, regardless, yet, in contrast.
Cause and Effect	because, consequently, thus, therefore, then, to this end, since, so, as a result, if... then, accordingly
Examples	for example, for instance, such as, to illustrate, indeed, in fact, specifically
Place	near, far, here, there, to the left/right, next to, above, below, beyond, opposite, beside
Repetition, Summary, or Conclusion	as mentioned earlier, as noted, in other words, in short, on the whole, to summarize, therefore, as a result, to conclude, in conclusion
Addition	and, also, furthermore, moreover

Review Video: Transition Words
Visit mometrix.com/academy and enter code: 707563

CONCLUSION

The conclusion of a composition should summarize the central idea and show that it has been explained well. A good conclusion shows the reader why the author's central idea is meaningful and important and how the supporting details should help the reader understand the central idea. The conclusion should also give the reader something to think about that is related to the central idea. For example, in the conclusion, the author can invite readers to think about how they feel or what they think after reading the composition. Some things to avoid when writing conclusions include:

- Introducing a completely new idea
- Apologizing for one's opinions or writing
- Repeating the central idea word for word rather than summarizing them
- Using the conclusion to summarize every detail in the composition

Review Video: Drafting Conclusions
Visit mometrix.com/academy and enter code: 209408

Grammar

Subjects and Predicates

Subjects

Every sentence needs a subject and a predicate. The **subject** of a sentence names who or what the sentence is about. The subject may be directly stated in a sentence, or the subject may be implied. The **complete subject** includes the simple subject and any **modifiers**, such as adjectives, articles, prepositions, and adverbs, that go with it. To find the complete subject, ask *Who* or *What* before the verb to complete the question. The answer, including any modifiers, is the complete subject. To find the **simple subject**, remove all of the modifiers in the complete subject.

Examples:

simple subject
The small, red car is the one that he wants for Christmas.
complete subject

simple subject
The young artist is coming over for dinner.
complete subject

Review Video: Subjects in English
Visit mometrix.com/academy and enter code: 444771

An imperative sentence is a sentence that gives someone instructions or makes a request to someone. In **imperative** sentences, the verb's subject is understood, but is not actually present in the sentence. For example, this about the sentence *Drive to the store*. This sentence is a command, and the subject is *you*. If the subject were directly stated, the sentence would be *You, drive to the store*. Another fact to consider is that, normally, the subject comes before the verb. However, the subject comes after the verb in sentences that begin with *There are* or *There was*.

Direct:

John knows the way to the park.	Who knows the way to the park?	John
The cookies need ten more minutes.	What needs ten minutes?	The cookies
By five o'clock, Bill will need to leave.	Who needs to leave?	Bill
There are five letters on the table for him.	What is on the table?	Five letters
There were coffee and doughnuts in the house.	What was in the house?	Coffee and doughnuts

Implied:

Go to the post office for me.	Who is going to the post office?	You
Come and sit with me, please?	Who needs to come and sit?	You

Predicates

In a sentence, there is always a predicate and a subject. The subject tells what the sentence is about, and the **predicate** explains or describes the subject.

Think about the sentence *He sings*. In this sentence, we have a subject, *He*, and a predicate, *sings*. This is all that is needed for a sentence to be complete. Most sentences contain more information, but if this is all the information that is given in a sentence, then it is a complete sentence.

Now, let's look at another sentence: *John and Jane sing on Tuesday nights at the dance hall.*

subject: John and Jane | predicate: sing on Tuesday nights at the dance hall.

John and Jane sing on Tuesday nights at the dance hall.

Subject-Verb Agreement

Verbs **agree** with their subjects in number. In other words, singular subjects need singular verbs. Plural subjects need plural verbs. **Singular** is for **one** person, place, or thing. **Plural** is for **more than one** person, place, or thing. Subjects and verbs must also share the same point of view, as in first, second, or third person.

Review Video: Subject-Verb Agreement
Visit mometrix.com/academy and enter code: 479190

Number Agreement Examples:

Single Subject and Verb: Dan (singular subject) calls (singular verb) home.

Dan is one person. So, the singular verb *calls* is needed.

Plural Subject and Verb: Dan and Bob (plural subject) call (plural verb) home.

More than one person needs the plural verb *call*.

Person Agreement Examples:

First Person: I *am* walking.

Second Person: You *are* walking.

Third Person: He *is* walking.

Complications with Subject-Verb Agreement

Words Between Subject and Verb

Words that come between the simple subject and the verb do not affect subject-verb agreement.

Examples:

The joy (singular subject) of my life returns (singular verb) home tonight.

The phrase *of my life* does not affect the verb *returns.*

The question (singular subject) that still remains unanswered is (singular verb) "Who are you?"

Don't let the phrase "*that still remains…*" confuse you. The subject *question* goes with the verb *is.*

Compound Subjects

A compound subject is formed when two or more nouns joined by *and, or,* or *nor* act together as the subject of the sentence.

Joined by And

When a compound subject is joined by *and,* it is treated as a plural subject and requires a plural verb.

Examples:

You and Jon (plural subject) are (plural verb) invited to come to my house.

The pencil and paper (plural subject) belong (plural verb) to me.

Joined by Or/Nor

For a compound subject joined by *or* or *nor,* the verb must agree in number with the part of the subject that is closest to the verb.

Examples:

Today or tomorrow (subject) is (verb) the day.

Stan or Phil (subject) wants (verb) to read the book.

Neither the pen nor the book (subject) is (verb) on the desk.

Either the blanket or pillows (subject) arrive (verb) this afternoon.

INDEFINITE PRONOUNS AS SUBJECT

An indefinite pronoun is a pronoun that does not refer to a specific noun. Different indefinite pronouns are used as a singular noun, a plural noun, or change depending on how they are used.

ALWAYS SINGULAR

Pronouns such as *each*, *either*, *everybody*, *anybody*, *somebody*, and *nobody* are always singular. This is because these pronouns always stand in for one person, place, or thing.

Examples:

Each (singular subject) of the runners has (singular verb) a different bib number.

Is (singular verb) either (singular subject) of you ready for the game?

Note: The words *each* and *either* can also be used as adjectives. For example, *each* person is unique. When one of these adjectives modifies the subject of a sentence, it is always a singular subject.

Everybody (singular subject) grows (singular verb) a day older every day.

Anybody (singular subject) is (singular verb) welcome to bring a tent.

ALWAYS PLURAL

Pronouns such as *both*, *several*, and *many* are always plural. This is because these pronouns always stand in for more than one person, place, thing, or idea.

Examples:

Both (plural subject) of the siblings were (plural verb) too tired to argue.

Many (plural subject) have tried (plural verb), but none have succeeded.

DEPEND ON CONTEXT

Pronouns such as *some*, *any*, *all*, *none*, *more*, and *most* can be either singular or plural depending on what they are representing in the context of the sentence.

Examples:

All (singular subject) of my dog's food was (singular verb) still there in his bowl.

By the end of the night, all (plural subject) of my guests were (plural verb) already excited about coming to my next party.

Other Cases Involving Plural or Irregular Form

Some nouns are **singular in meaning but plural in form**: news, mathematics, physics, and economics.

> The *news is* coming on now.
>
> *Mathematics is* my favorite class.

Some nouns are plural in form and meaning, and have **no singular equivalent**: scissors and pants.

> Do these *pants come* with a shirt?
>
> The *scissors are* for my project.

Note: Look to your **dictionary** for help when you aren't sure whether a noun with a plural form has a singular or plural meaning.

Example

Which word should go in the blank?

> If Kelly if going to the party, Joan and Susan ____ going to the store.

a. Is
b. Are
c. Am
d. Was

Try using each choice in the sentence. Choice A, *is*, forms this sentence: If Kelly is going to the party, Joan and Susan is going to the store. There are two people, Joan and Susan, who are going to the store. This makes the subject of the clause plural. *Is* is a singular verb, meaning it does not agree with the subject and cannot be the answer.

Choice B, *are*, forms this sentence: If Kelly is going to the party, Joan and Susan are going to the store. The subject of the clause is still plural. But *are* is a plural verb! The subject and verb agree, so *are* is the correct answer.

Choice C, *am*, forms this sentence: If Kelly is going to the party, Joan and Susan am going to the store. *Am* is a singular verb, and it is also only used in first person, when the writer or speaker is referring to themself. The subject of the clause is plural, and the sentence is in third person, so *am* is not the correct answer.

Choice D, *was*, forms this sentence: If Kelly is going to the party, Joan and Susan was going to the store. *Was* is a singular verb, so it does not agree with the plural subject in this clause.

Complements

A complement is a noun, pronoun, or adjective that is used to give more information about the subject or verb in the sentence.

DIRECT OBJECTS

A direct object is a noun or pronoun that takes or receives the **action** of a verb. A complete sentence does not need a direct object, so not all sentences will have them. When you are looking for a direct object, find the verb and ask *who* or *what.*

Examples:

> I took *the blanket.*
>
> Jane read *books.*

INDIRECT OBJECTS

An indirect object is a word or group of words that show how an action had an **influence** on someone or something. If there is an indirect object in a sentence, then you always have a direct object in the sentence. When you are looking for the indirect object, find the verb and ask *to, for, whom*, or *what.*

Examples:

> We taught [the old dog]_{indirect object} [a new trick.]_{direct object}
>
> I gave [them]_{indirect object} [a math lesson.]_{direct object}

Review Video: Direct and Indirect Objects
Visit mometrix.com/academy and enter code: 817385

PRONOUN-ANTECEDENT AGREEMENT

The **antecedent** is the noun that has been replaced by a pronoun. A pronoun and its antecedent **agree** when they have the same number (singular or plural) and gender (male, female, or neutral).

Examples:

> **Singular agreement**: [John]_{antecedent} came into town, and [he]_{pronoun} played for us.
>
> **Plural agreement**: [John and Rick]_{antecedent} came into town, and [they]_{pronoun} played for us.

To determine which is the correct pronoun to use in a compound subject or object, try each pronoun **alone** in place of the compound in the sentence. Your knowledge of pronouns will tell you which one is correct.

Example:

Bob and (I, me) will be going.

Test: (1) *I will be going* or (2) *Me will be going*. The second choice cannot be correct because *me* cannot be used as the subject of a sentence. Instead, *me* is used as an object.

Answer: Bob and I will be going.

When a pronoun is used with a noun immediately following (as in "we boys"), try the sentence **without the added noun**.

Example:

(We/Us) boys played football last year.

Test: (1) *We played football last yea*r or (2) *Us played football last year*. Again, the second choice cannot be correct because *us* cannot be used as a subject of a sentence. Instead, *us* is used as an object.

Answer: We boys played football last year.

Review Video: Pronoun Usage
Visit mometrix.com/academy and enter code: 666500

Review Video: Pronoun-Antecedent Agreement
Visit mometrix.com/academy and enter code: 919704

A pronoun should point clearly to the **antecedent**. Here is how a pronoun reference can be unhelpful if it is puzzling or not directly stated.

Unhelpful: Ron and Jim (antecedent) went to the store, and he (pronoun) bought soda.

Who bought soda? Ron or Jim?

Helpful: Jim (antecedent) went to the store, and he (pronoun) bought soda.

The sentence is clear. Jim bought the soda.

Example

Tom printed his ticket to the concert, but he forgot ____ at home.

Which pronoun should go in the blank?

a. It
b. Them
c. Him
d. He

What is the antecedent that the missing pronoun must match? There are only four nouns in the sentence. They are *Tom, ticket, concert*, and *home*. Which one should the missing pronoun refer to? Tom is the one who forgot something, so the pronoun does not refer to Tom. The concert is not at Tom's home, so he cannot forget the concert at home. It is also not logical to say that Tom forgot his home at home The antecedent must be *ticket*.

Choice A says that the missing pronoun is *it*. The pronoun refers to *ticket*, which is a singular noun. A ticket is also a nonliving thing. The missing pronoun is also the object in the second clause. *It* is singular, refers to nonliving nouns, and can be used as the object. Choice A is correct.

Choice B says that the missing pronoun is *them*. The pronoun refers to the singular noun *ticket*. While *them* can be used to refer to nonliving nouns and can be the object of a sentence, it is a plural pronoun. Choice B is incorrect.

Choice C says that the missing pronoun is *him*. The missing pronoun refers to a nonliving thing, not a human or animal. *Him* is an objective personal pronoun and is singular, but it only refers to living nouns. *Him* cannot represent *ticket*, so choice C is incorrect.

Choice D says that the missing pronoun is *he*. The missing pronoun refers to a nonliving noun and is the object of the second sentence. While *he* is a singular pronoun, it can only be used as the subject of a sentence and only refers to living nouns. Choice D is incorrect.

PHRASES

A phrase is a group of words that functions as a single part of speech, usually a noun, adjective, or adverb. A **phrase** is not a complete thought, and does not contain a subject, but it adds detail or explanation to a sentence, or renames something within the sentence.

CLAUSES

A clause is a group of words that contains both a subject and a predicate (verb). There are two types of clauses: independent and dependent. An **independent clause** contains a complete thought, while a **dependent (or subordinate) clause** does not. A dependent clause includes a subject and a verb, and may also contain additional information, but it cannot stand as a complete thought without being joined to an independent clause. Dependent clauses function within sentences as adjectives, adverbs, or nouns.

Example:

independent clause: I am running | dependent clause: because I want to stay in shape.

I am running because I want to stay in shape.

The clause *I am running* is an independent clause: it has a subject and a verb, and it gives a complete thought. The clause *because I want to stay in shape* is a dependent clause: it has a subject and a verb, but it does not express a complete thought. This is due to the fact that it begins with *because*, which shows that there is more information needed to complete the thought. This dependent clause adds detail to the independent clause to which it is attached.

Review Video: Independent and Dependent Clauses
Visit mometrix.com/academy and enter code: 556903

SENTENCE STRUCTURE

Sentence structure is based on the type and number of clauses in the sentence. Two common sentence structures are simple sentences and compound sentences:

Simple: A simple sentence has one independent clause with no dependent clauses. A simple sentence may have a **compound subject** or a **compound verb**, or both.

Examples:

single subject | single verb

Judy watered the lawn.

compound subject | single verb

Judy and Alan watered the lawn.

single subject | compound verb | compound verb

Judy watered the lawn and pulled weeds.

compound subject | compound verb | compound verb

Judy and Alan watered the lawn and pulled weeds.

Compound: A compound sentence has two or more independent clauses with no dependent clauses. Usually, the independent clauses are joined with a comma and a coordinating conjunction or with a semicolon.

Examples:

independent clause | independent clause

The time has come, and we are ready.

independent clause | independent clause

I woke up at dawn ; the sun was just coming up.

Complex: A complex sentence has one independent clause and at least one dependent clause.

Examples:

dependent clause | independent clause

Although he had the flu, Harry went to work.

independent clause | dependent clause

Marcia got married after she finished college.

Review Video: Sentence Structure
Visit mometrix.com/academy and enter code: 700478

SENTENCE FRAGMENTS

Recall that a group of words must contain at least one **independent clause** in order to be considered a sentence. If it doesn't contain even one independent clause, it is called a **sentence fragment**.

Choosing the best steps for **repairing** a sentence fragment depends on what type of fragment it is. If the fragment is a dependent clause, it can sometimes be fixed by simply removing a subordinating word, such as *when*, *because*, or *if*, from the beginning of the fragment. Alternatively, a dependent clause can be joined to a closely related neighboring sentence. If the fragment is missing some required part, like a subject or a verb, it may be fixed by simply adding the missing part.

Examples:

> **Fragment**: Because he wanted to sail the Mediterranean.
>
> **Removed subordinating word**: He wanted to sail the Mediterranean.
>
> **Combined with another sentence**: Because he wanted to sail the Mediterranean, he booked a Greek island cruise.

EXAMPLE

Which of the following changes will NOT correct this sentence fragment?

> Although she had found the coin first.

a. Remove *Although.*
b. Add a comma and *she let her brother keep it* after *first.*
c. Add *She let her brother keep the coin* before *although.*
d. Remove *first.*

Choice A suggests removing the word *although* to form the following sentence: She found the coin first. This option removes the subordinating conjunction to make the clause independent. The resulting sentence is complete, so removing *although* is an acceptable way to correct the fragment. Choice A is incorrect.

Choice B forms the following sentence: Although she had found the coin first, she let her brother keep it. A comma and an independent clause have been added to the sentence fragment to form a complex sentence. The resulting sentence is complete and written correctly, so choice B is incorrect.

Choice C forms the following sentence: She let her brother keep the coin although she had found the coin first. An independent clause has been added before the sentence fragment to form a complex sentence. This sentence is correctly written and complete, so choice C is an acceptable way to correct the fragment. Choice C is incorrect.

Choice D removes the word *first*, leaving *Although she had found the coin.* This is still a sentence fragment, since it is a single dependent clause. Choice D does not correct the fragment, so D is correct.

RUN-ON SENTENCES

Run-on sentences consist of multiple independent clauses that have not been joined together properly. Run-on sentences can be corrected in several different ways:

Join clauses properly: This can be done with a comma and coordinating conjunction, with a semicolon, or with a colon or dash if the second clause is explaining something in the first clause.

Example:

> **Incorrect**: I went on the trip, we visited lots of castles.
>
> **Corrected**: I went on the trip, and we visited lots of castles.

Split into separate sentences: This correction is best to use when the independent clauses are very long or when they are not closely related.

Example:

> **Incorrect**: The drive to New York takes ten hours, my uncle lives in Boston.
>
> **Corrected**: The drive to New York takes ten hours. My uncle lives in Boston.

Make one clause dependent: This is the easiest way to make the sentence correct and more interesting at the same time. It's often as simple as adding a subordinating word between the two clauses or before the first clause.

Example:

> **Incorrect**: I finally made it to the store and I bought some eggs.
>
> **Corrected**: When I finally made it to the store, I bought some eggs.

Reduce to one clause with a compound verb: If both clauses have the same subject, remove the subject from the second clause, and you now have just one clause with a compound verb.

Example:

> **Incorrect**: The drive to New York takes ten hours, it makes me very tired.
>
> **Corrected**: The drive to New York takes ten hours and makes me very tired.

Note: While these are the simplest ways to correct a run-on sentence, often the best way is to completely reorganize the thoughts in the sentence and rewrite it.

COMMA SPLICES

A comma splice is a specific error that may appear in a run-on sentence. When a sentence has two independent clauses, but the clauses are joined with only a comma, a **comma splice** is formed. Remember that if two independent clauses are joined with a comma, a coordinating conjunction is also needed. Most of the solutions for fixing run-on sentences can also be used to correct a comma splice.

Review Video: Fragments and Run-on Sentences
Visit mometrix.com/academy and enter code: 541989

EXAMPLE

> Rick wants to go see a movie tomorrow he would miss his sister's recital.

Identify the change that would NOT correct this run-on sentence.

a. Add a comma after *tomorrow*.
b. Split it into two sentences between *tomorrow* and *he*.
c. Add a comma and *but* after *tomorrow*.
d. Add a subordinating conjunction to make one of the clauses dependent.

Choice A says to add a comma after *tomorrow*. This forms the following sentence: Rick wants to go see a movie tomorrow, he would miss his sister's recital. A comma has been used to join two independent clauses, but there is no coordinating conjunction. This choice forms a comma splice, so it is not an acceptable correction for this sentence. Choice A is the correct answer.

Choice B says to split the sentence into two sentences. This forms the following two sentences: Rick wants to go see a movie tomorrow. He would miss his sister's recital. Both of these sentences are complete. This is an acceptable way to correct the run-on sentence, so choice B is incorrect.

Choice C says to add a coordinating conjunction after *tomorrow*. This forms the following sentence: Rick wants to go see a movie tomorrow, but he would miss his sister's recital. A comma and a coordinating conjunction have been added between the two independent clauses. This is an acceptable way to correct a run-on sentence. Choice C is incorrect.

Choice D says to add a subordinating conjunction to make one of the sentences dependent. There are many new sentences that could be created by adding a subordinating conjunction. For example, consider the following sentence: Although Rick wants to go see a movie tomorrow, he would miss his sister's recital. Alternatively, the following sentence could also be created: Rick wants to go see a movie tomorrow even though he would miss his sister's recital. Both of these sentences have an independent clause and a dependent clause. These sentences are both complete and written correctly, so choice D is incorrect.

EXAMPLE

Identify the sentence that has a comma splice.

a. Tom stopped at the store to buy supplies and his family met him at the campsite.
b. The ball rolled into the living room quietly, but it still startled the dog.
c. Theresa brought her mom some flowers, her mom did not have a vase.
d. Sweet potatoes, pecans, and brown sugar are all ingredients in my cousin's sweet potato casserole.

Choice A has two independent clauses joined by a coordinating conjunction. This is incorrect because there should be a comma before the coordinating conjunction. While the sentence is written incorrectly, there is no comma, so this sentence does not have a comma splice. Choice A is incorrect.

Choice B has two independent clauses joined by a comma and a coordinating conjunction. This is the correct way to write a compound sentence, so there is no error here. Choice B is incorrect.

Choice C has two independent clauses joined by a comma. This is incorrect because independent clauses should be joined together by a comma and a coordinating conjunction. When the comma is present without a coordinating conjunction between two independent clauses, a comma splice is formed. This means that choice C is correct.

Choice D is a simple sentence that contains one independent clause. The only commas used in this sentence are used to separate items in a list. There are no clauses that need to be joined or errors related to commas, so choice D does not contain a comma splice. Choice D is incorrect.

THE EIGHT PARTS OF SPEECH

NOUNS

When you talk about a person, place, thing, or idea, you are talking about a **noun**. The two main types of nouns are **common** and **proper** nouns.

Common Nouns

Common nouns are generic names for people, places, and things. Common nouns are not usually capitalized.

Examples of common nouns:

People: boy, girl, worker, manager

Places: school, bank, library, home

Things: dog, cat, truck, car

Proper Nouns

Proper nouns name specific people, places, or things. All proper nouns are capitalized.

Examples of proper nouns:

People: Abraham Lincoln, George Washington, Martin Luther King, Jr.

Places: Los Angeles, California; New York; Asia

Things: Statue of Liberty, Earth, Lincoln Memorial

Note: When referring to the planet that we live on, capitalize *Earth*. When referring to the dirt, rocks, or land, lowercase *earth*.

Singular and Plural Nouns

Singular nouns name **one** person, place, thing, or idea. **Plural nouns** name **more than one** person, place, thing, or idea. Most nouns have both a singular and plural form. Many plural nouns are spelled like the singular noun with an *-s* at the end, but this is not true for all plural nouns. Singular nouns that already end in an *s*, *o*, *ch*, *sh*, or *x* usually end in *-es* when they are in the plural form. Singular nouns that end in a consonant followed by the letter *y* will usually lose the *y* and end in *-ies* in the plural form, and words that end with the letter *f* or *fe* will usually lose the *f* and end in *-ves*.

Some plural nouns have much different spellings than their singular form, and some plural nouns are spelled the same as their singular form. There are more rules for spelling plural nouns, but these are the most common spelling changes.

Examples of singular nouns:

Typical nouns: dog, pencil, girl, store, hope, stingray

Nouns ending in *s*, *o*, *ch*, *sh*, or *x*: mass, hero, lunch, polish, fox

Nouns ending in a consonant and *y*: puppy, baby, fairy, sky

Nouns ending in *f* or *fe*: self, life, calf, hoof

Examples of plural nouns:

Typical nouns: dogs, pencils, girls, stores, hopes, stingrays

Nouns ending in *s*, *o*, *ch*, *sh*, or *x*: masses, heroes, lunches, polishes, foxes

Nouns ending in a consonant and *y*: puppies, babies, fairies, skies

Nouns ending in a vowel and *f* or *fe*: selves, lives, calves, hooves

Collective Nouns

Collective nouns are the names for a group of people, places, or things that function like singular nouns. The following are examples of collective nouns: *class, company, dozen, group, herd, team,* and *public.* Collective nouns usually require an article, such as *a, an,* and *the*, which shows that the noun is a single unit. For example, a choir is a group of singers. Even though there are many singers in a choir, the word choir describes a single group. If we refer to the members of the group, and not the group itself, it is no longer a collective noun.

Incorrect: The *choir are* going to compete nationally this year.

Correct: The *choir is* going to compete nationally this year.

Incorrect: The *members* of the choir *is* competing nationally this year.

Correct: The *members* of the choir *are* competing nationally this year.

Pronouns

Pronouns are words that are used to stand in for nouns. There are several different types of pronouns, but the two main types are subjective and objective pronouns. **Subjective** nouns and pronouns that those that are the subject of a sentence. **Objective** nouns and pronouns are those that are an object in a sentence. Another important type of pronoun is the personal pronoun, which refers to people. Personal pronouns can be subjective or objective. **Possessive** nouns and pronouns show possession or ownership. Pronouns can also be singular or plural.

Singular

Subjective	Objective	Possessive
I	Me	My, Mine
You	You	Your, Yours
He	Him	His
She	Her	Her, hers
It	It	Its
Who	Whom	Whose

Plural

Subjective	Objective	Possessive
we	us	our, ours
you	you	your, yours
they	them	their, theirs

Reflexive: Reflexive pronouns are pronouns that function as the object of a sentence and refer to the subject. Examples of reflexive pronouns include *myself, yourself, himself, herself, itself, ourselves, yourselves*, and *themselves.*

Indefinite: Indefinite pronouns are used to refer to multiple nouns or an undefined noun. Examples of indefinite nouns include *all, any, each, everyone, either/neither, one, some*, and *several.*

Relative: Relative pronouns are used to connect relative clauses that specify or describe a noun to the rest of the sentence. Examples of relative pronouns include *which, who, whom,* and *whose.*

> **Review Video: Nouns and Pronouns**
> Visit mometrix.com/academy and enter code: 312073

VERBS

If you want to write a sentence, then you need a verb. Without a verb, you have no sentence. The verb of a sentence indicates action or being. In other words, the verb shows something's action or state of being or the action that has been done to something.

ACTION VERBS AND LINKING VERBS

Action verbs show what the subject is doing. In other words, an action verb shows action. **Linking verbs** link the subject of a sentence to a noun or pronoun. They can also link a subject to an adjective, so the linking verb helps create a description. You always need a verb if you want a complete sentence. However, linking verbs on their own cannot be a complete sentence. Any verb that shows a condition and connects to a noun, pronoun, or adjective that describes the subject of a sentence is a linking verb.

Action: He sings. | Run! | Go! | I talk with him every day. | She reads.

Linking:

Incorrect: I am.

Correct: I am John. | I smell roses. | I feel tired.

> **Review Video: Action Verbs and Linking Verbs**
> Visit mometrix.com/academy and enter code: 743142

VERB TENSES

A verb **tense** shows the different form of a verb to point to the time of an action. The present and past tense are indicated by the verb's form. An action in the present, *I talk,* can change form for the past: *I talked.* However, for future tense, an auxiliary, or helping, verb is sometimes needed to show the change in form. When writing a composition, it is important to use verb tenses consistently. Choose the best tense for the composition and do not switch to a different tense unless it is necessary or appropriate for a particular sentence or paragraph.

Present: I talk
Past: I talked
Future: I will talk

Present: The action happens at the current time.

Example: He *walks* to the store every morning.

Past: The action happened in the past.

Example: He *walked* to the store an hour ago.

Future: The action is going to happen later.

Example: I *will walk* to the store tomorrow.

Review Video: Verb Tenses
Visit mometrix.com/academy and enter code: 269472

Irregular Verbs

While most verbs gain the suffix -ed when used in the past tense, irregular verbs receive different spelling changes when they are written in the past tense. For example, *walk* is a regular verb, and it becomes *walked* when written in the past tense. However, *run* is an irregular verb because it becomes *ran* when written in the past tense.

Example

My mother _____ me about the big nest of ants near the sandbox. I thanked her for telling me!

Which of the following verbs should go in the blank?

a. Warn
b. Warned
c. Will warn
d. Warns

First, look at the sentences. The first sentence does not have enough information to show which tense it is in. However, the second sentence says that the child thanked the mother. The verb here is *thanked*, which is the past-tense form of *thank*. Because the second sentence is in the past tense, it makes sense to say that the first sentence is also in past tense.

Choice A says that the missing verb is *warn*. *Warn* is a present-tense verb, but it can be used in the future tense if a helping verb is present. However, this sentence is in past tense, so it needs a past-tense verb. Choice A is wrong.

Choice B says that the missing verb is *warned*. *Warned* is a past-tense verb, and it logically completes the sentence. Choice B is correct!

Choice C says that the missing verb is *will warn*. *Will warn* is a future-tense verb, meaning that it describes an action that will occur in the future. However, since the speaker already thanked his or her mother for the warning, it is not logical to use a future-tense verb in the blank. Choice C is incorrect.

Choice D says that the missing verb is *warns*. *Warn* is usually used with plural subjects, and *warns* used with single subjects. *Warns* can be used in the future or present tense, but it cannot be used in the past tense. Since the sentence is in the past tense, it needs a past-tense verb, so D is incorrect.

ADJECTIVES

An **adjective** is a word that is used to modify a noun or pronoun. An adjective answers a question: *Which one? What kind?* or *How many?* Usually, adjectives come before the words that they modify, but they may also come after a linking verb.

Which one? The *third* suit is my favorite.

What kind? This suit is *navy blue*.

How many? I am going to buy *four* pairs of socks to match the suit.

Review Video: Descriptive Text
Visit mometrix.com/academy and enter code: 174903

COMPARISON WITH ADJECTIVES

Some adjectives are relative, and other adjectives are absolute. Adjectives that are **relative** can show the comparison between things. **Absolute** adjectives can also show comparison, but they do so in a different way. Let's say that you are reading two books. You think that one book is perfect, and the other book is not exactly perfect. It is not possible for one book to be more perfect than the other. Either you think that the book is perfect, or you think that the book is imperfect. In this case, perfect and imperfect are absolute adjectives.

Relative adjectives will show the different **degrees** of something or someone to something else or someone else. The three degrees of adjectives include positive, comparative, and superlative.

The **positive** degree is the normal form of an adjective.

Example: This work is *difficult*. | She is *smart*.

The **comparative** degree compares one person or thing to another person or thing.

Example: This work is *more difficult* than your work. | She is *smarter* than me.

The **superlative** degree compares more than two people or things.

Example: This is the *most difficult* work of my life. | She is the *smartest* lady in school.

Review Video: Adjectives
Visit mometrix.com/academy and enter code: 470154

ADVERBS

An **adverb** is a word that is used to **modify,** or describe, a verb, adjective, or another adverb. Usually, adverbs answer one of these questions: *When? Where? How?* and *Why?* The negatives *not* and *never* are considered adverbs. Adverbs that modify adjectives or other adverbs **strengthen** or **weaken** the words that they modify.

Examples:

He walks *quickly* through the crowd.

The water flows *smoothly* on the rocks.

Note: Adverbs are usually indicated by the suffix *-ly*, which has been added to the root word. For instance, *quick* can be made into an adverb by adding *-ly* to construct *quickly*. Some words that end in *-ly* do not follow this rule and can function as other parts of speech. Examples of adjectives ending in *-ly* include: *early, friendly, holy, lonely, silly*, and *ugly*. To know if a word that ends in *-ly* is an adjective or adverb, check your dictionary. Also, while many adverbs end in *-ly*, you need to remember that not all adverbs end in *-ly*.

Examples:

He is *never* angry.

You are *too* irresponsible to travel alone.

Types of Adverbs

Different types of adverbs are used to describe particular aspects of a verb, adjective, or other adverb. The following are examples of common types of adverbs:

Time: Some adverbs show when something was done, such as *yesterday, today*, or *in two days.*

Manner: Some adverbs show the way something was done, such as *hurriedly, neatly, grumpily*, or *loudly.*

Frequency: Some adverbs show how often something was done, such as *seldom, often, never*, or *often.*

Degree: Some adverbs show how much or to what degree something was done, such as *completely, barely, highly*, or *halfway.*

Conjunctive: Conjunctive adverbs are used similarly to conjunctions, as they connect different ideas, but they can connect ideas from different clauses or sentences. Some examples of conjunctive adverbs are *however, alternatively, likewise*, and *then.*

Comparison with Adverbs

The rules for comparing adverbs are the same as the rules for adjectives.

The **positive** degree is the standard form of an adverb.

Example: He arrives *soon.* | She speaks *softly* to her friends.

The **comparative** degree compares one person or thing to another person or thing.

Example: He arrives *sooner* than Sarah. | She speaks *more softly* than him.

The **superlative** degree compares more than two people or things.

Example: He arrives *soonest* of the group. | She speaks the *most softly* of any of her friends.

Review Video: Adverbs
Visit mometrix.com/academy and enter code: 713951

Example

Identify the conjunctive adverb in the following sentences.

Every night, Savannah's brother loudly gets up to get a glass of water. Consequently, she has started sleeping with earmuffs on so that he does not wake her up at night.

a. Every night
b. Loudly
c. Consequently
d. At night

Choice A says that *every night* is a conjunctive adverb. What does *every night* describe in this sentence? It describes how often Savannah's brother loudly gets a glass of water. This means that *every night* shows the frequency that Savannah's brother does this action. Since *every night* is an adverb that shows frequency, choice A is incorrect.

Choice B says that *loudly* is a conjunctive adverb. In this sentence, what does *loudly* describe? It describes the way that Savannah's brother gets a glass of water each night. This means that *loudly* is an adverb that shows manner. *Loudly* is not a conjunctive adverb, so choice B is incorrect.

Choice C says that *consequently* is a conjunctive adverb. What function does *consequently* have in this sentence? It shows the reason that Savannah started wearing earmuffs while she sleeps. It also shows a connection between the information in the first sentence and the information in the second sentence. Since *consequently* connects the ideas in these sentences, it is a conjunctive adverb. Choice C is correct.

Choice D says that *at night* is a conjunctive adverb. *At* and *night* work together to form an adverbial phrase. Which type of adverb do they form? In this sentence, *at night* shows when Savannah wants to avoid being woken up by her brother. This makes *at night* an adverb that shows time, meaning that *at night* is not a conjunctive adverb and choice D is incorrect.

Prepositions

A **preposition** is a word placed before a noun or pronoun that shows the relationship between an object and another word in the sentence.

Common prepositions:

about	before	during	on	under
after	beneath	for	over	until
against	between	from	past	up
among	beyond	in	through	with
around	by	of	to	within
at	down	off	toward	without

Examples:

The napkin is *in* the drawer.

The Earth rotates *around* the Sun.

The needle is *beneath* the haystack.

Can you find "me" *among* the words?

Prepositional Phrases

One important thing to know about prepositions is that they form special phrases, called prepositional phrases. A **prepositional phrase** begins with a preposition and ends with a noun or pronoun that is the object of the preposition. Normally, the prepositional phrase functions as an **adjective** or an **adverb** within the sentence.

Examples:

The picinic is on the blanket. (prepositional phrase: *on the blanket*)

I am sick with a fever today. (prepositional phrase: *with a fever*)

Among the many flowers, John found a four-leaf clover. (prepositional phrase: *Among the many flowers*)

Be careful not to mistake the object in a prepositional phrase as the subject of a sentence. The subject of the sentence will not be found in a prepositional phrase because a prepositional phrase is used to describe how an object is related to the subject. Prepositional phrases do not influence subject-verb agreement.

Review Video: Prepositions
Visit mometrix.com/academy and enter code: 946763

EXAMPLE

Which of the following could NOT complete the sentence?

She went ____ the cave.

a. Sadly
b. Into
c. From
d. Through

Choice A says that the missing word is *sadly*. The blank is between *went* and *the cave*, meaning that the missing word will connect these pieces of the sentence. While *sadly* could be used here to show how the girl felt, there would still be missing information. A preposition is needed here to show whether she entered, exited, or stood outside of the cave. *Sadly* is an adverb, so A is the correct answer.

Choice B says that *into* would complete the sentence. Does *into* complete the sentence without leaving missing information? To say *she went into the cave* is a logical, complete sentence. Choice B is incorrect.

Choice C says that the missing word is *from*. This creates the sentence *she went from the cave*. Since she could have left the cave to go somewhere else, this is also a logical, complete sentence. Choice C is incorrect.

Choice D says that *through* would complete the sentence. The sentence would read *she went through the cave*. Since she could have explored the whole cave or found an exit on the other side of it, *through* can logically complete the sentence. Choice D is incorrect.

EXAMPLE

Identify the prepositional phrase in the following sentence.

Mable visited the store to buy some vegetables.

a. To buy
b. Visited the store
c. The store to buy
d. To buy some vegetables

Remember the pieces of a prepositional phrase. Prepositional phrases should begin with a preposition and end with a noun or pronoun. Considering these rules, can any of the answer choices be eliminated? Choice B and choice C can be eliminated because neither choice begins with a preposition!

That leaves choices A and D. Choice A says that the prepositional phrase is *to buy*. This does start with a preposition, and it does give more information about Mable's trip to the store. However, it does not end with a noun or pronoun. Choice D says that the prepositional phrase is *to buy some vegetables*. Choice D begins with a preposition and ends with a noun, and it explains why Mabel went to the store.

Choice D is the only choice that has all of the pieces of a prepositional phrase, so D is correct!

EXAMPLE

Read the sentence below and answer the following question.

A band with 15 members _____ performing at my restaurant tonight.

Identify the verb that best completes the sentence.

a. Were
b. Is
c. Are
d. Are not

This question is asking which verb should go in the blank. There are a couple of reasons why choosing the correct verb for this sentence may be confusing. First of all, there are two nouns that appear before the verb. Second, one of these nouns is singular and one is plural.

The first step is to determine which noun goes with the verb. The two nouns are *band* and *members*. While *members* is closest to the blank, it is part of a prepositional phrase that describes *band*. The subject of the sentence is *band*, so the verb must agree with *band*.

Is *band* singular or plural? The sentence says that the band has multiple members, but there is only one band. *Band* is a collective noun, meaning that it is a singular noun. This means that the correct verb will also be singular. With this in mind, can any of the answer choices be eliminated?

Choices A, C, and D are all plural verbs. Even though the blank appears after a plural noun, this noun is part of a prepositional phrase. The verb should match the singular subject *band*. The only choice with a singular verb is choice B, so B is the correct answer.

CONJUNCTIONS

Conjunctions join words, phrases, or clauses and they show the connection between the joined pieces. **Coordinating conjunctions** connect equal parts of sentences. Coordinating conjunctions can also be used to create compound subjects and compound predicates, in addition to compound sentences.

COORDINATING CONJUNCTIONS

The **coordinating conjunctions** include: *and, but, yet, or, nor, for,* and *so*

Compound Subjects:

compound subject
Terry *and* Marissa went to the movies last Saturday.

compund subject
Either pumpkin pie *or* apple pie would be a good dessert to bring to Thanksgiving dinner.

compound subject
Neither the clownfish *nor* the goldfish liked the new fish food very much.

Compound Predicates:

compound predicate
Veronica left school *and* picked up her sister from soccer practice.

compound predicate
The cat did not take a nap *or* play with the dog yesterday.

Compound Sentences:

The rock was small, *but* it was heavy.

She drove in the night, *and* he drove in the day.

Bill dressed nicely today, *for* he must give an important presentation this afternoon.

CORRELATIVE CONJUNCTIONS

Some examples of **correlative conjunctions** are: *either...or* | *neither...nor* | *not only...but also*. When one correlative conjunction is used, its matching correlative conjunction will be used later in the sentence.

Examples:

Either you are coming *or* you are staying.

He *not only* ran three miles *but also* swam 200 yards.

Review Video: Coordinating and Correlative Conjunctions
Visit mometrix.com/academy and enter code: 390329

Subordinating Conjunctions

Subordinating conjunctions link dependent clauses, clauses with either a subject or a predicate, to independent clauses, clauses with both a subject and a predicate, to form a complex sentence. The subordinating conjunction will always be at the beginning of the dependent clause. When the dependent clause is at the beginning of the sentence, it will end with a comma. When the independent clause is at the beginning of the sentence, no comma is needed.

Common **subordinating conjunctions** include:

after	since	whenever
although	so that	where
because	unless	wherever
before	until	whether
in order that	when	while

Examples:

I am hungry *because* I did not eat breakfast.

He went home *when* everyone left.

While her brother ate dinner, she played his favorite video game.

Review Video: Subordinating Conjunctions
Visit mometrix.com/academy and enter code: 958913

Example

Which of the following is a complex sentence?

a. Joseph went grocery shopping and put all of the groceries away at home.
b. Joseph went grocery shopping, and he put all of the groceries away at home.
c. Joseph went grocery shopping and put all of the groceries away when he got home.
d. Joseph went grocery shopping; he put all of the groceries away at home.

Choice A contains one subject and a compound predicate. Because there is only one subject, Joseph, there is only one clause. Since the sentence is made of one independent clause and a prepositional phrase, it is a simple sentence, and choice A is incorrect.

Choice B contains two clauses. The clauses are separated by a comma and a coordinating conjunction, and both are independent clauses. This sentence contains a prepositional phrase and two independent clauses, so it is a compound sentence. Choice B is incorrect.

Choice C contains two clauses. There are two subjects in the sentence, *Joseph* and *he*. Even though one clause is much shorter than the other, these subjects each go with a different clause. The first clause is independent. The second clause is dependent, as it begins with the word *when*. Since the sentence is made of one independent clause and one dependent clause, it is a complex sentence. Choice C is correct.

Choice D contains two clauses. They are both independent clauses, because they both contain a subject and a predicate, and they both form complete thoughts. Since there is no coordinating conjunction, they are linked by a semicolon. Since the sentence is made from two independent clauses, it is a compound sentence. Choice D is incorrect.

EXAMPLE

Identify the sentence that contains correlative conjunctions.

a. She can wait for her friend's letter to arrive, or she can call her now.
b. He must leave now, or he will end up in heavy traffic when he gets on the highway.
c. When your grandfather gets here, you can greet him with a handshake or a hug.
d. I can't decide whether to go to my brother's concert or to study for my test tomorrow.

Read the answer choices carefully. Remember that correlative conjunctions appear in pairs, so there will be at least two conjunctions in the sentence. Additionally, these conjunctions will go together. The information given immediately after the first conjunction will make little sense without the information that comes after the second conjunction.

Choice A contains the conjunction *or*. Though *or* can be a correlative conjunction, in this sentence, it is used by itself to connect two independent clauses. This means it is a coordinating conjunction. There are no correlative conjunctions in this sentence, so choice A is incorrect.

Choice B contains the conjunctions *or* and *when*. Again, *or* can be a correlative conjunction. However, the sentence could end after *traffic*. The information beginning with *when* is not needed to complete the thought, and *or* and *when* do not form a pair of correlative conjunctions. Choice B is incorrect.

Choice C contains the conjunctions *when* and *or*. *When* is used to begin a dependent clause. *Or* is used to form a compound object by linking *handshake* and *hug*. These conjunctions do not work together in this sentence, so they are not correlative conjunctions. Choice C is incorrect.

Choice D contains the conjunctions *whether* and *or*. *Whether* is used to introduce one choice the speaker can make, and *or* is used to introduce an alternative choice. If the sentence ended before *or*, it would be an incomplete thought. The conjunctions *whether* and *or* go together in this sentence, and they are correlative conjunctions. Choice D is correct.

END PUNCTUATION

PERIODS

Use a period to end all sentences except direct questions and exclamations. Periods are also used for abbreviations.

Examples: 3 p.m. | 2 a.m. | Mr. Jones | Mrs. Stevens | Dr. Smith | Bill, Jr. | Pennsylvania Ave.

Note: An abbreviation is a shortened form of a word or phrase.

QUESTION MARKS

Question marks should be used following a **direct question**. A polite request can be followed by a period instead of a question mark.

Direct Question: What is for lunch today? | How are you? | Why is that the answer?

Polite Requests: Can you please send me the item tomorrow. | Will you please walk with me on the track.

Review Video: Question Marks
Visit mometrix.com/academy and enter code: 118471

Exclamation Marks

Exclamation marks are used after a word group or sentence that shows much feeling or has special importance. Exclamation marks should not be overused. They are saved for proper **exclamatory interjections**.

Example: We're going to the finals! | You have a beautiful car! | "That's crazy!" she yelled.

Review Video: Exclamation Points
Visit mometrix.com/academy and enter code: 199367

Commas

The comma is a punctuation mark that can help you understand connections in a sentence. Not every sentence needs a comma. However, if a sentence needs a comma, you need to put it in the right place. A comma in the wrong place or a missing comma will make a sentence's meaning unclear. These are some of the rules for commas:

Use Case	Example
Before a **coordinating conjunction** joining independent clauses in compound sentences	Bob caught three fish, and I caught two fish.
Between **items in a series**	I will bring the turkey, the pie, and the coffee.
After a **dependent clause** that **begins a complex sentence**	Before she left, Ashley turned off all of the lights in her house.
After **transition words**	Consequently, Joel's mother grounded him.
After an **introductory phrase**	After the final out, we went to a restaurant to celebrate.
After a **prepositional phrase** at the **beginning of a sentence**	At 10 in the evening, Georgia finally arrived home from work.
After an **adverbial clause**	Studying the stars, I was awed by the beauty of the sky.
Before and after **nonessential modifiers**	John Frank, who coaches the team, was promoted today.
Before and after **nonessential appositives**	Thomas Edison, an American inventor, was born in Ohio.
Before and after **nonrestrictive phrases** or **clauses**	His favorite movie, which premiered before he was born, is over three hours long.
After **absolute phrases**	Relieved the test was over, Leah dropped her pencil and slouched in her chair.

Commas for Setting Off Nonessential Words, Phrases, and Clauses

Identifying where to place commas for nonessential words, phrases, and clauses is sometimes tricky. If the word, phrase, or clause is necessary for the sentence to be complete or logical, then it is essential, or restrictive. Additionally, if the word, phrase, or clause cannot be removed without changing the meaning of the sentence, then it is essential. Nonessential words, phrases, and clauses are those that give unnecessary information or do not flow smoothly with the rest of the words in the sentence. These words usually can also be logically placed in more than one spot in the sentence. **Appositives** are often nonessential words or phrases. They are most often used to specify which person or thing is being discussed. An appositive is an additional name or description that may be essential or nonessential.

Review Video: When To Use a Comma
Visit mometrix.com/academy and enter code: 786797

EXAMPLE

Ella's favorite stuffed animal Rory used to be her mother's.

Which word in the sentence is nonessential and should be set off by commas?

a. Be
b. Stuffed
c. Her
d. Rory

Choice A says that *be* should be set off by commas. Since *be* is a verb, it is unlikely that it is a nonessential word. In this sentence, the subject is *stuffed animal*, and *be* is the verb that shows the subject's action. *Be* is essential to the sentence, so choice A is incorrect.

Choice B says that *stuffed* should be set off by commas. *Stuffed* is an adjective, so it may be nonessential. However, it affects the meaning of this sentence. The word *stuffed* shows that the sentence is about a toy, not a live animal. *Stuffed* is essential to the meaning of the sentence, so choice B is incorrect.

Choice C says that *her* should be set off by commas. *Her* is a personal pronoun, so it is unlikely that it is nonessential. This sentence uses the word *her* to identify whose mother previously owned the stuffed animal. *Her* is essential to show who is being discussed. Choice C is incorrect.

Choice D says that *Rory* should be set off by commas. *Rory* is a name, so it could be a nonessential word, or even an appositive. In this sentence, the word tells the reader the name of Ella's favorite stuffed animal. The sentence can only be about one stuffed animal, because Ella can only have one favorite. This means that the stuffed animal's name is extra, or nonessential, information. *Rory* is a nonessential appositive, so choice D is correct.

EXAMPLE

The singer growing more exhausted with every song decided to stop dancing and stood still while singing.

Identify the nonrestrictive phrase that should be set off by commas in the above sentence.

a. The singer growing more exhausted
b. Decided to stop dancing
c. Growing more exhausted with every song
d. Stop dancing and stood still

Choice A says that *the singer growing more exhausted* is the nonrestrictive phrase. Is the sentence still a complete sentence without this phrase? No, because choice A includes the subject, *the singer*. Choice A is not the nonrestrictive phrase.

Choice B says that *decided to stop dancing* is the nonrestrictive phrase. Does the sentence make sense without this phrase? No, removing this phrase leaves the following sentence: The singer growing more exhausted with every song and stood still while singing. This is not a logical sentence, so choice B is not the nonrestrictive phrase.

Choice C says that *growing more exhausted with every song* is the nonrestrictive phrase. Removing this phrase leaves the following sentence: The singer decided to stop dancing and stood still while singing. This sentence makes sense and has the same meaning as the original sentence. This phrase gives extra information that is not essential to the sentence, so choice C is the nonrestrictive phrase. Choice C is correct.

Choice D says that *stop dancing and stood still* is the nonrestrictive phrase. Removing this phrase leaves the following sentence: The singer growing more exhausted with every song decided to while singing.

This sentence is now missing important information. What did the singer decide to do while singing? The remaining sentence is now missing the verb. Removing choice D makes the sentence incomplete, so choice D is not the nonrestrictive phrase.

Example

Where should a comma be added in the following sentence?

Though the mountain is very steep he is not afraid to scale it.

a. After *Though*
b. After *mountain*
c. After *steep*
d. After *afraid*

Choice A says there should be a comma after *though*. In this sentence, *though* is a subordinating conjunction that begins a dependent clause. Remember that a comma goes at the end of a dependent clause that appears at the beginning of a sentence. *Though* is at the beginning of the clause, and there is no other need for a comma right after it. Choice A is incorrect.

Choice B says there should be a comma after *mountain. Mountain* is the subject of the dependent clause in this sentence. The comma should go at the end of the dependent clause. *Mountain* appears in the middle of the dependent clause, not at the end of it. Choice B is incorrect.

Choice C says there should be a comma after *steep. Steep* is the last word in the dependent clause that begins the sentence. Adding a comma here would correctly separate the dependent clause from the following independent clause. This is the correct place for the comma, so choice C is correct.

Choice D says there should be a comma after *afraid. Afraid* is the verb in the independent clause, and there is no need to separate it from the rest of the sentence. Choice D is incorrect.

Semicolons

The semicolon is used to connect major sentence pieces of equal value. Some rules for semicolons include:

Use Case	Example
Between closely connected independent clauses **not connected with a coordinating conjunction**	You are right; we should go with your plan.
Between independent clauses **linked with a transitional word**	I think that we can agree on this; however, I am not sure about my friends.
Between items in a **series that has internal punctuation**	I have visited New York, New York; Augusta, Maine; and Baltimore, Maryland.

Review Video: How to Use Semicolons
Visit mometrix.com/academy and enter code: 370605

Example

Which of the following sentences is NOT written correctly?

a. My sister burned the lasagna we were going to eat for dinner; we went out to eat instead of cooking something else.
b. The ball rolled into the ditch, therefore, it was muddy and wet when he retrieved it.
c. She has lived in many cities, including Nashville, Tennessee; San Diego, California; and Salt Lake City, Utah.
d. He hung the picture in the wrong spot; now there is a distracting hole in the wall.

Choice A is a compound sentence. The semicolon is used to separate two independent clauses. There is no coordinating conjunction in the sentence. This sentence correctly uses a semicolon, so choice A is incorrect.

Choice B is a compound sentence. In a compound sentence, either a coordinating conjunction or a semicolon can be used to separate the independent clauses. This sentence includes a transitional word, but it uses neither a semicolon nor a coordinating conjunction. To revise this sentence, *therefore* can be replaced by a coordinating conjunction, or the first comma can be replaced with a semicolon This sentence is written incorrectly, so choice B is the correct answer.

Choice C is a sentence that includes a list. Remember that semicolons can be used to separate items in a list when at least one of the items includes a comma. In this sentence, a list of cities is given. Since a comma is required to separate the name of a city from the name of the state it is in, each of the items in the list contain a comma. This means that each full city name must be separated by a semicolon. This sentence is written correctly, so choice C is incorrect.

Choice D is a compound sentence and does not contain a coordinating conjunction. Semicolons can be used to separate independent clauses in a compound sentence instead of a coordinating conjunction. This sentence uses a semicolon correctly, so choice D is incorrect.

Quotation Marks

Use quotation marks to close off **direct quotations** of a person's written or spoken words, which are also called **dialogue**. Do not use quotation marks around indirect quotations. An indirect quotation gives someone's message without using the person's exact words. Use **single quotation marks** to close off a quotation inside a quotation.

> **Direct Quote**: Nancy said, "I am waiting for Henry to arrive."
>
> **Indirect Quote**: Henry said that he is going to be late to the meeting.
>
> **Quote inside a Quote**: The teacher asked, "Has everyone read Martin Luther King's 'I Have a Dream' speech?"

Quotation marks should be used around the titles of **short works**: newspaper and magazine articles, poems, short stories, songs, television episodes, and radio programs. Titles of **long works** should be italicized when they are part of a typed composition or underlined when they are part of a handwritten composition.

Examples:

> "Rip Van Winkle" (short story by Washington Irving)
>
> "O Captain! My Captain!" (poem by Walt Whitman)

Review Video: Quotation Marks
Visit mometrix.com/academy and enter code: 884918

APOSTROPHES

An apostrophe is used to show **possession** or the **deletion of letters in contractions**. An apostrophe is not needed with the possessive pronouns *his, hers, its, ours, theirs, whose,* and *yours.*

Singular Nouns: David's car | a book's theme | my brother's board game

Plural Nouns that end with -*s*: the scissors' handle | boys' basketball

Plural Nouns that end without -*s*: Men's department | the people's adventure

Review Video: Apostrophes
Visit mometrix.com/academy and enter code: 213068

Review Video: Punctuation Errors in Possessive Pronouns
Visit mometrix.com/academy and enter code: 221438

APOSTROPHES IN CONTRACTIONS

Contractions are combinations of words. Contractions involve taking two words, removing at least one letter from one of the words, putting an apostrophe in its place, and removing the space. For example, *does not* can be written as the contraction *doesn't*. The *o* is removed from *not* and is replaced with an apostrophe, which represents the removed letter, so it appears as *n't*. The space after does is then removed, turning *does not* into the contraction *doesn't*. Some more examples of contractions are listed below.

First Word	Second Word	Contraction
Can	Not	Can't
Do	Not	Don't
She	Will	She'll
They	Will	They'll
He	Is	He's
It	Is	It's
They	Are	They're
I	Am	I'm

Not all words can be used to form contractions, but many small, commonly used words can.

CAPITALIZATION

One important part of using correct grammar is properly capitalizing words. Usually, only nouns will be capitalized, but there are some exceptions. The most important capitalization rule is that the first word of every sentence, no matter what part of speech it is, should be capitalized. Another exception is that the pronoun *I* should always be capitalized.

Proper nouns are always capitalized, but sometimes it can be tricky to decide whether or not a noun is a proper noun. Some words that are usually common nouns may become proper nouns when used with other words or phrases. Also, when words that are not nouns are used with a noun, or when a group of words are used together as one noun, those words may also need to be capitalized.

TITLES OF BOOKS, STORIES, AND ESSAYS

Most of the words in titles of things like books, stories, and essays should be capitalized, but some should not. The very first word in a title should always be capitalized. Any other word in a title that is a noun, pronoun, adjective, verb or adverb should be capitalized. Articles, such as *a* or *the*, should not be capitalized. Short conjunctions and prepositions are usually not capitalized.

Abbreviations, Initials, and Acronyms

Abbreviations are shortened versions of other words. When an abbreviation shortens, or abbreviates, a word that should be capitalized, the abbreviation's first letter should also be capitalized. When the shortened word is a noun that is not capitalized, the abbreviation should be in lowercase. Initials are usually written using the first letter from multiple words. For example, John Fitzgerald Kennedy is commonly referred to by his initials, JFK. Acronyms also use the first letter from multiple words, but they are different from initials because they form words on their own. For example, NASA is an acronym for National Aeronautics and Space Administration. Some acronyms, like NASA, omit small words, such as *and*, *of*, and *for*. When initials and acronyms are used for proper nouns, each letter should be capitalized.

The types of words and phrases in the chart below are proper nouns and should always be capitalized:

	Description	**Example**
Historical Periods	A range of time in history that is related to specific events or circumstances	During the Romantic Period, many authors and poets wrote about their emotions.
Historical Events	Names of important events that happened in history	Napoleon Bonaparte led France after the French Revolution.
Historical Documents	Titles of important papers or compositions that are connected to historical events	The Mayflower Compact was written to create rules and expectations for the colony in Plymouth.
Languages	Names of the different languages that people speak	I want to learn to speak Cantonese, Spanish, and German.
Races and Ethnicities	Words often used to describe a person's heritage or cultural group	Malia taught her granddaughter how to hula so she could share a tradition of her Native Hawaiian heritage with her.
Nationalities	Words that describe which country a person is from	My teacher who moved to Canada last year is Romanian.
Organizations	Titles of official groups formed by people	Fewer than half of the states in America have a team in the National Basketball Association.

Example

> Allison and Claire enjoy studying art from the beginning of the renaissance. They started a club so they and other students can learn more about it. Allison and Claire named the club Early Renaissance Art Club, which can be abbreviated to ERA Club. The students that joined elected Claire as the president and Allison as the vice president. The club's first meeting will take place after Christmas vacation.

Which of the following changes should be made in the passage?

a. In the first sentence, *Renaissance* should be capitalized.
b. In the third sentence, *ERA* should be written as *Era*.
c. In the fourth sentence, *president* and *vice president* should be capitalized.
d. In the last sentence, *Christmas* should be in lowercase.

Choice A says that *Renaissance* should be capitalized in the first sentence of the passage. The Renaissance is a historical period, so *Renaissance* is a proper noun that should always be capitalized. Choice A is correct.

Choice B says that *ERA* should be written as *Era*. In the third sentence of the passage, the word *era* is used as an acronym. Remember that all letters in an acronym should be capitalized. The correct capitalization is *ERA*, so choice B is incorrect.

Choice C says that *president* and *vice president* should be capitalized. Titles for people are capitalized when they are used as part of a person's name or in the place of a person's name. In this passage, these titles are not used as part of anyone's name or in place of anyone's name, so they should be in lowercase. Choice C is incorrect.

Choice D says that *Christmas* should be in lowercase. The passage says that the first meeting will be held after Christmas break. Even though *Christmas* is used to describe when the students are getting a vacation from school, it is the name of a holiday. Names of holidays are always capitalized, so choice D is incorrect.

Word Confusion

To, Too, and Two

To can be an adverb or a preposition for showing direction, purpose, and relationship. A dictionary can also be used to see the many other ways to use *to* in a sentence.

> Examples: I went to the store. | I want to go with you.

Too is an adverb that means *also, as well, very,* or *in excess.*

> Examples: I can walk a mile too. | You have eaten too much.

Two is a number.

> Example: You have two minutes left.

There, Their, and They're

There can be an adjective, adverb, or pronoun. Often, *there* is used to show a place or to start a sentence.

> Examples: I went there yesterday. | There is something in his pocket.

Their is a pronoun that is used to show ownership.

> Examples: He is their father. | This is their fourth apology this week.

They're is a contraction of *they are.*

> Example: Did you know that they're in town?

Its and It's

Its is a possessive pronoun that shows ownership.

> Example: The guitar is in its case.

It's is a contraction of *it is.*

> Example: It's an honor and a privilege to meet you.

Affect and Effect

There are two main reasons that *affect* and *effect* are so often confused: 1) both words can be used as either a noun or a verb, and 2) unlike most homophones, their usage and meanings are closely related to each other. Here is a quick explanation of the four usage options:

Affect (n): feeling, emotion, or mood that is displayed

> Example: The patient had a flat *affect.* (i.e., his face showed little or no emotion)

Affect (v): to alter, to change, to influence

> Example: The sunshine *affects* the plant's growth.

Effect (n): a result, a consequence

> Example: What *effect* will this weather have on our schedule?

Effect (v): to bring about, to cause to be

> Example: These new rules will *effect* order in the office.

Example

Choose the correct spelling from each pair of homophones in the following passage.

> I found a unique tree in the forest. (It's/Its) trunk is blue, and it has (two/too) many branches to count. I brought some of my friends to see it, but the tree did not seem to (affect/effect) them. While (their/they're) not fascinated by the strange tree, I am!

The first pair of homophones is *it's* and *its.* Remember that the contraction *it's* is used in place of *it is. Its* is a possessive pronoun that shows a thing's ownership or possession. An easy way to decide whether *it's* or *its* is correct is to see how the sentence sounds with *it is*, instead. *It is trunk is blue* does not make sense. *Its trunk is blue* means that the tree has a blue trunk, so *its* is the correct choice.

The next pair of homophones is *two* and *too. Two* only means the number two. *Too* can mean *also* or *in excess.* Which of these makes the most sense in this sentence? *Two many branches to count* or *too many branches to count*? The correct meaning is that there is an abundance of branches, so *too* is the correct choice for this pair.

The third pair of homophones is *affect* and *effect.* Since both of these words can be used as a noun or verb, identifying the correct part of speech is a helpful first step. The part of speech is a verb, since the correct word will show what *the tree* does to *them. Affect* as a verb means to change or influence. *Effect* as a verb means to lead to or cause something to happen. Replace the homophone with these synonyms. Seeing the tree cannot cause or lead the speaker's friends to exist, but it can change them or influence them. *Affect* is the correct choice for this pair.

The last pair of homophones is *their* and *they're. Their* is a possessive pronoun used to show that multiple people or things own something. *They're* is a contraction used in place of *they are.* Replace the homophone with *they are.* Does the sentence make sense? It does because they, the speaker's friends, are not fascinated by the tree. Saying *their not fascinated* does not make sense. *They're* is the correct choice for this pair.

Vocabulary

Word Roots and Prefixes and Suffixes

Affixes

Affixes in the English language are morphemes that are added to words to create related but different words. Derivational affixes form new words based on and related to the original words. For example, the affix *–ness* added to the end of the adjective *happy* forms the noun *happiness.* Inflectional affixes form different grammatical versions of words. For example, the plural affix *–s* changes the singular noun *book* to the plural noun *books,* and the past tense affix *–ed* changes the present tense verb *look* to the past tense *looked.* Prefixes are affixes placed in front of words. For example, *heat* means to make hot; *preheat* means to heat in advance. Suffixes are affixes placed at the ends of words. The *happiness* example above contains the suffix *–ness.* Circumfixes add parts both before and after words, such as how *light* becomes *enlighten* with the prefix *en-* and the suffix *-en.* Interfixes create compound words via central affixes: *speed* and *meter* become *speedometer* via the interfix *–o–*.

Review Video: Affixes
Visit mometrix.com/academy and enter code: 782422

Word Roots, Prefixes, and Suffixes to Help Determine Meanings of Words

Many English words were formed from combining multiple sources. For example, the Latin *habēre* means "to have," and the prefixes *in-* and *im-* mean a lack or prevention of something, as in *insufficient* and *imperfect.* Latin combined *in-* with *habēre* to form *inhibēre,* whose past participle was *inhibitus*. This is the origin of the English word *inhibit,* meaning to prevent from having. Hence by knowing the meanings of both the prefix and the root, one can decipher the word meaning. In Greek, the root *enkephalo-* refers to the brain. Many medical terms are based on this root, such as encephalitis and hydrocephalus. Understanding the prefix and suffix meanings (*-itis* means inflammation; *hydro-* means water) allows a person to deduce that encephalitis refers to brain inflammation and hydrocephalus refers to water (or other fluid) in the brain.

Review Video: Root Words in English
Visit mometrix.com/academy and enter code: 896380

Review Video: Determining Word Meanings
Visit mometrix.com/academy and enter code: 894894

Prefixes

Knowing common prefixes is helpful for all readers as they try to determining meanings or definitions of unfamiliar words. For example, a common word used when cooking is *preheat.* Knowing that *pre-* means in advance can also inform them that *presume* means to assume in advance, that *prejudice* means advance judgment, and that this understanding can be applied to many other words beginning with *pre-*. Knowing that the prefix *dis-* indicates opposition informs the meanings of words like *disbar, disagree, disestablish,* and many more. Knowing *dys-* means bad, impaired, abnormal, or difficult informs *dyslogistic, dysfunctional, dysphagia,* and *dysplasia.*

Suffixes

In English, certain suffixes generally indicate both that a word is a noun, and that the noun represents a state of being or quality. For example, *-ness* is commonly used to change an adjective into its noun form, as with *happy* and *happiness, nice* and *niceness,* and so on. The suffix *–tion* is commonly used to transform a verb into its noun form, as with *converse* and *conversation or move* and *motion*. Thus, if readers are unfamiliar with the second form of a word, knowing the meaning of the transforming suffix can help them determine meaning.

Prefixes for Numbers

Prefix	Definition	Examples
bi-	two	bisect, biennial
mono-	one, single	monogamy, monologue
poly-	many	polymorphous, polygamous
semi-	half, partly	semicircle, semicolon
uni-	one	uniform, unity

Prefixes for Time, Direction, and Space

Prefix	Definition	Examples
a-	in, on, of, up, to	abed, afoot
ab-	from, away, off	abdicate, abjure
ad-	to, toward	advance, adventure
ante-	before, previous	antecedent, antedate
anti-	against, opposing	antipathy, antidote
cata-	down, away, thoroughly	catastrophe, cataclysm
circum-	around	circumspect, circumference
com-	with, together, very	commotion, complicate
contra-	against, opposing	contradict, contravene
de-	from	depart
dia-	through, across, apart	diameter, diagnose
dis-	away, off, down, not	dissent, disappear
epi-	upon	epilogue
ex-	out	extract, excerpt
hypo-	under, beneath	hypodermic, hypothesis
inter-	among, between	intercede, interrupt
intra-	within	intramural, intrastate
ob-	against, opposing	objection
per-	through	perceive, permit
peri-	around	periscope, perimeter
post-	after, following	postpone, postscript
pre-	before, previous	prevent, preclude
pro-	forward, in place of	propel, pronoun
retro-	back, backward	retrospect, retrograde
sub-	under, beneath	subjugate, substitute
super-	above, extra	supersede, supernumerary
trans-	across, beyond, over	transact, transport
ultra-	beyond, excessively	ultramodern, ultrasonic

Negative Prefixes

Prefix	Definition	Examples
a-	without, lacking	atheist, agnostic
in-	not, opposing	incapable, ineligible
non-	not	nonentity, nonsense
un-	not, reverse of	unhappy, unlock

Extra Prefixes

Prefix	Definition	Examples
for-	away, off, from	forget, forswear
fore-	previous	foretell, forefathers
homo-	same, equal	homogenized, homonym
hyper-	excessive, over	hypercritical, hypertension
in-	in, into	intrude, invade
mal-	bad, poorly, not	malfunction, malpractice
mis-	bad, poorly, not	misspell, misfire
neo-	new	Neolithic, neoconservative
omni-	all, everywhere	omniscient, omnivore
ortho-	right, straight	orthogonal, orthodox
over-	above	overbearing, oversight
pan-	all, entire	panorama, pandemonium
para-	beside, beyond	parallel, paradox
re-	backward, again	revoke, recur
sym-	with, together	sympathy, symphony

Below is a list of common suffixes and their meanings:

Adjective Suffixes

Suffix	Definition	Examples
-able (-ible)	capable of being	toler*able*, ed*ible*
-esque	in the style of, like	picturesque, grotesque
-ful	filled with, marked by	thankful, zestful
-ific	make, cause	terrific, beatific
-ish	suggesting, like	churlish, childish
-less	lacking, without	hopeless, countless
-ous	marked by, given to	religious, riotous

Noun Suffixes

Suffix	Definition	Examples
-acy	state, condition	accuracy, privacy
-ance	act, condition, fact	acceptance, vigilance
-ard	one that does excessively	drunkard, sluggard
-ation	action, state, result	occupation, starvation
-dom	state, rank, condition	serfdom, wisdom
-er (-or)	office, action	teach*er*, elevat*or*, hon*or*
-ess	feminine	waitress, duchess
-hood	state, condition	manhood, statehood
-ion	action, result, state	union, fusion
-ism	act, manner, doctrine	barbarism, socialism
-ist	worker, follower	monopolist, socialist
-ity (-ty)	state, quality, condition	acid*ity*, civil*ity*, twen*ty*
-ment	result, action	Refreshment

Suffix	Definition	Examples
-ness	quality, state	greatness, tallness
-ship	position	internship, statesmanship
-sion (-tion)	state, result	revi*sion*, expedi*tion*
-th	act, state, quality	warmth, width
-tude	quality, state, result	magnitude, fortitude

VERB SUFFIXES

Suffix	Definition	Examples
-ate	having, showing	separate, desolate
-en	cause to be, become	deepen, strengthen
-fy	make, cause to have	glorify, fortify
-ize	cause to be, treat with	sterilize, mechanize

NUANCE AND WORD MEANINGS

SYNONYMS AND ANTONYMS

When you understand how words relate to each other, you will discover more in a passage. This is explained by understanding **synonyms** (e.g., words that mean the same thing) and **antonyms** (e.g., words that mean the opposite of one another). As an example, *dry* and *arid* are synonyms, and *dry* and *wet* are antonyms.

There are many pairs of words in English that can be considered synonyms, despite having slightly different definitions. For instance, the words *friendly* and *collegial* can both be used to describe a warm interpersonal relationship, and one would be correct to call them synonyms. However, *collegial* (kin to *colleague*) is often used in reference to professional or academic relationships, and *friendly* has no such connotation.

If the difference between the two words is too great, then they should not be called synonyms. *Hot* and *warm* are not synonyms because their meanings are too distinct. A good way to determine whether two words are synonyms is to substitute one word for the other word and verify that the meaning of the sentence has not changed. Substituting *warm* for *hot* in a sentence would convey a different meaning. Although warm and hot may seem close in meaning, warm generally means that the temperature is moderate, and hot generally means that the temperature is excessively high.

Antonyms are words with opposite meanings. *Light* and *dark*, *up* and *down*, *right* and *left*, *good* and *bad*: these are all sets of antonyms. Be careful to distinguish between antonyms and pairs of words that are simply different. *Black* and *gray*, for instance, are not antonyms because gray is not the opposite of black. *Black* and *white*, on the other hand, are antonyms.

Not every word has an antonym. For instance, many nouns do not. What would be the antonym of *chair*? During your exam, the questions related to antonyms are more likely to concern adjectives. You will recall that adjectives are words that describe a noun. Some common adjectives include *purple*, *fast*, *skinny*, and *sweet*. From those four adjectives, *purple* is the item that lacks a group of obvious antonyms.

Review Video: Synonyms and Antonyms Visit mometrix.com/academy and enter code: 105612

DENOTATIVE VS. CONNOTATIVE MEANING

The **denotative** meaning of a word is the literal meaning. The **connotative** meaning goes beyond the denotative meaning to include the emotional reaction that a word may invoke. The connotative meaning often takes the denotative meaning a step further due to associations the reader makes with the denotative meaning. Readers can differentiate between the denotative and connotative meanings by first recognizing how authors use each meaning. Most non-fiction, for example, is fact-based and authors do not use flowery, figurative language. The reader can assume that the writer is using the denotative meaning of words. In fiction, the author may use the connotative meaning. Readers can determine whether the author is using the denotative or connotative meaning of a word by implementing context clues.

Review Video: Connotation and Denotation
Visit mometrix.com/academy and enter code: 310092

Nuances of Word Meaning Relative to Connotation, Denotation, Diction, and Usage

A word's denotation is simply its objective dictionary definition. However, its connotation refers to the subjective associations, often emotional, that specific words evoke in listeners and readers. Two or more words can have the same dictionary meaning, but very different connotations. Writers use diction (word choice) to convey various nuances of thought and emotion by selecting synonyms for other words that best communicate the associations they want to trigger for readers. For example, a car engine is naturally greasy; in this sense, "greasy" is a neutral term. But when a person's smile, appearance, or clothing is described as "greasy," it has a negative connotation. Some words have even gained additional or different meanings over time. For example, *awful* used to be used to describe things that evoked a sense of awe. When *awful* is separated into its root word, awe, and suffix, -ful, it can be understood to mean "full of awe." However, the word is now commonly used to describe things that evoke repulsion, terror, or another intense, negative reaction.

Review Video: Word Usage in Sentences
Visit mometrix.com/academy and enter code: 197863

Using Context to Determine Meaning

Context Clues

Readers of all levels will encounter words that they have either never seen or have encountered only on a limited basis. The best way to define a word in **context** is to look for nearby words that can assist in revealing the meaning of the word. For instance, unfamiliar nouns are often accompanied by examples that provide a definition. Consider the following sentence: *Dave arrived at the party in hilarious garb: a leopard-print shirt, buckskin trousers, and bright green sneakers.* If a reader was unfamiliar with the meaning of garb, he or she could read the examples (i.e., a leopard-print shirt, buckskin trousers, and bright green sneakers) and quickly determine that the word means *clothing*. Examples will not always be this obvious. Consider this sentence: *Parsley, lemon, and flowers were just a few of the items he used as garnishes.* Here, the word *garnishes* is exemplified by parsley, lemon, and flowers. Readers who have eaten in a variety of restaurants will probably be able to identify a garnish as something used to decorate a plate.

Review Video: Reading Comprehension: Using Context Clues
Visit mometrix.com/academy and enter code: 613660

Using Contrast in Context Clues

In addition to looking at the context of a passage, readers can use contrast to define an unfamiliar word in context. In many sentences, the author will not describe the unfamiliar word directly; instead, he or she will describe the opposite of the unfamiliar word. Thus, you are provided with some information that will bring you closer to defining the word. Consider the following example: *Despite his intelligence, Hector's low brow and bad posture made him look obtuse.* The author writes that Hector's appearance does not convey intelligence. Therefore, *obtuse* must mean unintelligent. Here is another example: *Despite the horrible weather, we were beatific about our trip to Alaska*. The word *despite* indicates that the speaker's feelings were at odds with the weather. Since the weather is described as *horrible*, then *beatific* must mean something positive.

Substitution to Find Meaning

In some cases, there will be very few contextual clues to help a reader define the meaning of an unfamiliar word. When this happens, one strategy that readers may employ is **substitution**. A good reader will brainstorm some possible synonyms for the given word, and he or she will substitute these words into the sentence. If the sentence and the surrounding passage continue to make sense, then the substitution has revealed at least some information about the unfamiliar word. Consider the sentence: *Frank's admonition rang in her ears as she climbed the mountain.* A reader unfamiliar with *admonition* might come up with some substitutions like *vow, promise, advice, complaint*, or *compliment.* All of these words make general sense of the sentence, though their meanings are diverse. However, this process has suggested that an admonition is some sort of message. The substitution strategy is rarely able to pinpoint a precise definition, but this process can be effective as a last resort.

Occasionally, you will be able to define an unfamiliar word by looking at the descriptive words in the context. Consider the following sentence: *Fred dragged the recalcitrant boy kicking and screaming up the stairs.* The words *dragged, kicking*, and *screaming* all suggest that the boy does not want to go up the stairs. The reader may assume that *recalcitrant* means something like unwilling or protesting. In this example, an unfamiliar adjective was identified.

Additionally, using description to define an unfamiliar noun is a common practice compared to unfamiliar adjectives, as in this sentence: *Don's wrinkled frown and constantly shaking fist identified him as a curmudgeon of the first order.* Don is described as having a *wrinkled frown and constantly shaking fist*, suggesting that a *curmudgeon* must be a grumpy person. Contrasts do not always provide detailed information about the unfamiliar word, but they at least give the reader some clues.

Words with Multiple Meanings

When a word has more than one meaning, readers can have difficulty determining how the word is being used in a given sentence. For instance, the verb *cleave*, can mean either *join* or *separate*. When readers come upon this word, they will have to select the definition that makes the most sense. Consider the following sentence: *Hermione's knife cleaved the bread cleanly*. Since a knife cannot join bread together, the word must indicate separation. A slightly more difficult example would be the sentence: *The birds cleaved to one another as they flew from the oak tree.* Immediately, the presence of the words *to one another* should suggest that in this sentence *cleave* is being used to mean *join*. Discovering the intent of a word with multiple meanings requires the same tricks as defining an unknown word: look for contextual clues and evaluate the substituted words.

Context Clues to Help Determine Meanings of Words

If readers simply bypass unknown words, they can reach unclear conclusions about what they read. However, looking for the definition of every unfamiliar word in the dictionary can slow their reading progress. Moreover, the dictionary may list multiple definitions for a word, so readers must search the word's context for meaning. Hence context is important to new vocabulary regardless of reader methods. Four types of context clues are examples, definitions, descriptive words, and opposites. Authors may use a certain word, and then follow it with several different examples of what it describes. Sometimes authors actually supply a definition of a word they use, which is especially true in informational and technical texts. Authors may use descriptive words that elaborate upon a vocabulary word they just used. Authors may also use opposites with negation that help define meaning.

Examples and Definitions

An author may use a word and then give examples that illustrate its meaning. Consider this text: "Teachers who do not know how to use sign language can help students who are deaf or hard of hearing understand certain instructions by using gestures instead, like pointing their fingers to indicate which direction to look or go; holding up a hand, palm outward, to indicate stopping; holding the hands flat, palms up, curling a finger toward oneself in a beckoning motion to indicate 'come here'; or curling all fingers toward oneself repeatedly to indicate 'come on', 'more', or 'continue.'" The author of this text has used the word "gestures" and then followed it with examples, so a reader unfamiliar with the word could deduce from the examples that "gestures" means "hand motions." Readers can find examples by looking for signal words "for example," "for instance," "like," "such as," and "e.g."

While readers sometimes have to look for definitions of unfamiliar words in a dictionary or do some work to determine a word's meaning from its surrounding context, at other times an author may make it easier for readers by defining certain words. For example, an author may write, "The company did not have sufficient capital, that is, available money, to continue operations." The author defined "capital" as "available money," and heralded the definition with the phrase "that is." Another way that authors supply word definitions is with appositives. Rather than being introduced by a signal phrase like "that is," "namely," or "meaning," an appositive comes after the vocabulary word it defines and is enclosed within two commas. For example, an author may write, "The Indians introduced the Pilgrims to pemmican, cakes they made of lean meat dried and mixed with fat, which proved greatly beneficial to keep settlers from starving while trapping." In this example, the appositive phrase following "pemmican" and preceding "which" defines the word "pemmican."

DESCRIPTIONS

When readers encounter a word they do not recognize in a text, the author may expand on that word to illustrate it better. While the author may do this to make the prose more picturesque and vivid, the reader can also take advantage of this description to provide context clues to the meaning of the unfamiliar word. For example, an author may write, "The man sitting next to me on the airplane was obese. His shirt stretched across his vast expanse of flesh, strained almost to bursting." The descriptive second sentence elaborates on and helps to define the previous sentence's word "obese" to mean extremely fat. A reader unfamiliar with the word "repugnant" can decipher its meaning through an author's accompanying description: "The way the child grimaced and shuddered as he swallowed the medicine showed that its taste was particularly repugnant."

OPPOSITES

Text authors sometimes introduce a contrasting or opposing idea before or after a concept they present. They may do this to emphasize or heighten the idea they present by contrasting it with something that is the reverse. However, readers can also use these context clues to understand familiar words. For example, an author may write, "Our conversation was not cheery. We sat and talked very solemnly about his experience and a number of similar events." The reader who is not familiar with the word "solemnly" can deduce by the author's preceding use of "not cheery" that "solemn" means the opposite of cheery or happy, so it must mean serious or sad. Or if someone writes, "Don't condemn his entire project because you couldn't find anything good to say about it," readers unfamiliar with "condemn" can understand from the sentence structure that it means the opposite of saying anything good, so it must mean reject, dismiss, or disapprove. "Entire" adds another context clue, meaning total or complete rejection.

SYNTAX TO DETERMINE PART OF SPEECH AND MEANINGS OF WORDS

Syntax refers to sentence structure and word order. Suppose that a reader encounters an unfamiliar word when reading a text. To illustrate, consider an invented word like "splunch." If this word is used in a sentence like "Please splunch that ball to me," the reader can assume from syntactic context that "splunch" is a verb. We would not use a noun, adjective, adverb, or preposition with the object "that ball," and the prepositional phrase "to me" further indicates "splunch" represents an action. However, in the sentence, "Please hand that splunch to me," the reader can assume that "splunch" is a noun. Demonstrative adjectives like "that" modify nouns. Also, we hand someone some*thing*—a thing being a noun; we do not hand someone a verb, adjective, or adverb. Some sentences contain further clues. For example, from the sentence, "The princess wore the glittering splunch on her head," the reader can deduce that it is a crown, tiara, or something similar from the syntactic context, without knowing the word.

Syntax to Indicate Different Meanings of Similar Sentences

The syntax, or structure, of a sentence affords grammatical cues that aid readers in comprehending the meanings of words, phrases, and sentences in the texts that they read. Seemingly minor differences in how the words or phrases in a sentence are ordered can make major differences in meaning. For example, two sentences can use exactly the same words but have different meanings based on the word order:

- "The man with a broken arm sat in a chair."
- "The man sat in a chair with a broken arm."

While both sentences indicate that a man sat in a chair, differing syntax indicates whether the man's or chair's arm was broken.

Review Video: Syntax
Visit mometrix.com/academy and enter code: 242280

Determining Meaning of Phrases and Paragraphs

Like unknown words, the meanings of phrases, paragraphs, and entire works can also be difficult to discern. Each of these can be better understood with added context. However, for larger groups of words, more context is needed. Unclear phrases are similar to unclear words, and the same methods can be used to understand their meaning. However, it is also important to consider how the individual words in the phrase work together. Paragraphs are a bit more complicated. Just as words must be compared to other words in a sentence, paragraphs must be compared to other paragraphs in a composition or a section.

Determining Meaning in Various Types of Compositions

To understand the meaning of an entire composition, the type of composition must be considered. **Expository writing** is generally organized so that each paragraph focuses on explaining one idea, or part of an idea, and its relevance. **Persuasive writing** uses paragraphs for different purposes to organize the parts of the argument. **Unclear paragraphs** must be read in the context of the paragraphs around them for their meaning to be fully understood. The meaning of full texts can also be unclear at times. The purpose of composition is also important for understanding the meaning of a text. To quickly understand the broad meaning of a text, look to the introductory and concluding paragraphs. Fictional texts are different. Some fictional works have implicit meanings, but some do not. The target audience must be considered for understanding texts that do have an implicit meaning, as most children's fiction will clearly state any lessons or morals. For other fiction, the application of literary theories and criticism may be helpful for understanding the text.

Resources for Determining Word Meaning and Usage

While these strategies are useful for determining the meaning of unknown words and phrases, sometimes additional resources are needed to properly use the terms in different contexts. Some words have multiple definitions, and some words are inappropriate in particular contexts or modes of writing. The following tools are helpful for understanding all meanings and proper uses for words and phrases.

- **Dictionaries** provide the meaning of a multitude of words in a language. Many dictionaries include additional information about each word, such as its etymology, its synonyms, or variations of the word.
- **Glossaries** are similar to dictionaries, as they provide the meanings of a variety of terms. However, while dictionaries typically feature an extensive list of words and comprise an entire

publication, glossaries are often included at the end of a text and only include terms and definitions that are relevant to the text they follow.

- **Spell Checkers** are used to detect spelling errors in typed text. Some spell checkers may also detect the misuse of plural or singular nouns, verb tenses, or capitalization. While spell checkers are a helpful tool, they are not always reliable or attuned to the author's intent, so it is important to review the spell checker's suggestions before accepting them.
- **Style Manuals** are guidelines on the preferred punctuation, format, and grammar usage according to different fields or organizations. For example, the Associated Press Stylebook is a style guide often used for media writing. The guidelines within a style guide are not always applicable across different contexts and usages, as the guidelines often cover grammatical or formatting situations that are not objectively correct or incorrect.

Types of Essays

Essays

Essays usually focus on one topic, subject, or goal. There are several types of essays, including informative, persuasive, and narrative. An essay's structure and formality depend on the type of essay and its goal. While narrative essays typically do not include outside sources, other types of essays often require some research and the use of primary and secondary sources.

The basic format of an essay typically has three major parts: the introduction, the body, and the conclusion. The body is further divided into the writer's main points. Most essays will have at least three main points, but essays that go into more depth can have almost any number of main points.

An essay's introduction should answer three questions:

1. What is the **subject** of the essay?

   If an essay is about a book, the answer would include the title and author of the book, as well as any additional information needed, such as the subject or argument of the book.

2. How does the essay **discuss** the subject?

   To answer this, the writer briefly summarizes the main points and the evidence supporting them to let readers know how the essay is organized and what information they can expect to read.

3. What will the essay **prove**?

   This information is in the thesis statement, usually the opening paragraph's last sentence, which clearly states the writer's message.

The body elaborates on all the main points related to the thesis, introducing one main point at a time, and includes supporting evidence with each main point. Each body paragraph should state the point in a topic sentence, which is usually the first sentence in the paragraph. The paragraph should then explain the point's meaning, support it with quotations or other evidence, and then explain how this point and the evidence are related to the thesis. The writer should then repeat this procedure in a new paragraph for each additional main point.

The conclusion restates the content of the introduction, including the thesis, to remind the reader of the essay's main argument or subject. The essay writer may also summarize the highlights of the argument or description contained in the body of the essay, following the same organization originally used in the body. For example, a conclusion might look like: Point 1 + Point 2 + Point 3 = Thesis, or Point 1 → Point 2

→ Point 3 → Thesis Proof. Good organization makes essays easier for writers to compose and provides a guide for readers to follow. Well-organized essays hold attention better and are more likely to get readers to believe or agree with the writer.

Using Sources in Essays

Sometimes writers use information from others in their work. This is most common in expository and persuasive writing. For an expository essay, a writer may not know all of the information that he or she needs to finish the composition. The writer may use other people's work to find the missing information and complete the composition. Persuasive writers may do research to find facts or statements from others that support their own beliefs and make their writing more persuasive. In both cases, research helps the writer find information that **supports** his or her **original work**.

Outside information must be relevant, true, and helpful to be appropriate for a composition. Writers must also be careful not to use too much outside information, since this can make the composition unoriginal. If a writer does use outside information, it is extremely important that the writer mention in the composition where the information came from. If the writer forgets or chooses not to say where the information came from, he or she has stolen someone else's work and presented it as their own. Doing this is called **plagiarism**.

Informational Texts

Informational texts, also called instructional or expository texts, are compositions written to inform the reader about a specific topic. An informational essay can inform readers in a variety of ways, such as giving them instructions, telling them facts about the topic, or teaching them why something happens. Informational texts should be logical, meaning that they should present information in an order that the reader can easily understand, and they should include the right amount of information so the writer successfully informs his or her audience of new information.

Informational texts should also focus on a **central idea**. In the introduction of an informational text, there may be a sentence or two that clearly state the essay's central idea. This sentence, or sentences, is called a **thesis statement**. The central idea should be clear throughout the composition. By emphasizing the central idea in the introduction, body, and conclusion, the writer can ensure that the central idea is clear. One way to make sure that the central idea is emphasized is to think about the purpose of each part of the essay. The introduction prepares the reader by telling them what the rest of the essay is about, so the central idea should be **introduced** in this section. The body tells the reader the information the writer wants to tell the audience, so this **explains** the central idea and facts about it to the reader. The conclusion is used to **remind** the reader of how the information in the body is related and **restates** the central idea one final time.

Structures or Organizational Patterns in Informational Texts

Informational text can be **descriptive**, meaning that it gives information that can be experienced through the five senses, or it answers the questions what, who, when, where, and why. One common method of organizing informational text is to put it in a certain sequence, or order. **Chronological** texts include events in the order that they occurred, from start to finish. **How-to**, or **instructional**, texts organize information into a series of instructions in the order in which the steps should be followed. **Comparison-contrast** structures of informational text describe different ideas to their readers by pointing out how things or ideas are similar and how they are different. **Cause and effect** structures of informational text describe events that occurred and the causes or reasons for those events. **Problem and solution** structures of informational texts introduce and describe problems and offer one or more solutions for each problem described.

Review Video: Organizational Methods to Structure Text
Visit mometrix.com/academy and enter code: 606263

ARGUMENTATIVE WRITING

In argumentative writing, the writer expresses a belief or opinion that he or she wants to lead readers to agree with. When writing an argumentative composition, the writer should first identify the **topic** his or her opinion is about. The topic may be serious or fun, as long as there is one clear topic in the composition. The next step is for the writer to determine his or her opinion on the topic and determine why he or she holds that opinion. In order to persuade others to agree with their opinion, the writer must be able to give readers reasons to support the opinion. If the writer does not know why he or she has an opinion, it will be difficult to convince readers to agree. In addition to having reasons that support their opinion, writers should prepare examples that support each of these reasons in order to strengthen their composition.

Once the writer has determined his or her topic, opinion, and reasons for having the opinion, he or she is ready to begin writing an argumentative essay. In the introduction, the writer should capture the reader's interest, introduce the topic, and reveal his or her opinion about the topic. In the body of the composition, the writer should remind the reader of the opinion and give his or her reasons for holding the opinion. If the writer has any examples, facts, or other information that supports his or her opinion or reasons for believing it, these should also be included in the body. Writers may also use a body paragraph to mention opposing opinions or beliefs and explain why they disagree with them. As in other compositions, the conclusion should remind the reader of the essay's topic and purpose, as well as remind the reader how the opinion has been explained and supported. The conclusion should also invite the reader to continue thinking about the topic and writer's opinion. This can be done through questions or statements that lead readers to consider whether or not they agree with the author's opinion or what their own opinions are.

Review Video: Argumentative Writing
Visit mometrix.com/academy and enter code: 561544

INFORMATIVE VS. PERSUASIVE WRITING

Informative writing, also called explanatory or expository writing, is written to show that something is true or factual, while **persuasive** writing is written to lead the reader to agree with something that may or may not be true or factual. While persuasive text is written to **persuade** readers to agree with the author's position, informative text simply **provides information** to readers. Informative writing **informs** readers about why or how something is as it is. This can include offering new information, explaining how a process works, or describing a concept for readers.

Review Video: Informational Text
Visit mometrix.com/academy and enter code: 924964

FACTS AND OPINIONS

Writers and readers must always be aware of the difference between fact and opinion. A **fact** can be tested and proven to be true. An **opinion**, on the other hand, is someone's personal thoughts or feelings. Opinions are often not changed by information. If an author writes that a newborn elephant is about five times taller than a newborn giraffe, then he or she is stating a fact. If the author writes that giraffes are more interesting than elephants, then he or she is giving an opinion because this cannot be proven to be true or false. Opinions are often supported by facts. For instance, the author might use a comparison between the way that giraffes eat and the way elephants eat as evidence of how giraffes are more interesting. An opinion supported by facts tends to be more convincing. On the other hand, when authors support their opinions with other opinions, readers should seriously think about and read the argument carefully to see whether it is logical and trustworthy.

Review Video: Distinguishing Fact and Opinion
Visit mometrix.com/academy and enter code: 870899

Narrative Writing

Put simply, **narrative** writing tells a story. Narratives should tell stories in such a way that the readers learn something or gain understanding about a related topic or idea. Personal narratives are narratives writers create about personal experiences that were meaningful to them. Narratives should start with the story's actions or events, rather than long descriptions or introductions. However, the narrative should still include descriptions at points where they will entertain the reader or help the reader visualize or better understand the scene. To write an effective description, writers should include sensory details, asking themselves what they saw, heard, felt or touched, smelled, and tasted during the experiences they describe. In narrative writing, the details should be **concrete** rather than **abstract**. Concrete details are those that can be experienced through one of the five senses, while abstract details are not able to be experienced in this way. Using concrete details enables readers to imagine everything that the writer describes. Writers should make sure that there is a point to each story by describing what they learned from the experience they narrate.

Personal Narratives

A **personal narrative** is a story about something that happened to the writer. **Personal narrative essays** are structured the same as other types of essays, as they have an introduction, body paragraphs, and a conclusion. Like other essays, the introduction of a personal narrative should contain a hook, or an opening sentence that interests the reader and prompts them to read the rest of the narrative. The introduction may also provide context for the story told in the personal narrative. One significant difference between personal narratives and other essays is that the body paragraphs of a personal narrative should contain sensory details, or imagery. A good personal narrative will give the reader a clear picture of the events and engage their emotions, and sensory details are effective at achieving these goals. The body should describe the events in chronological order, and the story should be completed in the last body paragraph. The conclusion will summarize the main idea of the personal narrative and may include information such as the writer's brief reflection on the events, how the events taught or changed the writer, or any relevant events that have happened since the events in the narrative.

Sensory Details

Writers need to use vivid descriptions when writing descriptive essays. Narratives should also include descriptions of characters, things, and events. Writers should remember to describe not only the visual detail of what someone or something looks like, but details from other senses, as well. For example, they can contrast the feeling of a sea breeze to the feeling of a mountain breeze, describe how they think something inedible would taste, and compare sounds they hear in the same location at different times of day and night. Readers have trouble visualizing images or imagining sensory impressions and feelings from abstract descriptions, so concrete descriptions make these more real.

Informational Text Example

Below is a prompt for an informational text. There is also an example of an essay that addresses the prompt. There are multiple drafts of this essay to show what kinds of changes a writer may make during the writing process to improve his or her work.

PROMPT:

Do you ever dream of going to a new city, state, or even country? Write about one place you want to travel to on vacation. Be sure to share why you would like to visit that place.

Rough Draft

Imagine traveling into the city or the beach and being transported back in time. This is what it must be like to live in Greece. The old buildings, beautiful beaches, and Greek foods are reasons I want to visit Greece.

Several buildings from ancient Greece are still standing, and they can easily be enjoyed by visitors and the people of Greece today. Some of the most famous ones, like the Parthenon, are located throughout the capital. This means that even when you are sitting in an air-conditioned restaurant in Athens, you can still see what is left of history. There are also tours that teach visitors more about these structures and the events that happened at each one. Though seeing these structures is not the only reason I would like to visit Greece, they would be enough of a reason for me to visit.

In addition to the scenery, another reason to visit Greece is to try real Greek and Mediterranean foods. I have tried a few Greek foods, like baklava and pita bread, and I enjoyed them. While these foods are available in America, I think they are probably made a little differently in Greece. I am interested in seeing what the differences are and trying new things. I hope I can visit Greece soon, because I am getting hungry just thinking about the food there!

Greece has a variety of beaches, as some are small with rocky structures and some look like normal beaches. The water is also different from some American waters because Greece is next to the Mediterranean Sea. Also, many historical events and myths took place on some of the beaches. I would love to sit on one of those beaches and try to imagine ships or characters from myths coming to the shore! The beaches in Greece are beautiful, but I think they also sound fun and interesting!

Walking through historical structures, visiting unique beaches, and eating new foods there is my dream. If I only ever have the chance to go on one vacation, I hope it is to Greece!

Revised Draft

Imagine traveling into the city or the beach and being transported back in time. This is what it must be like to live in Greece. <u>The remaining historical sites that are still there allow visitors to see two cultures side by side.</u> The old buildings, beautiful beaches, and Greek foods are reasons I want to visit Greece.

Several buildings from ancient Greece are still standing, and they can easily be enjoyed by visitors and the people of Greece today. Some of the most famous ones, like the Parthenon, are located throughout the capital. This means that even when you are sitting in an air-conditioned restaurant in Athens, you can still see what is left of history. There are also tours that teach visitors more about these structures and the events that happened at each one. Though seeing these structures is not the only reason I would like to visit Greece, they would be enough of a reason for me to visit.

Greece has a variety of beaches, as some are small with rocky structures and some look like normal beaches. The water is also different from some American waters because Greece is next to the Mediterranean Sea. Also, many historical events and myths took place on some of the beaches. I would love to sit on one of those beaches and try to imagine ships or characters from myths coming to the shore! The beaches in Greece are beautiful, but I think they also sound fun and interesting!

In addition to the scenery, a third reason to visit Greece is to try real Greek and Mediterranean foods. I have tried a few Greek foods, like baklava and pita bread, and I enjoyed them. While these foods are available in America, I think they are probably made a little differently in Greece. I am interested in seeing what the differences are and trying new things. I hope I can visit Greece soon, because I am getting hungry just thinking about the food there!

<u>Greece is a special place where the old and the new come together.</u> Walking through historical structures, visiting unique beaches, and eating new foods there is my dream. If I only ever have the chance to go on one vacation, I hope it is to Greece!

Revised Draft Notes

Remember the purpose of the revising stage of the writing process. When revising, it is important to look at the whole composition. Do all of the paragraphs strengthen the composition? Do the introduction and conclusion help the reader understand the central idea and main points?

In this revision, nothing has been removed, but there are some additions. Look at the underlined words. In the introduction, a sentence has been added. Why? Previously, the introduction had only a hook and a thesis. The sentences were well written, but the writer did not provide a connection between the hook and the thesis. The new sentence connects the ideas in both sentences and introduces some of the main points the writer will discuss in the essay.

In the conclusion, another sentence has been added. This sentence strengthens the composition by creating a transition from the body to the conclusion. Before, the conclusion began abruptly by listing the three main points from the body of the essay. This sentence makes the essay flow better by giving the reader a transition from the body to the conclusion. This sentence reminds the reader of composition's central idea before repeating the writer's main points and sharing his or her hopes.

Finally, the third and fourth paragraphs have been switched. Why is that? Before, the writer discussed ancient buildings, then food, then the beaches. This revised draft discusses buildings, then beaches, then food. This new order puts the more closely related points, the scenery of the buildings and beaches, closer together in the essay. This helps the reader by making the organization of the essay more logical.

EDITED DRAFT

Imagine traveling into the city or the beach and being transported back in time. This is what it must be like to live in Greece, since the remaining historical sites ~~that are still there~~ allow visitors to see two cultures side by side. The ~~old~~ ancient buildings, beautiful beaches, and Greek foods are reasons I want to visit Greece.

Several buildings from ancient Greece are still standing, and they can easily be enjoyed by visitors and the people of Greece today. Some of the most famous ones, like the Parthenon, are located throughout the capital. This means that even when you are sitting in an air-conditioned restaurant in Athens, you can still see ~~what is left~~ glimpses of history. There are also tours that teach visitors more about these structures and the events that happened at each one. ~~Though seeing these structures is not the only reason I would like to visit Greece, they would be enough of a reason for me to visit.~~ Seeing these structures alone is enough of a reason for me to visit Greece!

Another reason I want to travel to Greece is to see the beaches there. There are a variety of beaches, as some are small with rocky structures and some look like ~~normal~~ typical beaches. The water is also different from some American waters because Greece is next to the Mediterranean Sea. Also, many historical events and myths took place on some of the beaches. I would love to sit on one of those beaches and try to imagine ships or characters from myths coming to the shore! The beaches in Greece are beautiful, but I think they also sound fun and interesting!

In addition to the scenery, a third reason to visit Greece is to try ~~real~~ authentic Greek and Mediterranean foods. I have tried a few Greek foods, like baklava and pita bread, and I enjoyed them. While these foods are available in America, I think they are probably made a little differently in Greece, so I am interested in seeing what the differences are and trying new things. I hope I can visit Greece soon, because I am getting hungry just thinking about the food there!

Greece is a special place where the old and the new come together. Walking through historical structures, visiting unique beaches, and eating new foods there is my dream. If I only ever have the chance to go on one vacation, I hope it is to Greece!

Edited Draft Notes

Since the writer has revised his or her work, the next step is to edit the composition. Remember that editing is very similar to revising, but editing usually includes paying attention to each paragraph, instead of the whole composition. Look at the changes that were made to each paragraph.

There are small changes throughout this draft. First, look at the introduction. Before, the introduction had four sentences that were about the same length. In this draft, the second and third sentences have been combined to make a longer sentence. This creates more sentence variety in the introduction, which makes the composition more entertaining for the writer's audience. A few words have been crossed out, as well. *That are still there* has been replaced with *remaining*. This change makes the writing more concise and formal. Also, *old* has been replaced with *ancient*. This clarifies what kind of buildings the writer is describing by using a word that more specifically describes the age of the buildings.

In the next paragraph, *what is left* has been replaced with *glimpses*. This change makes the writing more concise by using one word instead of three. Furthermore, this change makes the writing more interesting and entertaining by using a better vocabulary word. At the end of the paragraph, the last sentence has been condensed. Most of the sentences in this paragraph are long. Shortening this sentence adds sentence variety to this paragraph and makes the concluding sentence more concise. Overall, these changes make the paragraph easier to read by eliminating unnecessary words and using better vocabulary.

There are a few more changes left in the third and fourth paragraphs. A transition has been added to the beginning of the third paragraph. Now, the writer introduces the next main point before describing the beaches. This makes the essay flow better overall and making it easier for the writer's audience to read. *Normal* has been replaced with *typical*. Since there are so many different beaches in the world, there are not really any normal beaches. *Typical* is a much clearer word. Now, the reader knows that the writer is trying to distinguish the beaches in Greece from the type of beaches that he or she sees most often.

In the next paragraph, *real* has been replaced with *authentic*. The food the writer has tried in America has been real food, not fake food, so this is poor word choice. Now, *authentic* clarifies the writer's meaning that the food will be closer to its original Greek or Mediterranean style. These changes in word choice improve the clarity of the essay by using specific words that better communicate the writer's points. Finally, the third and fourth sentences have been joined together. This increases sentence variety by adding a longer sentence to this paragraph.

Final Draft

Imagine traveling into the city or the beach and being transported back in time. This is what it must be like to live in Greece, since the remaining historical sites allow visitors to see two cultures side by side. The ancient buildings, beautiful beaches, and Greek foods are reasons I want to visit Greece.

Several buildings from ancient Greece are still standing, and they can easily be enjoyed by visitors and the people of Greece today. Some of the most famous ones, like the Parthenon, are located throughout the capital. This means that even when you are sitting in an air-conditioned restaurant in Athens, you can still see glimpses of history. There are also tours that teach visitors more about these structures and the events that happened at each one. Seeing these structures alone is enough of a reason for me to visit Greece!

Another reason I want to travel to Greece is to see the beaches there. There are a variety of beaches, as some are small with rocky structures and some look like typical beaches. The water is also different from some American waters because Greece is next to the Mediterranean Sea. Also, many historical events and myths took place on some of the beaches. I would love to sit on one of those beaches and try to imagine ships or characters from myths coming to the shore! The beaches in Greece are beautiful, but I think they also sound fun and interesting!

In addition to the scenery, a third reason to visit Greece is to try authentic Greek and Mediterranean foods. I have tried a few Greek foods, like baklava and pita bread, and I enjoyed them. While these foods are available in America, I think they are probably made a little differently in Greece, so I am interested in seeing what the differences are and trying new things. I hope I can visit Greece soon, because I am getting hungry just thinking about the food there!

Greece is a special place where the old and the new come together. Walking through historical structures, visiting unique beaches, and eating new foods there is my dream. If I only ever have the chance to go on one vacation, I hope it is to Greece!

Final Draft Evaluation

The essay answers the prompt and is on topic throughout the composition. The central idea is clear and is stated in the introduction, supported in the body, and restated in the conclusion. The thesis statement restates parts of the prompt and gives the reader a preview of the rest of the essay. The body uses well-structured paragraphs to explain the supporting details and examples and connects them to the central idea. The conclusion also emphasizes the central idea and supporting details and invites the reader to consider what they have read.

The essay is also interesting and written with a variety of sentence types. It uses transitions and good paragraph structure to make the essay easy for the reader to understand. The introduction also uses a hook to get the reader's attention and help him or her relate to the information in the essay. Not only does this essay answer the prompt and have appropriate structure, but it also makes use of good, engaging, and interesting details.

Reading Practice Test #1

Refer to the passage "Summer's Heat" to answer questions 1-9.

Summer's Heat

(1) I remember the day as if it were yesterday. It was Saturday afternoon and cloudless. The Sun beat down upon my face through the chain-link fenced dugout. It was so hot that I could feel my skin burning, and I was sweating, even though I wasn't on the field. I sat on the bench with a jug of water at my feet and a fistful of sunflower seeds. We were losing, three to one. I looked at our right fielder, Johnny, who was fanning his face with his glove as he was getting ready for the play.

(2) The ball was hit to the third basemen, and he got the last out of the inning at first base. The team ran into a huddle, and our coach told us to keep our eye on the ball. "Concentrate," he said.

(3) Philip hit the ball to the fence and was stopped on second base by the coaches. We were all shouting and very happy with his double. The next batter bunted the ball to the pitcher and moved Philip to third base. Johnny then came to the plate and hit a double. Philip scored, and we were one run away from tying the game.

(4) "Max!" the coach shouted.

(5) I turned my head and was shocked to see that I wasn't imagining things. Coach was pointing right at me.

(6) "You're up," he said.

(7) I threw my sunflower seeds to the ground, stuffed my helmet onto my head, and grabbed my favorite bat. I took two practice swings and was ready for the pitcher.

(8) I hit two foul balls over the side fences. They were hard and flew for a long time before ever hitting the ground. I was going to do it. I was going to get Johnny to home plate. I just needed one good pitch.

(9) The pitcher looked down at his feet and then stared into my eyes. I stared back. It was like there was no one else on the field. It was just us. He started his windup, and I dug my feet into the ground and adjusted my grip on the bat. The ball came in, and I swung as hard as I could.

(10) I was confused. I didn't feel anything.

(11) "Strike three!" the umpire yelled behind me. I was out.

(12) Bradley came up after me and we ended up losing the game, three to two.

(13) The coaches told us we played a good game. They said that it was a team effort and that we should be proud of ourselves. My mom tried to comfort me. "It was no one's fault," she said. "It's just a game."

(14) But it was not just a game to me. I felt like I had let everyone down and disappointed all of my teammates. It was the last game of the season, and we lost.

(15) I decided at that moment to spend my summer vacation training. I was going to do nothing but practice baseball. I spent two weeks outside, with just my baseball bat and a bucket of balls. I hit until it was dark and my mom forced me to come inside and eat dinner. When I asked her if we could install some lights in the backyard so that I could see and practice more, she looked at me with a very stern face and said the most horrible sentence.

(16) "No more baseball for the rest of the summer."

(17) My heart dropped. I felt sick to my stomach and filled with anger.

(18) "How can you do this to me?" I shouted.

(19) "There is more to life than baseball," she said. "I want you to enjoy spending the summer playing with your friends."

(20) She then grounded me for the weekend for shouting at her.

(21) After a few days without baseball, I realized how fun it was to be a regular kid and spend time with my friends, swimming in the pool, fishing in the lake, and climbing trees. Once, someone suggested we play some baseball, and we gathered some of our friends together and played a game in the park. We didn't keep score, and had fun just playing. It was a great summer.

(22) When baseball season came around again, I played center field. My first time up to bat, I smiled. I was having fun. The pitch came and I swung hard. The ball landed on the other side of the fence, and I ran around the bases to cheers after hitting my first homerun.

1. Based on paragraphs 21 and 22, what can the reader predict about the narrator's upcoming baseball season?

a. He will have a better overall batting average this season.
b. He will enjoy the season regardless of his performance.
c. He will play centerfield more often this season.
d. He will be less excited to play this season.

2. What does the first-person point of view used in this passage help the reader understand?

a. The narrator thought the team's loss was his fault.
b. The team felt disappointed when the narrator struck out.
c. The narrator's mother told the narrator that he could not practice anymore.
d. The narrator and his friends decided to play baseball without keeping score.

3. How does paragraph 9 impact the plot?

a. Paragraph 9 foreshadows the fact the narrator's mother will make him stop playing baseball later in the passage.
b. Paragraph 9 creates a plot twist by having the narrator be surprised that he is being called to bat.
c. Paragraph 9 leaves the readers on a cliffhanger by describing an event that is not related to the one in paragraph 8.
d. Paragraph 9 uses suspense to build tension and push the story towards the outcome of an important event.

4. What key idea is supported by paragraph 19?

a. The narrator's mother does not like that her son plays baseball and would rather he spend time with friends.
b. The narrator's mother wants her son to spend more time playing baseball with friends instead of by himself.
c. The narrator's mother is concerned her son is too worried about his baseball skills and is missing out on time with his friends.
d. The narrator's mother believes that her son does not need to practice to become better at baseball.

5. What do paragraphs 4 and 5 help the reader understand about the narrator?

a. He is not often called on to bat when there is someone in a scoring position.
b. He was startled by the coach yelling calling his name, and this caused his confusion.
c. He imagines things while waiting, which is why he thought he imagined his coach talking.
d. He did not want to go up to bat and was hoping that it had been in his head.

6. How does the setting of paragraph 15 contribute to the narrator's character development?

a. It shows the conditions in which the narrator is practicing.
b. It proves that the narrator's mother's reaction was right.
c. It increases the pressure the narrator feels to be successful in batting.
d. It reveals the narrator's dedication to improving his skills.

7. Why did Max think he was imagining things?

a. It was so hot outside.
b. He could not believe his team was losing.
c. The coach was calling his name to come into the game to bat.
d. He was surprised to see that Philip scored.

8. In paragraph 9, what kind of mood does the author create?

a. A tense mood
b. An angry mood
c. A comforting mood
d. A sad mood

Refer to the passage "The Responsibilities of Bees" to answer questions 9-16.

The Responsibilities of Bees

(1) While some people see bees as a nuisance or just another insect, they are a crucial part of the global ecosystem and survival. They support human and animal life through their role in food production and help maintain healthy habitats in a variety of ecosystems. Their ability to pollinate plants, provide resources for animals, and support biodiversity are their most important roles.

(2) Bats, birds, and a variety of insects pollinate plants, but bees are responsible for around 80% of global pollination. Pollinators transfer pollen from the male organs of one plant to the female organs of another. Pollination occurs when plants become fertilized and develop seeds. Fruits and vegetables then develop around the seed and grow into the produce that we find at grocery stores and farmer's markets. Bees are one of the most important pollinators. They move from flower to flower transferring pollen while they search for nectar. Without bees, food as we know it would change. Many of

the fruits and vegetables we enjoy rely on bees to grow, so without bees the amount of food grown would significantly decrease.

(3) Not only would this impact us by reducing the amount of available food, but it would also hurt farmers economically. If the amount of food a farmer was able to grow decreased because of a decline in the bee population, they would not make enough money to support their farm. Even though there are other animals and insects that help with pollination, they aren't as effective as bees. If there were no more bees, most plants would have to be pollinated by hand to compensate for all of the work they do. The pollen would need to be manually transferred from one plant to another. This would take a lot of time, manpower, and money. The low supply of food would drive up the cost, hurting the consumers as well.

(4) We aren't the only ones who enjoy the fruits and vegetables bees help grow! Many animals eat fruits and vegetables just like us, so they need bees to keep pollinating too. Bees also play a direct role in supporting animal life and habitats. While we need an abundance of bees for our crops to thrive, it is necessary that some are eaten by birds, small mammals, and other insects as part of the food web. If the bee population were to disappear, an important food source for these animals would too. This could cause animals that rely on the bees to begin starving to death or consuming other insects and animals, further disrupting the ecosystem. Changes in food webs are capable of decimating entire species and ecosystems.

(5) Biodiversity is the variety of life found on Earth. This doesn't just include people and animals, but plants, insects, and all living organisms. Bees' role in supporting biodiversity is highlighted in the foods they help produce and the animals they help support, but it also goes beyond that. The seeds produced by the fertilized plants that were mentioned earlier continue to spread and grow new plants, allowing plant life cycles to continue. Sometimes bees help with spreading these seeds in a process known as seed dispersal. The seeds become attached to the bees while they collect nectar and fall off as they fly to another plant. This helps the seeds spread to new places. Not only does this create food for animals, but also habitats. The plants that grow as a result of seed dispersal create grassy, plant-filled homes for animals in a variety of ecosystems like meadows, forests, and grasslands.

(6) Even though bees are not the only pollinators, they're the most important ones. Bees keep our food sources and ecosystems stable! We need to maintain the bee population in order to keep the Earth and its inhabitants safe, healthy, and happy.

9. Based on the information in the passage, what can the reader infer about bees?

a. The total loss of bees is not preventable.
b. Pollinators can be completely replaced by people.
c. Bees are capable of destroying crops.
d. Protecting bees is beneficial to everyone.

10. Which sentence from the passage best supports the idea that bees support biodiversity?

a. They move from flower to flower transferring pollen while they search for nectar.
b. The plants that grow as a result of seed dispersal create grassy, plant-filled homes for animals in a variety of ecosystems like meadows, forests, and grasslands.
c. Many animals eat fruits and vegetables just like us, so they need bees to keep pollinating too.
d. Many of the fruits and vegetables we enjoy rely on bees to grow, so without bees the amount of food grown would significantly decrease.

11. What is the most likely reason that the author uses a cause-and-effect structure in paragraph 3?

a. To illustrate the financial impact that the loss of bees can have
b. To reveal the importance of bees in many food webs
c. To outline the process for manual pollination
d. To suggest solutions for increasing the bee population

12. What is the most likely reason the author wrote "The Responsibilities of Bees"?

a. To highlight the ways that bees are harmful
b. To describe the importance of bee movement
c. To highlight the worldwide impact of bees
d. To show why so many people appreciate bees

13. What is the controlling idea of this passage?

a. Pollination by bees is required for crops to grow on their own.
b. How diverse a habitat is depends on how many bees are present.
c. Bees support the survival of plants and animals worldwide.
d. Bees are the most efficient pollinators in most ecosystems.

14. Which detail from the selection supports the key idea that bees are an essential part of Earth's global ecosystem?

a. If the amount of food a farmer was able to grow decreased because of a decline in the bee population, they would not make enough money to support their farm.
b. Bats, birds, and a variety of insects pollinate plants, but bees are responsible for around 80% of global pollination.
c. Bees' role in supporting biodiversity is highlighted in the foods they help produce and the animals they help support, but it also goes beyond that.
d. Sometimes bees help with spreading these seeds in a process known as seed dispersal.

15. What is the best summary of this passage?

a. Bees are the most important pollinator. They pollinate the majority of the Earth's plant life. Without them, the cost of producing food would increase. This would harm the economy.
b. Bees are an important part of the global ecosystem. They support animal and human life and maintain a balance in a variety of habitats. Without them, the world as we know it would be very different.
c. Bees help seeds from plants spread across large areas. They then grow and develop into habitats that support biodiversity. Without bees, many organisms would not have homes or food.
d. Bees are a part of the food web in several different habitats. This means that animals and other insects eat them as a source of energy. If bees went extinct, the food web would not be complete.

16. Why did the author most likely use a cause-and-effect structure in this passage?

a. To show the connections between humans and animals
b. To highlight the possible effect of a decline in the bee population
c. To present bees as solutions to pollination problems
d. To demonstrate how animals and humans rely on bees differently

Refer to the passage "The Road Not Taken" to answer questions 17-19.

The Road Not Taken

by Robert Frost

Two roads diverged in a yellow wood,
And sorry I could not travel both
And be one traveler, long I stood
And looked down one as far as I could
To where it bent in the undergrowth;
Then took the other, as just as fair,
And having perhaps the better claim,
Because it was grassy and wanted wear;
Though as for that the passing there
Had worn them really about the same,
And both that morning equally lay
In leaves no step had trodden black.
Oh, I kept the first for another day!
Yet knowing how way leads on to way,
I doubted if I should ever come back.
I shall be telling this with a sigh
Somewhere ages and ages hence:
Two roads diverged in a wood, and I—
I took the one less travelled by,
And that has made all the difference.

17. Read lines 18-20 from the poem.

Two roads diverged in a wood, and I—
I took the one less travelled by,
And that has made all the difference.

What can the reader infer from these sentences?

a. The speaker wants to follow the crowd and be the same as others.
b. The decision the speaker made had a large impact on his life.
c. The roads would have both led the speaker to the same outcome.
d. The speaker likes to make travel plans as he goes, not beforehand.

18. Read line 8 from the poem.

Because it was grassy and wanted wear;

Part A: What type of figurative language is used in this description of the path?

a. Hyperbole
b. Metaphor
c. Simile
d. Personification

Part B: Why is figurative language used in this description of the path?

a. To support the speaker's decision to take the more worn path
b. To describe the unique qualities of the grassier path
c. To emphasize that the path was not commonly taken by others
d. To describe the physical qualities of the woods being traveled

19. Which of the following themes is clearly present in this poem?

a. Deciding which road to take while on a hike is difficult.
b. A person can make different choices than the majority of others.
c. It is challenging to make the best of a bad decision.
d. Wondering about the choices that others have made is tempting.

Refer to the passage "The Right Thing to Do" to answer questions 20-23.

The Right Thing to Do

Cast of Characters

Cast of Characters

- Jessica: A sixth-grade girl, Amy's friend
- Amy: A sixth-grade girl, Jessica's friend
- Sales Clerk: a clerk in the store Amy and Jessica visit

Scene 1

(1) [JESSICA *stands with a group of friends on the school steps. The group is chatting and laughing.* AMY *approaches from stage right.]*

(2) AMY: Jessica! Jessica!

(3) JESSICA: [*turning away from her friends and taking a step toward* AMY] Hi, Amy. What's up?

(4) AMY: I'm headed to the mall, and I thought you might want to come.

(5) JESSICA: Why me? I thought we weren't friends anymore.

(6) AMY: [*waving her hand and shaking her head*] That old fight? Ancient history. So... do you want to come or not?

(7) JESSICA: [*glancing back at her friends*] Sure. I'll come. Just give me a minute.

(8)[JESSICA *runs back and talks with her friends for a moment, then rejoins* AMY. AMY *and* JESSICA *exit stage right.*]

Scene 2

(9) [*Amy and Jessica are looking at a shelf full of lipstick in a cosmetics store in the mall.*]

(10) AMY: [*picking up a lipstick tube*] Look at this one, Jess. Don't you just love this color?

(11) JESSICA: [*picking up a different lipstick tube*] It's nice, but I like this one better.

(12) A sales clerk enters from stage left.

(13) SALES CLERK: [*stopping by the girls*] Can I help you ladies find something?

(14) AMY: Oh, no. We're just looking.

(15) JESSICA: Thank you, though.

(16) SALES CLERK: Okay. Well, let me know if you need anything.

(17) [SALES CLERK exits stage right.]

(18) AMY: So, which one are you going to get?

(19) JESSICA: [*shaking her head*] I'm not getting one. They're a little pricy for me. Besides, I'm saving up for something special.

(20) AMY: [laughing] Who said anything about money? I didn't ask you which one you were going to buy. I asked which one you were going to get. So, which one will it be?

(21) JESSICA: But—but—that's stealing!

(22) AMY: Look at all these tubes of lipstick. They'll never miss a couple.

(23) JESSICA: [*looking around nervously*] What if that sales clerk comes back and catches us?

(24) AMY: [*Picking up two tubes of lipstick*] You worry too much. Now, was this the one you liked? Or was it this one? Never mind. We'll take them both.

(25) [AMY *slips both tubes into her pocket.*]

(26) JESSICA: Amy! This is wrong. We shouldn't be doing this.

(27) AMY: [*glaring at* JESSICA] Do you even want to be my friend again? It sure doesn't sound like it.

(28) JESSICA: Of course I want to be your friend. It's just—

(29) AMY: Then come on. Let's go. [AMY *starts to walk away, and then turns and looks back.*] Are you coming?

(30) JESSICA: Fine. [*She follows* AMY.] But what if the alarm goes off?

(31) AMY: For a couple of tubes of lipstick? Not gonna happen. Now, follow me. And for heaven's sake, don't look so nervous.

(32) The girls exit stage right.

Scene 3

(33) [JESSICA *reenters the cosmetics store from stage right. She stops at the shelf of lipsticks and looks around.* SALES CLERK *enters from stage left.*]

(34) JESSICA: Excuse me ...

(35) SALES CLERK: [*stopping*] Did you need help with something?

(36) JESSICA: Yes. [*She looks at the floor.*] My friend who was just with me, um, she took—well, actually, she stole two tubes of lipstick. I'm not okay with that. So, um, I wanted to pay for them.

(37) SALES CLERK: That's impressive. I've never seen that happen before. And kids take stuff from this store all the time. What made you come back?

(38) JESSICA: [*shrugging*] I don't know. I guess it was just the right thing to do.

20. Which word from the passage best helps the reader understand the meaning of the term *cosmetics*, which is used in line 9?

a. Mall
b. Stealing
c. Lipstick
d. Color

21. How do Jessica's character traits impact the outcome of the play?

a. Her optimism allows her to see past her friend's mistakes and forgive her.
b. Her integrity allows her to return the lipstick and make things right.
c. Her carefree personality allows her to fit in with her friends.
d. Her stubbornness allows her to confront her friend.

22. Which two characteristics of this passage show that it is realistic fiction? Select all that apply.

a. The play takes place in a location that could be real.
b. The dialogue sounds normal and natural.
c. The play includes several stage directions.
d. The events in the story are possible.
e. The play includes more than one character.

23. What does the conversation in lines 20 through 28 reveal about Amy?

a. Amy disagrees with the decision being made by the clerk.
b. Amy has a strong moral compass and makes good choices.
c. Amy wants to be liked by her peers regardless of the consequences.
d. Amy is manipulative and pressures others into doing what she wants.

Refer to the passages "The Road Not Taken" and "The Right Thing to Do" to answer questions 24-26.

24. What theme is found in both "The Road Not Taken" and "The Right Thing to Do"?

a. Doing the right thing is always beneficial.
b. Sometimes we must do what others do not.
c. There is conflict between good and bad.
d. Appearances can be deceiving.

25. Compare scene 3 of "The Right Thing to Do" with lines 14 and 15 of "The Road Not Taken." How are the actions of the characters different?

a. Jessica is able to make up for something that has been done, while the speaker in the poem wants to but cannot.
b. The speaker in the poem does not return to the start of the woods to change his decision, while Jessica returns to do what she had decided is right.
c. Jessica is able to explain why she made the choice she did, while the speaker of the poem is not able to do so.
d. The speaker in the poem cannot control his own actions, while Jessica cannot control the actions of her friend.

26. Which idea is suggested by the writer of "The Road Not Taken" and the author of "The Right Thing to Do"?

a. Doing as others do is usually the best choice.
b. It is sometimes better not to conform.
c. Rules do not apply evenly to all people.
d. Decisions should be simple to make.

Refer to the passage "Adventure Land Chase" to answer questions 27-35.

Adventure Land Chase

(1) Saturday was the day that Adventure Land was opening. It was going to be the largest theme park in three states, have massive rollercoasters that travel at super speed and loop three times, and a full water park. But it wasn't just the grand opening of Adventure Land about which I was excited. Saturday was also my best friend Riley's birthday. To celebrate, she was having her party at Adventure Land.

(2) I woke up very early Saturday morning because I could not sleep. I kept thinking about all the rides that we would go on and the games we were going to play, but, more than anything, spending time with all of my friends. While I was eating my cereal, my mom packed us a large bag filled with things she said we were going to need at the theme park all day. She packed sunscreen, sunglasses, and water bottles. I didn't pay attention because I was still too excited about the biggest rollercoaster, the Slithering Cobra. It was the one that shot up really high and had three loops. It was going to be so much fun!

(3) When we first got to the park, my first thought was that it was a lot bigger than I thought it was going to be. It was huge! I could see the tops of the rollercoasters from the car in the parking lot. Inside, everything was made to look like a jungle. There were lots of different kinds of trees, both real and fake; long green vines draped across the park like telephone lines; and workers dressed up as if they were going on safari. The park was so big, and there was so much to do, but then I noticed one huge problem: there were so many people in the park. Everywhere I looked, there were more people. I was even bumped a few times while we stood at the entrance.

(4) Riley's mom gave all of us wristbands and said that we had to stay with one of our friends at all times. "Have a buddy," she said. "If anyone gets lost, come to the food court. We will meet at Lickin' Fried Chicken at one o'clock."

(5) Riley was my buddy, and we immediately ran off to go ride the Slithering Cobra.

(6) "Wait up," Charlotte and Ryan called. "We want to come too!"

(7) We stood in line for the ride for over half an hour. There were so many people, and more people kept coming.

(8) "I'm hot," Riley said.

(9) "This is boring," Ryan complained.

(10) When we were finally at the front of the line, the gates opened, and we were allowed to take our seats. Since it was Riley's birthday, they let us ride in the front seats. The rollercoaster took off really fast and went straight into the air. It stopped at the top of the tracks, and it felt as if we were going to fall out of our seats! The rollercoaster tipped over the edge, and soon we were rushing toward the ground. Riley put her arms up, and we both started screaming. The coaster then went straight up and into the three loops. Before we knew it, we were back at the platform, and the ride was over.

(11) "That was awesome!" Charlotte yelled.

(12) "I want to go again!" Ryan added.

(13) We looked at the line, and it had doubled since we had gotten there.

(14) "Maybe later," I said.

(15) When we got off the ride and were walking toward the arcade, our friend Natalie came running up to us. She looked really worried. "I've lost him," she said. "I lost George! I wasn't supposed to leave him, but I went to the bathroom and now I can't find him!"

(16) "Did you go to the food court?" Ryan asked.

(17) "Yes, and he wasn't there!" she said.

(18) I didn't know what to do. The park was so big, and there were so many people.

(19) "We will have to retrace your steps," Charlotte said. "Where were you the last time you saw him?"

(20) "In the arcade. Playing Skee-Ball."

(21) We all started running toward the arcade, which was shaped like a giant tiger. "Make sure we all stay together!" Ryan called.

(22) It was really hot, and the sun was beating down right on our faces. I probably should have thought about putting on my sunglasses, but all I could think of was George.

(23) "Who is George?" Riley asked me while we were running.

(24) "I thought you knew!" I said. "I have no idea. Maybe her brother?"

(25) It felt really nice to be inside of the arcade. It looked just like a jungle, too. I kept thinking there was no way we were going to find him, but we had to try. We ran up a flight of stairs and across the room to the Skee-Ball games.

(26) "There he is!" Natalie pointed forward. We didn't see anything. She ran to one of the alleys and picked up a large stuffed monkey. It was George, the stuffed animal from our homeroom that one student has to take home every weekend and write a story about their adventures. We were bewildered.

(27) "That's the George you were talking about?" Riley whined.

(28) "Of course. Mrs. Miller would have killed me if I lost him! But now I have a great adventure to write about!" she said.

(29) We all laughed, relieved.

(30) "Let's go on another ride," I said, and we all started walking back into the jungle.

27. How did Charlotte's reaction to the announcement that George was missing impact the story's outcome?

a. She was ready to act and helped the group solve the problem.
b. She did not take the problem seriously and made it worse.
c. She showed selfishness and failed to help the others.
d. She acted harshly and questioned whether they needed to find George.

28. How does the setting influence the plot of the story?

a. The amusement park is frightening, which makes it easy for the characters to panic.
b. The amusement park is open and nearly empty, so the characters can ride any ride.
c. The amusement park is an exciting place where the characters can have fun.
d. The amusement park is busy and crowded, making it easy to get lost or lose things.

29. Which sentences from the passage foreshadow that something bad may happen at the amusement park?

a. Saturday was the day that Adventure Land was opening. It was going to be the largest theme park in three states, have massive rollercoasters that travel at super speed and loop three times, and a full water park.
b. She looked really worried. "I've lost him," she said. "I lost George! I wasn't supposed to leave him, but I went to the bathroom and now I can't find him!"
c. The park was so big, and there was so much to do, but then I noticed one huge problem: there were so many people in the park.
d. "Have a buddy," she said. "If anyone gets lost, come to the food court. We will meet at Lickin' Fried Chicken at one o'clock."

30. Based on paragraph 2, what can the reader predict about the trip to the amusement park?

a. That the narrator was ready to go to the park.
b. That Riley will have the perfect birthday.
c. That the park will not be entertaining.
d. That the weather will be hot and sunny.

31. What is the best summary of this passage?

a. A group of friends' fun is quickly put to an end when one friend goes missing at the amusement park.
b. A group of friends attend an exciting celebration but encounter a problem along the way.
c. A group of friends make their way through a crowded amusement park on a hot summer day.
d. A group of friends have to stop celebrating and split up to find a missing stuffed animal.

32. What does the first-person point of view used in this passage help the reader understand?

a. How much Natalie cares for the stuffed monkey George
b. How thrilled Riley is about her birthday celebration
c. How worried Riley's mother is about someone getting lost
d. How much the narrator is looking forward to the amusement park

33. In paragraph 3, what type of mood does the author create?

a. A mood of anger
b. A mood of frustration
c. A mood of unease
d. A mood of excitement

34. Why does the narrator discuss the number of people at the park in paragraph 3?

a. To explain why it was important to not get lost
b. To highlight the popularity of the park
c. To support her complaints about waiting in line
d. To show that it was hot

35. How is the conflict of the story resolved?

a. The children find George
b. The lines on the rides become shorter
c. The children don't care about a stuffed animal
d. The children leave the park

Refer to the passage "The Royal Scenery" to answer questions 36-39.

The Royal Scenery

(1) To celebrate their fifteenth wedding anniversary, my parents decided to take our family on vacation to London. This was the first time that I had ever been out of the country, and I was very excited. While in London, we discovered some really cool places, but my favorite was The Regent's Park in the City of Westminster in central London.

(2) The Regent's Park, which most people refer to as "Regent's Park," is one of the eight Royal Parks in Greater London. A Royal Park is land that was once owned by the royal monarchy, or crown, of the United Kingdom. A monarchy is a form of government where a monarch acts as the head of state.

(3) The parks were originally used as recreation for the royal family but have been opened to the general public over the last two centuries. The largest of the Royal Parks in Central London are the Regent's Park, Hyde Park, St. James's Park, Green Park, and Kensington Gardens, although the largest Royal Park in London is Richmond Park.

(4) Regent's Park is very big, and there are many attractions and things to do for both London citizens and travelers. Immediately, I was amazed with the beautiful scenery and the plethora of trees and ponds. It is also a very popular site for physical activities

and exercise. There are several fields known as "sport pitches" that are used for soccer, cricket, rugby, and other sports. The park is lined with pedestrian trails, and there were many walkers and joggers.

(5) Regent's Park was my favorite park because it housed the London Zoo. In an attempt to create a close replica to the animals' natural environment, the animals were in the open, out of cages, in enclosed areas. My favorite attraction was the Galapagos Tortoise exhibit, as they were the largest tortoises I had ever seen.

A Galapagos Tortoise at the London Zoo

(6) We all had a great time in London, and I loved seeing all of the great London attractions. It surprised me that with everything available to do in London, my favorite part of the city was a Royal Park.

36. Which two of the following are the most likely reasons that the author included an image? Select all that apply.

a. To show the reader the enclosures in which the tortoises live
b. To show the reader what the author saw at his favorite part of the zoo
c. To show the reader where the tortoises were able to roam
d. To show the reader how safe the park was for tortoises
e. To show the reader the physical appearance of the tortoises

37. Which sentence best expresses the central idea of the passage?

a. The narrator learned about monarchies and how their land was used during his trip.
b. The narrator enjoyed his trip to London, specifically when he visited Regent's Park.
c. The narrator was awed by tortoises and the way they were able to roam Regent's Park.
d. The narrator developed a love for traveling after his trip to London with his family.

38. What is the most likely reason that the author chose a descriptive structure for this passage?

a. It allows him to express his reasons for liking Regent's Park.
b. It allows him to explain to readers why he visited Regent's Park.
c. It allows him to highlight a problem that happened on the trip.
d. It allows him to provide vivid details about traveling to London.

39. What does the word *replica* mean in paragraph 5?

a. Item
b. Family
c. Copy
d. Habitat

Refer to the passage "The Educational Market Town" to answer questions 40-41.

The Educational Market Town

(1) Aberystwyth is a market town on the West Coast of Wales within the United Kingdom. A market town refers to European areas that have the right to have markets, which differentiates it from a city or village. The town is located where two rivers meet, the River Ystwyth and River Rheidol, and is the best known as an educational center, housing an established university since 1872.

(2) The town is situated between North and South Wales and is a large vacation destination as well as tourist attraction. Constitution Hill on the north end of Aberystwyth provides excellent views of Cardigan Bay and is supported by the Aberystwyth Electric Cliff Railway. Although Aberystwyth is known as a modern Welsh town, it is home to several historic buildings, such as the remnants of a castle.

(3) Although there are several grocery, clothing, sporting goods, and various other miscellaneous shops, Aberystwyth is best known for its educational services. Aberystwyth University, formerly known as University College Wales, as well as the National Library of Wales, which is the legal deposit library for Wales and which houses all Welsh publications, are both located within Aberystwyth. The two main languages traditionally spoken in Aberystwyth are English and Welsh. With local live music, arts center, and educational opportunities in gorgeous scenery, Aberystwyth is a hidden luxury within the United Kingdom.

40. Read these sentences from paragraph 3.

Although there are several grocery, clothing, sporting goods, and various other miscellaneous shops, Aberystwyth is best known for its educational services. Aberystwyth University, formerly known as University College Wales, as well as the National Library of Wales, which is the legal deposit library for Wales and which houses all Welsh publications, are both located within Aberystwyth.

What central idea do these sentences help the reader understand?

a. The town of Aberystwyth has a lot to offer residents who live there year-round.
b. The town of Aberystwyth is a great place for tourists who plan to stay temporarily.
c. The town of Aberystwyth is an exceptional place for schooling as well as tourism.
d. The town of Aberystwyth hasn't changed much over time and will likely stay that way.

41. How does the descriptive structure of this passage support the author's purpose?

a. It allows the author to convince people to visit the town.
b. It allows the author to showcase the town as a hidden gem.
c. It allows the author to entertain readers with facts about the town.
d. It allows the author to downplay the draws of the town.

Refer to the passages "The Royal Scenery" and "The Educational Market Town" to answer questions 42-44.

42. What theme is present in both "The Royal Scenery "and "The Educational Market Town"?

a. Learning can be a delight.
b. Places can be special and admirable.
c. Travelling with family can be frustrating.
d. It is important to appreciate history.

43. What does "The Royal Scenery" achieve that "The Educational Market Town" does not?

a. It expresses a desire to return to a place.
b. It portrays the unique features of a town.
c. It mentions a city's landmarks and attractions.
d. It uses a casual, personal view of a destination.

44. Which idea is supported by both "The Royal Scenery" and "The Educational Market Town"?

a. Large animals should be given more space to roam about freely.
b. The qualities that are unique to an area are what make it worth visiting.
c. A city's worth goes beyond what it can offer to tourists who visit.
d. Language is an important part of the culture of a region.

Answer Key and Explanations for Reading Test #1

1. B: Based on paragraphs 21 and 22, the reader can predict that the main character will enjoy this season regardless of the outcome. In paragraph 21, the narrator expresses his joy while playing baseball during the summer in a casual setting. In paragraph 22, he writes that he was smiling and having fun. This shows that choice B is correct. Although the narrator hit his "first homerun" in paragraph 22, there is no suggestion in paragraphs 21 and 22 that this will continue throughout the season. This shows that choice A is incorrect. Paragraphs 21 and 22 do not discuss the narrator's performance in centerfield, so no prediction about this can be made and choice C is incorrect. Paragraphs 21 and 22 show that the narrator is excited and happy. Choice D suggests the opposite, so it is incorrect.

2. A: The narrator thinks that the team's loss was his fault. This is shown when he says "I felt like I had let everyone down and disappointed all of my teammates." Because he felt like this, he became overly committed to practicing. Choice B is incorrect because the passage does not tell the reader the thoughts or feelings of the other teammates. It only shows how the narrator thinks they feel. Choice C is incorrect because first-person point of view allows readers to understand the narrator's inner thoughts and feelings. The fact that the narrator's mother told her son to stop practicing could be told to the reader using any point of view. Choice D is incorrect for the same reason. The fact that they played baseball without keeping score could be known by the reader no matter which point of view was used to tell the story.

3. D: Paragraph 9 builds suspense by giving details about what occurred right before an important event in the story. In this case, the event is the result of the narrator's swing. This leads up to the moment that he realizes he missed the ball and struck out. Choice D is correct. This paragraph does not mention the narrator's mother or foreshadow that she will make him stop playing baseball. This means that choice A is incorrect. Choice B is incorrect because that narrator is called to bat in paragraph 6. Choice C is incorrect because paragraph 8 describes the narrator's first two swings. These events lead up to the event in paragraph 9, so they are not unrelated and they do not create a cliffhanger.

4. C: The narrator's mother explains that "there is more to life than baseball," which shows that she thinks her son is investing too much of his time in practicing baseball. She also explains that she would prefer that he spend "the summer playing with friends." This shows that she wants him to socialize with his friends. Choice C is correct. While the narrator's mother wants the narrator to spend more time with his friends, the passage does not show that she does not want him to play baseball. Choice A is incorrect. While the narrator's mother does want her son to spend more time with his friends, she does not want him to be focused on baseball, so choice B is incorrect. The passage does not show that the narrator's mother wants her son to stop practicing because she thinks he is already great at baseball. This makes choice D incorrect.

5. A: In paragraph 5, the narrator is shocked to have heard his coach call him up to bat. Since he is surprised by this, the reader can infer that this does not usually happen, so choice A is correct. Paragraphs 4 and 5 do not say that he was startled by the coach calling his name. They also do not say that the narrator was confused, so choice B is incorrect. Paragraphs 4 and 5 do not show that the narrator often imagines things, so choice C is incorrect. While the narrator thought he might have imagined the coach calling his name, these paragraphs do not show that he did not want to bat. They also do not show that he was hoping he had imagined the coach calling to him, so choice D is incorrect.

6. D: The fact that the narrator was playing until it was dark out and late enough for dinner shows that he was extremely dedicated to getting better at batting. This shows that choice D is correct. The paragraph does explain the conditions the narrator is practicing in. However, the conditions do not show the narrator's character development on their own, so choice A is incorrect. Choice B is incorrect because the setting does not prove that the mother's reaction was the right one to have. The setting is at the narrator's home, where his mother tells him to stop practicing. This does not increase the pressure on the narrator, so choice C is incorrect.

7. C: In paragraph 5, the narrator was shocked to see that he was not imagining the coach calling him up to bat. In the preceding paragraphs, the narrator shows the reader that there is tension at the baseball game. The next batter could help the team by scoring and making them more likely to win. However, the next batter could also hurt the team by striking out and making them more likely to lose. The next batter's success was very important. The reader can conclude that Max was surprised that the coach was calling him up to bat at such an important moment, so choice C is correct. Choice A is incorrect because the narrator does not suggest that the heat was so severe that it would cause confusion for the people outside. Choice B is incorrect because the narrator's reaction comes after the coach calls on him, not when he sees that his team is losing. Choice D is incorrect because the narrator does not give information that suggests that he did not expect Philip to score.

8. A: Max and the pitcher are both under pressure. Max wants to hit the ball and help his team, and the pitcher wants to help his own team by not letting Max hit the ball. The mood is tense because the author has created a situation that causes tension and pressure for the characters. Choices B and D are incorrect because none of the details in the passage suggest that the characters are angry or sad. Their emotions are not shown. Instead, they appear to be focused on the game. Choice C is incorrect because paragraph 9 describes a situation that is uncomfortable for the narrator and the pitcher, since they are under pressure.

9. D: This passage describes the roles that bees play and explains how they benefit the Earth's inhabitants. The passage shows that bees keep the systems that provide people with food stable, and that bees help flowers and animals get the things they need. Therefore, the reader can infer that protecting bees benefits everyone, so choice D is correct. Choice A is incorrect because the statements in the passage do not suggest that losing all bees is unpreventable. Choice B is also incorrect. The passage mentions that plants would have to be hand pollinated by humans if bees went extinct. However, the passage describes other roles that pollinators play, so it cannot be assumed that they can be replaced by people. Bees support crops by pollinating the plants and assisting in reproduction. The passage does not suggest that their behavior can destroy or harm crops, so choice C is incorrect.

10. B: The passage defines biodiversity as "the variety of life found on Earth" and explains that this refers to all living organisms. Bees' ability to help create supportive homes for a variety of living organisms through seed dispersal best demonstrates their role in supporting biodiversity. This makes choice B correct. Choice A defines the process of pollination. It does not show that bees support a wide variety of organisms, so it is incorrect. Choices C and D are incorrect as they only focus on bees' role in food production. These statements do not show that bees make it possible for a wide variety of organisms to live as clearly as choice B does, so choices C and D are incorrect.

11. A: The third paragraph uses a cause-and-effect structure to explain what would happen to farmers and the economy if the bee population declined. The loss of bees would cause fewer plants to grow, causing food prices to rise. It would also require farms to pay for plants to be manually pollinated. Choice B is incorrect. The importance of bees in food webs is explained in paragraph 4. Choice C is incorrect. While manual pollination is mentioned in paragraph 3, the structure of the paragraph does not outline the process. Paragraph 3 does not contain solutions for increasing the bee population, making choice D incorrect.

12. C: The author most likely wrote this passage to highlight the worldwide impact of bees. The passage explains how bees can support all forms of life, so choice C is correct. Choice A is incorrect. This passage does not explain any harmful, or otherwise negative, effects of bees. The movement of bees is discussed and explained as important in both pollinating and seed dispersal. However, this is not the main message of the passage. This makes choice B incorrect. The author does not discuss people's appreciation of bees in the passage. In fact, the author suggests that some people find them to be a nuisance, making choice D incorrect.

13. C: The passage explains why plants and animals are dependent on bees for survival. The introduction also states that bees support animal and plant life, so C is the best answer. Choice A comes from the third paragraph and does not show the purpose of the entire passage. Choice B refers to the biodiversity explained in paragraph five, which is also a detail and not the point of the whole passage. Choice D is incorrect. The efficiency of bees is referenced in the passage, but it is not what the passage is about.

14. B: The idea that bees are an essential part of the ecosystem is supported by the statement that bees are responsible for 80% of global pollination. This shows the widespread need for bees. Choice A shows that the loss of bees could have a financial impact on farmers, not the ecosystem. This makes choice A incorrect. Choice C shows that bees can support biodiversity, but it does not show that biodiversity and bees' role in it are essential to preserving the ecosystem. Choice C is incorrect. Choice D describes another important role bees play, but it is incorrect because it does not explain the global impact of seed dispersal.

15. B: Choice B best summarizes the passage. It covers the main ideas from the passage, including the fact that bees support human life, animal life, and habitats. It also explains that the world would be different without bees. Choice A is incorrect because it only focuses on the economic issues associated with the loss of bees. Choice C is incorrect because it is only focused on how bees support biodiversity. Choice D discusses the food web and the roles bees play, but doesn't mention any other ways bees support the environment, so it is incorrect. Choices A, C, and D only discuss one idea from the passage, while choice B summarizes all of these ideas.

16. B: The cause-and-effect structure shows the reader what effects a decline in the bee population may have. This allows the reader to understand what the world would be like without bees, so choice B is correct. While the passage describes connections between humans and animals, this is not the purpose of the passage. It is also not made clear by the cause-and-effect structure, so choice A is incorrect. Choice C is incorrect because the passage does not present bees as a solution to pollination problems. Instead, it describes changes in bee populations as the problem. Though the passage explains why bees are important to both humans and animals, this is not explained through causes and effects, so choice D incorrect.

17. B: The poem uses roads and traveling as metaphors for making decisions in life. The speaker had to choose between two life paths. In line 20, he states that the path he chose "made all the difference." This demonstrates that the path he chose impacted his life in a large way and that the outcome would likely have been different if he had chosen the other path. Line 19 states that the speaker "took the road less travelled by," meaning fewer people had taken that path than the other one. This shows that choice A is incorrect, since the speaker did not follow the crowd or want to be the same as others. Because the road he picked "made all the difference," choice C is incorrect. Choosing the other road would have had a different outcome. Choice D is incorrect because the traveling mentioned in the poem is not literal.

18. Part A: D: Personification is when human characteristics or qualities are attributed to non-human things or abstract concepts. The grassy path took on the human ability to want someone to use it.

Part B: C: The poet uses personification to describe the grassy path by saying it "wanted wear." The fact that it is both grassy and "wanting wear" shows that the path was not commonly walked by others, so choice C is correct. Choice A is incorrect. Later in the poem, the speaker decides to take the path less traveled, not the more worn path as indicated in the answer choice. Choice B is incorrect. While the statement does describe the physical qualities of the path, the poet's intent was to demonstrate that the path had not been heavily traveled. Similarly, the line is not intended to describe the woods being traveled, making choice D incorrect.

19. B: This poem describes a speaker choosing to walk down a path that has not been walked by many others. This means that the speaker has chosen an option that is not often chosen by other people. This supports the theme in choice B, so it is correct. Choice A is incorrect because the speaker does not have a difficult time choosing a path, though he thinks about each one for a while. The statement in choice A is also not a theme, since it is very specific and is not true for most people. Choice C is incorrect because the poem does not suggest that the speaker's decision was a bad one. Choice D is incorrect because the speaker does not give much thought to the choices others have made. He observes that most people have chosen the first path. However, he does not wonder about the choices they have made, and he is not tempted to do so.

20. C: In line 9, the girls enter a cosmetics store where they look at a shelf of lipstick. This helps the reader understand that lipstick is a type of cosmetic. From this, the reader may be able to tell that cosmetics are makeup or beauty products. Choice A is incorrect because a mall contains many different stores with different types of products, so the word *mall* does not tell the reader what cosmetics are. Choice B is incorrect because the fact that Amy steals something does not show the reader what cosmetics are. Choice D is incorrect because many different products have a color or come in different colors, so the word *color* does not show what cosmetics are.

21. B: In scene 3, Jessica returns to the store to pay for the lipstick her friend stole. This demonstrates her strong integrity, which means she does the right thing no matter what the consequences may be. Jessica is not portrayed as optimistic, and she does not overlook her friend's poor choices. This makes choice A incorrect. Choice C is incorrect. Jessica chooses not to conform to what her friend is doing when she returns to pay for the stolen lipstick. It is also clear that Amy's choice to steal the lipstick has upset her. This demonstrates that she is not carefree. Though Jessica confronted her friend about stealing, it was because she wanted to do what was right, not because she is stubborn. Therefore, choice D is incorrect.

22. A, D: Realistic fiction takes place in settings that can exist in real life. This play takes place at a mall, which is a commonly appearing location in real life, so choice A is correct. Stories in the genre of realistic fiction include events that could really happen to the average person. The events should be things that can occur in an everyday setting to believable characters. This makes choice D correct. While the passage and other realistic fiction works contain normal and natural dialogue, this is not only seen in realistic fiction. Normal-sounding dialogue can be found in many types of fiction writing, so B is incorrect. Stage directions are found in scripts for plays. They tell the person acting as the character what to do. Choice E is incorrect because stories in any genre may include more than one character.

23. D: In the conversation that takes place in lines 20 through 28, Amy is pressuring Jessica into stealing. She implies that they cannot be friends if Jessica stops her from stealing the lipstick. This shows that Amy is manipulative, as she tries to control others to get what she wants. No decisions made by the clerk are discussed in lines 20-28, which makes choice A incorrect. Because Amy is stealing and pressuring her friend to steal as well, she does not have strong morals or make good choices. This makes choice B incorrect. Choice C is incorrect. While it is clear that Amy is not worried about the consequences of stealing, it is not clear that she is stealing so that she will be liked by her peers.

24. B: In both passages, the main character decides to make a choice that others have not. The speaker in "The Road Not Taken" chooses to take the path that others do not. In "The Right Thing to Do," Jessica chooses not to steal, unlike Amy. She also returns to the store to make amends. This makes B the correct answer. In "The Road Not Taken," there is not a "right thing" to do like there is in the play. This makes choice A incorrect. Similarly, choosing either path is not morally good or bad in "The Road Not Taken," making choice C incorrect. Neither passage show things that are not as they appear, so choice D is incorrect.

25. B: In lines 14 and 15 of "The Road Not Taken," the speaker expresses that he will not return to the beginning of the path to walk the other one. In scene 3 of "The Right Thing to Do," Jessica returns to the store to do the right thing. These events show that choice B is correct. The speaker of the poem does not mention a desire to make up for something, so choice A is incorrect. Choice C is incorrect. Jessica is not able to explain exactly why she made the choice she did, while the speaker in the poem explains why he chose the less-travelled path. In the poem, the speaker can control his own actions, making choice D incorrect.

26. B: In both passages, a main character chooses to do something that is different from what others have often chosen. The speaker in "The Road Not Taken" decides to take a path that others do not. Jessica in "The Right Thing to Do" decides not to steal with her friend and reports the theft while offering to pay. The sales clerk also points out that Jessica's behavior is different from the behavior of other kids who visit the store. Both passages show a character who chooses not to conform, change their behaviors or choices to fit in, or do what others do or expect, so choice B is correct. This leads to the speaker in the poem making a major life decision and Jessica in the play being praised for her choices. Choice A is incorrect as it is contrary to what the speaker of the poem and Jessica chose. Neither character did as others had. Choice C is incorrect because neither passage mentions rules and how they apply to people. The decisions that had to be made were not simple to those making them, so choice D is incorrect.

27. A: When Natalie announced that George was missing, Charlotte told her to retrace her steps to where she saw him last. The group of children then ran to that location, the arcade, where they found George and resolved the story's problem. Charlotte's readiness to act and her quick thinking helped the group solve their problem, so choice A is correct. Choice B is incorrect because Charlotte did take the problem seriously and quickly suggested a way to fix the problem. Charlotte's solution led to the group finding George, so she was able to help others. Her actions were not selfish, and choice C is incorrect. There was never debate about whether George needed to be found, so choice D is incorrect.

28. D: Paragraph 3 shows that the amusement park is a busy, crowded environment congested with people. It is easy to get lost in a crowded setting, so this sets the scene for someone to go missing later on. The park does not frighten the characters, so choice A is incorrect. The park is described as crowded and full of people, and the characters have to wait in long lines to get on rides, so choice B is incorrect. Choice C is incorrect. While the park is a place where the characters can have fun, this does not impact the plot of the passage.

29. C: In choice C, the narrator is concerned about the size of the crowd in the park. The narrator states that the number of people is a problem and expresses unease after noticing how crowded it is. This choice most clearly foreshadows that something bad may happen while the characters are at the park. Choice A describes where the story will take place, but it does not suggest that anything bad will happen, so it is incorrect. Choice B is incorrect because it shows that something bad has happened. It does not suggest that something bad will happen. Choice D is also incorrect. Though it shows that Riley's mom is concerned about the children getting lost, it also shows that they are taking measures to prevent this and fix the problem if it does happen. This is a reasonable statement for Riley's mother to make, and her dialogue in these lines shows that getting lost can be easily corrected. This does not suggest that something bad will happen.

30. D: In paragraph two, the narrator's mom packs a back with supplies that will be needed for the day. This included sunscreen, sunglasses, and water bottles. From this, the reader can tell that it will most likely be a warm and sunny day, so choice D is correct. Because the narrator's mother was packing a bag and the narrator was eating breakfast, it can be assumed that the narrator was not ready to go yet, so choice A is incorrect. While the narrator is very excited to go to the park for Riley's birthday, there is not enough information about how Riley feels to predict that her birthday will be perfect. This makes choice B incorrect. The narrator repeatedly describes why the idea of going to the amusement park is exciting, so it cannot be assumed that the park will not be fun. This makes choice C incorrect.

31. B: The birthday celebration is very exciting as it is also the grand opening of the new amusement park. The children are having fun until one loses an important stuffed animal. Losing the stuffed animal is an obstacle they faced while celebrating at the park. This makes choice B correct. Choice A is incorrect. George is a stuffed animal, not a friend, and the group carries on about their fun immediately after locating George. While choice C is a fact about the passage, it is not the best summary as it leaves out a key detail of losing George. Choice D is incorrect because the group does not split up.

32. D: The first-person point of view used in the passage portrays the narrator's emotions. The first two paragraphs include details that show how excited the narrator is for the party at the amusement park. Choice A is incorrect. Natalie shows concern for George when he gets lost. However, it is not clear if this is because she cares for him or if it is because she fears getting in trouble. Choice B is incorrect because the passage does not portray Riley's emotions leading up to the event. Riley's mother is not portrayed as being overly worried about losing a child at the park. She simply provides a plan for what to do if someone gets lost. This makes choice C incorrect.

33. D: The narrator provides many examples of his excitement throughout paragraph 3. For example, the narrator shares that he could not sleep and was distracted when his mother was talking because he was thinking about all of the fun things he was going to do at the park. Choices A, B, and C are all incorrect because the narrator's behavior and word choice in paragraph 3 do not show anger, frustration, or unease.

34. A: The narrator mentions being lost several times throughout the passage, and the central conflict is created when the children think someone is lost. The narrator explains that there are many people in the park to show that it would be easy to get lost, so choice A is correct. Choice B is incorrect because the story takes place during the grand opening of the park. Because the park has opened recently, this description cannot be understood as a sign that the park is popular, since people are still trying it out. Choice C is incorrect because the narrator does not complain about waiting in line. Choice D is incorrect because the narrator shows that it was hot by listing what his mother packed in the bag in paragraph 2.

35. A: The conflict of the story is trying to find George, who is lost. The conflict is resolved when George is found, so choice A is correct. The passage does not show whether or not the lines become shorter, so choice B is incorrect. The children do care about George, who is a stuffed animal, because they need to return him to their teacher. This makes choice C incorrect. The conflict is not resolved by the children leaving the park, since George was lost inside of the park, so choice D is incorrect.

36. B, E: The image is provided after the paragraph that says the tortoises live in the park and are not in cages. The photo only shows a tortoise, not the park or enclosures. As such, it can be assumed that this image is meant to show readers what tortoises look like, so choice E is correct. Since this enclosure was also the author's favorite part of the zoo, choice B is also correct. Because the enclosures, park layout, and fencing are not shown, choices A, C, and D are incorrect.

37. B: The central idea of this passage is that the narrator enjoyed his trip to London. Because the narrator focused so heavily on his trip to Regent's Park, it can be assumed this was his favorite part, so choice B is correct. The narrator did learn about monarchies and how some royal land was used to create parks. However, this is the main idea of the second paragraph, not the passage as a whole, so choice A is incorrect. Choice C is incorrect for similar reasons. The tortoises are mentioned in a supporting detail in paragraph five. The central idea of the passage is not about the tortoises. The narrator did not express that this trip sparked a love for traveling, so choice D is incorrect.

38. A: The author used a descriptive structure to explain the aspects of Regent Park and why he enjoyed visiting it. Choice B is incorrect. If an author wanted to explain to readers why he or she went somewhere or did something, this would be best accomplished using a cause-and-effect structure of writing. Highlighting a problem on the trip would be best accomplished with a problem and solution style of writing, so choice C is incorrect. While vivid details could be provided in a passage that uses a descriptive structure, this passage does not contain enough sensory details for that to be the case. This makes choice D incorrect.

39. C: Replica means an exact copy of something, especially on a smaller scale. This can be understood based on the context in paragraph 5, which shows the reader that the zoo wanted to create something like the animals' environment. Choices A and B are incorrect because the description of how the zoo attempted to create a replica does not show actions that would result in the creation of an item or family. Choice D is incorrect because a habitat could be created whether or not the zoo aimed to make it similar to the tortoises' natural environment.

40. C: This paragraph makes it clear that the town of Aberystwyth is very well known for its educational services in addition to other, more tourist-focused features. Choice C rephrases this information but maintains the same main idea, so it is correct. This makes the area great for both residents and tourists, making choices A and B incorrect. The passage mentions remnants of castles, but it does not focus on how the area around them has changed. This makes choice D incorrect.

41. B: The author describes all of the positive and noteworthy aspects of the town in order to showcase how wonderful it is, so choice B is correct. To convince people to visit the town, the author would have written a persuasive essay. The passage is not written this way, so choice A is incorrect. While this passage does contain facts about the town, it is not meant to entertain, so choice C is incorrect. This passage does not downplay the draws of the town. Instead, it highlights the town's positive aspects, so choice D is incorrect.

42. B: Both passages express admiration for a city, so choice B is correct. "The Royal City" expresses admiration for London while "The Educational Market Town" expresses admiration for Aberystwyth. Education and learning are only discussed in "The Educational Market Town," making choice A incorrect. Neither passage discusses frustration while traveling, so choice C is incorrect. While both passages touch on the history of a city, neither focuses on appreciating a city's history, so choice D is incorrect.

43. D: "The Royal Scenery" is written using a casual, first-person point of view that describes the author's vacation experience. This is different from the more formal third-person point of view used in "The Educational Market Town." Neither passage expresses the author's desire to return to the location he or she wrote about, so choice A is incorrect. Both passages describe what makes the towns unique, so choice B is incorrect. Both passages discuss the landmarks and attractions in the area they are written about, so choice D is incorrect.

44. B: Both authors focus on the unique qualities of the area they are writing about. This implies that qualities that are unique to an area are what make it worth visiting. Only "The Royal Scenery" mentioned animals roaming freely, so choice A is incorrect. "The Royal Scenery" focuses primarily on things the author did as a tourist, while the author of "The Educational Market Town" discusses the town's appeal to both tourists and those interested in education opportunities. Additionally, neither passage discusses the worth or value of either place, so choice C is incorrect. Only "The Educational Market Town" discusses languages, so choice D is incorrect.

Language Practice Test #1

Questions 1-8 pertain to the following passage:

An American Hero

(1) In the year 1912, the unsinkable Titanic sank, the United States territory of Arizona became a state, and my Great Uncle Charlie was born. (2) Charlie was born in a small town in Kentucky. (3) On a farm. (4) He grew up learning about the seasons, when to plant the seeds, and when the crops were ripe for picking. (5) His mornings were spent with his hands in dirt as he tended to the growing corps.

(6) When Charlie was only 12, his father died. (7) He had to quit school to take care of his family. (8) While other children were learning and playing at school, Charlie worked in factories to help pay for his mother and sisters to eat. (9) Irregardless of how he felt about having to work, Charlie never complained.

(10) On December 7, 1941, Japan attacked the American naval base at Pearl Harbor. (11) Charlie enlisted in the army when he was 30 years old, and went to fight in the war. (12) He fought in six major battles, including landing in Normandy on D-Day. (13) While he was in the army, Charlie joined the United States horseshoe team and became the champion of the european allies. (14) After the war, Charlie returned to Kentucky married a woman named Bethany, and had three children.

(15) Today, Charlie can still be found with his hands in the dirt. (16) He loves to work in the small garden beside his front porch. (17) The bright colors of ripening strawberries, tomatoes, and ears of corn can be seen next to the house with Charlie walking though the rows of crops with his watering can. (18) He tends to them with love. (19) Charlie watches over his family like the crops in the garden, and that is why he is my hero.

1. What is the BEST way to explain the information in sentences 2 and 3?

a. Charlie was born in a small town in Kentucky. It was on a farm
b. Charlie was born in Kentucky. In a small town and on a farm
c. Charlie was born in a small town. In Kentucky, it was on a farm
d. Charlie was born in a small Kentucky town on a farm

2. What change, if any, should be made to sentence 5?

a. Change *corps* to *crops*
b. Change *were* to *was*
c. Insert a comma after *dirt*
d. Make no change

3. What change, if any, should be made to sentence 9?

a. Change *complained* to *complains*
b. Change *irregardless* to *regardless*
c. Delete the comma after *work*
d. Make no change

4. What sentence could BEST follow and support sentence 10?

a. Pearl Harbor is a naval base in Hawaii
b. The USS Arizona was one of the battleships that sank
c. This event directly led into the United States' involvement in World War II
d. Charlie had never been to Hawaii

5. What change, if any, should be made to sentence 13?

a. Change *european* to *European*
b. Change *became* to *becomes*
c. Insert a comma after *champion*
d. Make no change

6. What change, if any, should be made to sentence 14?

a. Change *returned* to *returns*
b. Insert a comma after *Kentucky*
c. Insert *and* after *Kentucky*
d. Make no change

7. What change, if any, should be made in sentence 16?

a. Change *loves* to *loved*
b. Insert a comma after *garden*
c. Change *beside* to *besides*
d. Make no change

8. What change, if any, should be made in sentence 17?

a. Change *colors* to *colours*
b. Delete the comma after *strawberries*
c. Change *though* to *through*
d. Make no change

Questions 9 – 16 pertain to the following story:

The Top Deck

(1) We walked outside through the sliding glass doors and waited in line for the large, double-decker red bus. (2) My family flew to London for a week in July to celebrate my sisters graduation. (3) She wore a blue cap and gown. (4) The sky was gray, and light puddles spotted the ground. (5) As the bus pulled up against the curb, dirty water splashed our feet.

(6) The driver's seat was on the opposite side of the bus, and the driver smiled at me when I showed him my ticket. (7) I looked out the window and realised that we were driving on the opposite side of the street. (8) All around us people who were on the wrong side of the street driving from what looked like the passenger seat. (9) The bus was filled with people. (10) Almost every seat was taken, and people were even standing in the aisle holding onto handrails and poles. (11) Their was a spiral staircase directly behind the driver, and we walked up to it to try to find more seats. (12) There were two rows of seats upstairs and a large window that looked onto the streets. (13) For seats were open near the front of the bus and we hurried to get them.

(14) The bus stopped every few seconds, and each time I had to hold onto my seat to keep from sliding into the aisle. (15) "What street are we looking for?" my dad asked my mom. (16) "Oxford" she replied. (17) I looked out the giant window. (18) We passed a large

building that was shaped like an egg, and we continued to travel. (19) The bus driver's voice came over the speakers. (20) "Now approaching Liverpool," he said

(21) My mom looked at my dad. (22) I grabbed my sister's arm, but she was busy taking pictures of the buildings out the window. (23) "Liverpool," my mom whispered with a worried look on her face. (24) "We're lost, aren't we?" my dad said.

9. What change, if any, should be made in sentence 2?

a. Change *flew* to *flied*
b. Change *week* to *weak*
c. Change *sisters* to *sister's*
d. Make no change

10. What change, if any, should be made in sentence 7?

a. Change *realised* to *realize*
b. Change *street* to *streat*
c. Change *looked* to *look*
d. Make no change

11. What change, if any, should be made in sentence 11?

a. Delete the comma after *driver*
b. Change *Their* to *There*
c. Change *staircase* to *stair case*
d. Make no change

12. What change should be made in sentence 13?

a. Change *open* to *opened*
b. Change *were* to *was*
c. Change *For* to *Four*
d. Change *hurried* to *hurried*

13. Which of the following is the BEST way to rewrite the ideas in sentence 8?

a. All around us people were driving from what looked like the passenger seat, and they were driving on the opposite side of the street
b. All around us people who were on the wrong side of the street, driving from what looked like the passenger seat
c. All around us people were driving on the wrong side of the street. Driving from what looked like the passenger seat
d. All around us people were driving from what looked like passenger seat, they were on the opposite side of the street

14. What change, if any, should be made in sentence 16?

a. Change *Oxford* to *oxford*
b. Insert a comma after *Oxford*
c. Insert a period after the quotation mark
d. Make no change

15. Which sentence does not belong in this essay?

a. Sentence 20
b. Sentence 6
c. Sentence 13
d. Sentence 3

16. What is the BEST transition word or phrase that could be added to the beginning of sentence 19?

a. However
b. Once in a while
c. Additionally
d. After a while

Questions 17 -24 pertain to the following story:

Longhorn Café

(1) Last Saturday night my dad took me to watch the Longhorns play football in Austin. (2) It was a cool evening, and the orange-painted stadium was filled with screaming fans. (3) Even though we live in San Antonio, my dad has always been a dedicated Longhorns fan, and he wears his orange proudly.

(4) We arrived in Austin early. (5) "Traffic," my dad said as his only explanation. (6) He parked the truck down a small side street and motions for me to get out and follow him. (7) "I want to take you someplace," he said. (8) "I used to come here all the time when I was in college. (9) We walked up to a small building with a large patio off to the side. (10) A large tree with low branches spread across the patio and connected with the roof. (11) The leaves were beginning to change colors, and it was like sitting under a leafy canopy.

(12) We sat at a table outside on a rusting rocking bench beside an abandoned bathtub. (13) Stands of colored lights hung across the patio. (14) Wrapped around the tree. (15) "What is this place?" I asked. (16) My dad smiled and pointed to a sign bordered with colored lights. (17) "Spider Café," he said. (18) All around us, people were drinking coffee and staring at them computer screens. (19) Our waiter was named Chris, and he had a long beard, wore a dirtied apron, and carried empty coffee mugs.

(20) The waited came up to us, and my dad ordered himself a latte and a sweet drink for me. (21) My dad looked around the patio and smiled. (22) He leaned into the bench and placed his hand on the side of the bathtub. (23) He didn't even mind when he spilled coffee onto his favorite orange shirt. (24) "You'll love it here," he said, "when you are a Longhorn football player?"

17. What change, if any, should be made in sentence 5?

a. Delete the comma after *traffic*
b. Insert a comma after *said*
c. Change *said* to *says*
d. Make no change

18. What change should be made in sentence 6?

a. Change *parked* to *park*
b. Change *street* to *Street*
c. Insert a comma after *street*
d. Change *motions* to *motioned*

19. What change, if any, should be made in sentence 8?

a. Change *come* to *came*
b. Change *to* to *too*
c. Insert a quotation mark after *college*
d. Make no change

20. What revision, if any, is needed in sentences 13 and 14?

a. Strands of colored lights hung across the patio wrapped, around the tree
b. Strands of colored lights hung across the patio and wrapped around the tree
c. Strands of colored lights hung. Across the patio, wrapped around the tree
d. No revision is needed

21. What change, if any, should be made in sentence 18?

a. Change *them* to *their*
b. Delete the comma after *us*
c. Insert a comma after *and*
d. Make no change

22. Where is the best placement for sentence 19?

a. After sentence 22
b. After sentence 20
c. Before sentence 18
d. No change is needed

Questions 23 – 25 pertain to the following story:

Strike Three

(1) As I stared down at the hitter in the batters box, I remembered what my dad had said to me. (2) "Shut everything out." (3) I focused on the glove in front of me. (4) I looked into the deep, blackened pocket, and sawed my target. (5) The batter tapped his bat against the sides of his cleats, and rested the bat on his shoulders. (6) With hard eyes, he stares back at me.

(7) I kicked the front of my cleat into the bright white rubber on the pitching mound and took a deep breath. (8) Shut everything out," he had said. (9) Slowly the noises disappeared. (10) I could no longer hear the shouts from the parents in the stands. (11) In my head, I silenced the cheers from both dugouts. (12) The umpire did not exist. (13) There were no players, no coaches, not even a catcher. (14) There was just me. (15) The ball and the glove.

(16) I took a deep breath and brought my hands together at my chest. (17) I looked over at first base, but there was no runner. (18) In one motion, my feet left the rubber and connected with ground. (19) Dirt flew in the air as my arm rotated forward and released the ball in front of me. (20) I watched as the ball spun and landed into glove with a hard crack. (21) The umpire shot up from his crouched position and pointed his finger to the right and yelled, "Strike Three!"

(22) The noises came back. (23) The crowd cheered in the stands and I could here stomping feet. (24) My teammate clapped his hand to its glove and ran toward me. (25) My coach raised a first into the air in celebration. (26) I was surrounded by my teammates, and they were patting me on the back. (27) My dad was sitting on a bleacher behind home plate. (28) He raised his thumb to me and smiled as I ran off the field with my teammates.

23. What change, if any, should be made in sentence 1?

a. Change *stared* to *starred*
b. Change *dad* to *Dad*
c. Change *batters* to *batter's*
d. Make no change

24. What change should be made in sentence 4?

a. Change *blackened* to *blacked*
b. Change *sawed* to *saw*
c. Delete the comma after *deep*
d. Change *into* to *in to*

25. What change, if any, should be made in sentence 6?

a. Change *stares* to *stared.*
b. Change *me* to *I*
c. Delete the comma after *eyes*
d. Make no change

Questions 26 – 30 pertain to the following passage:

Imagine a Better World

(1) My favorite song is "imagine" by John Lennon. (2) It was released in 1971. (3) It is one of the few famous songs that John Lennon recorded and sang alone. (4) For the majority of his career, John Lennon was a member of an iconic rock band called the Beatles, a band that changed the music industry. (5) The Beatles accepted a lot of success in their career, with popular songs such as "I Want to Hold Your Hand," "Come Together," "Let it Be," and "Here Comes the Sun." (6) After the band decided to separate, John Lennon became a solo artist as well as an promoter for peace.

(7) "Imagine" tells the story of Lennons dream of peace in the world. He asks the listener to imagine different situations. (8) He says to imagine that there are no countries, religions, or possessions. (9) He says, "I wonder if you can." (10) This line strikes me the most I try to imagine such a world. (11) When talking about no possessions, he continues and says, "No need for greed or hunger." (12) It is a great line. (13) Throughout the song, he says, "Imagine all the people." (14) And he gives examples. (15) At first he says, "living for today," and then moves on to say, "living life in peace," and finally, "sharing all the world."

(16) My favorite part of the song is the chorus. (17) Lennon says, "You may say I'm a dreamer, but I'm not the only one. (18) I hope someday you'll join us, and the world will be as one." (19) When I really listen to the words of this song, I realize that "Imagine" is so much more than something that sounds nicely. (20) Lennon is saying something very important and suggesting ways in which the world can live in peace. (21) Because of this song, I am a dreamer as well, and I join John Lennon in the fight for world peace.

26. What change, if any, should be made in sentence 1?

a. Change *favorite* to *favourite*
b. Change *imagine* to *Imagine*
c. Insert a comma after *song*
d. Make no change

27. What is the BEST verb to replace accepted in sentence 5?

a. Lasted
b. Liked
c. Had
d. Watched

28. What change should be made in sentence 6?

a. Change *separate* to *separated*
b. Insert a comma after *artist*
c. Change *solo* to *Solo*
d. Change *an* to *a*

29. What change, if any, should be made in sentence 7?

a. Change *Lennons* to *Lennon's*
b. Change *dream* to *dreamt*
c. Insert a comma after *peace*
d. Make no change

30. What is the BEST way to revise sentence 10?

a. This line strikes me the most as I try to imagine such a world.
b. This line strikes me the most, I try to imagine such a world.
c. This line strikes me, the most. I try to imagine such a world.
d. No revision needed.

Answer Key and Explanations for Language Test #1

1. D: because this sentence is the simplest way to explain where Charlie was born. A is not correct because two sentences are not necessary. The additional subject and verb are unnecessary to express the idea. B is not correct, because *In a small town and on a farm* is a fragment. C is not correct, because the sentences contain awkward wording. The sentences need to be combined in order to express the idea in the simplest form.

2. A: because in this sentence, *crops* has been misspelled as *corps.* B is not correct, because the subject of the sentence, *mornings,* is plural. Therefore, the verb also must be plural for correct subject verb agreement. C is not correct, because this sentence does not need a comma.

3. B: because irregardless is not a word. The correct word is *regardless.* A is not correct because *complains* is in the present tense, while the rest of the paragraph is in the past tense. C is not correct, because a comma is needed after an introductory clause.

4. C: because this sentence supports both sentence 10 and sentence 11. The sentence supports the cause and effect idea that the attack on Pearl Harbor prompted the United States to become involved in the war, which caused Charlie to enlist in the army. A is not correct. Although this sentence provides new information, it does not link and support sentences 10 and 11. B is not correct. Although this sentence provides new information, it does not link and support sentences 10 and 11. D is not correct. Although this sentence provides new information, it does not link and support sentences 10 and 11.

5. A: because *European* is a proper noun and must be capitalized. B is not correct, because *becomes* is in the present tense, and the rest of the paragraph is written in the past tense. C is not correct, because a comma is not needed after *champion.*

6. B: because this sentence uses commas in a series as it lists aspects of Charlie's life after the war. Both *returned to Kentucky* and *married a woman named Bethany* are events that have happened and therefore need to be separated by a comma. A is not correct. *Returns* is in the present tense, and the rest of the paragraph is written in the past tense. C is not correct. The correct sentence uses commas in a series, and therefore only uses one *and* in the sentence.

7. D: because the sentence is correct as written. A is not correct. Although the rest of the essay is written in the past tense, the last paragraph begins with *Today* and is written in the present tense. Therefore, *loves* is correct. B is not correct, because this sentence does not need a comma. C is not correct. Both *beside* and *besides* are prepositions, but *beside* means "next to" and *besides* means "in addition to" or "other than." *Beside* is used in this sentence as "next to."

8. C: because in this sentence, *through* has been misspelled as *though.* A is not correct, because *colors* is spelled correctly. B is not correct, because this sentence needs a comma after *strawberries,* since the sentence contains a list and uses commas in a series.

9. C: In this sentence, *Sister's* is possessive and requires an apostrophe. A is not correct. *Flew* is the correct past tense of *fly.* B is not correct, because *week* is a noun and is spelled correctly.

10. A: because *realized* is misspelled in this sentence. B is not correct, because *street* is spelled correctly. C is not correct, because *look* is in the present tense, while the essay is written in past tense.

11. B: because a homonym has been misused. *There* is used to indicate a physical or abstract place, while *their* is used to indicate possession. A is not correct, because this sentence has two independent clauses joined by the conjunction *and*, and a comma is used before the conjunction. C is not correct, because *staircase* is one word.

12. C: because a homonym has been misused. *Four* is a number. A is not correct, because in this sentence *open* is used as a noun rather than a verb and does not need to be in the past tense. B is not correct. *Were* is plural, and *was* is singular. The subject of the sentence, *seats*, is plural; therefore, the verb also must be plural for correct subject verb agreement. D is not correct, because *hurried* is spelled correctly.

13. A: because this rewording of this sentence makes the meaning clear and is grammatically correct. B is not correct because this sentence is a fragment. C is not correct because the second sentence is a fragment. D is not correct because this sentence is a run-on sentence.

14. B: because a comma is needed before the closing quotation when the sentence is not completed with the quotation. A is not correct because *Oxford* is a proper noun and must be capitalized. C is not correct. The sentence does not end with the quotation; therefore, a comma, rather than a period, goes before the quotation mark.

15. D: because this sentence this sentence provides new information that is not important to the rest of the essay. Answers A, B, and C are incorrect, because all of these sentences present content that is important to the essay.

16. D: In the previous sentence, the phrase *we continued to travel*, suggests a passage of time. A proper transition into the next sentence would involve the acknowledgement that time has passed. A is not correct because *however* is not a good transition into the sentence. B is not correct. Although *once in a while* relates to time, it does not transition well into the sentence given the context of the previous sentence. C is not correct. *Additionally* is not a good transition into the sentence because it does not indicate a passage of time.

17. D: because the sentence is correct as written. A is not correct, because a comma is needed before the closing quotation when the sentence is not completed with the quotation. B is not correct because this sentence does not need a comma. C is not correct because *says* is in the present tense, and the essay is written in the past tense.

18. D: because *motions* is in the present tense, and the rest of the essay is written in the past tense. B is not correct because *street* is not used in this sentence as a proper noun and does not need to be capitalized. C is not correct. A comma is unnecessary because the second sentence is not an independent clause.

19. C: because a quotation mark is needed to end dialogue. A is incorrect because *come* is in the present tense, and the essay is written in the past tense. B is not correct. *Too* means "also" or an indication of excess.

20. B: because this sentence is grammatically correct as written. A is not correct. The comma is misplaced and disrupts the sentence. C is not correct because the second sentence is a fragment. D is not correct because sentence 14 is a fragment.

21. A: because *their* indicates possession; *them* does not. *Computer screens* belong to the subject, *people*. B is not correct. *All around us* is an introductory clause and needs a comma. C is not correct. *Staring at them computer screens* is not an independent clause and therefore does not need a comma.

22. B: because the sentence provides additional information about the waiter. The sentence should be placed after the waiter has been introduced in sentence 20. A is not correct. The subject of the paragraph has shifted to the father at sentence 21, and therefore a sentence involving information about the waiter would be out of place after sentence 22. C is not correct. Sentence 18 provides setting information. A sentence involving information about the waiter before this sentence would be out of place. D is not correct. This sentence provides additional information about the waiter and should not conclude a paragraph.

23. C: In this sentence, *batter's* is possessive and needs an apostrophe. A is not correct because *stared*, the past tense of the verb, *stare*, is spelled correctly. B is not correct. In this sentence, *dad* is not a proper noun, since it is not used as a name. *My* before *dad* indicates that it is not a proper noun.

24. B: because *saw* is the correct past tense of the verb, *see*. A is not correct because *blackened* is the correct adjective. C is not correct. A comma is needed to separate adjectives when each adjective separately describes the noun. D is not correct. *Into* is spelled correctly.

25. A: because *stares* is in the present tense, and the rest of the essay is in the past tense. *Stared* is the correct past tense of *stare*. B is not correct. *Me* is the object of the sentence because it is the recipient of the action, *stares*. I is traditionally used as a subject. C is not correct. *With hard eyes* is an introductory clause, and a comma is needed after the clause.

26. B: because *imagine* is a proper noun. As the title of a song, it requires capitalization. A is not correct. *Favorite* is spelled correctly. C is not correct. *My favorite song* is not an introductory clause, so a comma is not needed.

27. C: because the missing verb in this sentence must have something to do with possession, since it discusses the band's success. *Had* indicates possession. A, B, and D are incorrect, because these verbs do not fit within the sentence.

28. D: It is correct because in the sentence, the article *an* is followed by a noun, *promoter*. *Promoter* begins with a consonant and a consonant sound and therefore must be followed by the article *a*. A is not correct. The verb in this sentence is *decided*, not *separate*, and therefore *separate* does not need to be in the past tense like the rest of the paragraph. B is not correct because the comma is unnecessary. C is not correct. *Solo* is not a proper noun and does not need to be capitalized.

29. A: because *Lennon* is possessive in this sentence; therefore, it requires an apostrophe. B is not correct. In this sentence, *dream* is a noun rather than a verb, so it does not need to be in the past tense. C is not correct, because a comma is unnecessary.

30. A: because the sentence is missing the article *as*. This is the simplest way to express the idea of the sentence. B is incorrect because this sentence is not grammatically correct. C is incorrect because the first sentence is grammatically incorrect.

Reading Practice Test #2

Refer to the passage "'The Ettrick Shepherd'" to answer questions 1-8.

"The Ettrick Shepherd"

by James Baldwin

(1) In Scotland there once lived a poor shepherd whose name was James Hogg. His father and grandfather and great-grandfather had all been shepherds.

(2) It was his business to take care of the sheep which belonged to a rich landholder by the Ettrick Water. Sometimes he had several hundreds of lambs to look after. He drove these to the pastures on the hills and watched them day after day while they fed on the short green grass.

(3) He had a dog which he called Sirrah. This dog helped him watch the sheep. He would drive them from place to place as his master wished. Sometimes he would take care of the whole flock while the shepherd was resting or eating his dinner.

(4) One dark night James Hogg was on the hilltop with a flock of seven hundred lambs. Sirrah was with him. Suddenly a storm came up. There was thunder and lightning; the wind blew hard; the rain poured.

(5) The poor lambs were frightened. The shepherd and his dog could not keep them together. Some of them ran towards the east, some towards the west, and some towards the south.

(6) The shepherd soon lost sight of them in the darkness. With his lighted lantern in his hand, he went up and down the rough hills calling for his lambs.

(7) Two or three other shepherds joined him in the search. All night long they sought for the lambs.

(8) Morning came and still they sought. They looked, as they thought, in every place where the lambs might have taken shelter.

(9) At last James Hogg said, "It's of no use; all we can do is to go home and tell the master that we have lost his whole flock."

(10) They had walked a mile or two towards home, when they came to the edge of a narrow and deep ravine. They looked down, and at the bottom they saw some lambs huddled together among the rocks. And there was Sirrah standing guard over them and looking all around for help. "These must be the lambs that rushed off towards the south," said James Hogg.

(11) The men hurried down and soon saw that the flock was a large one.

(12) "I really believe they are all here," said one.

(13) They counted them and were surprised to find that not one lamb of the great flock of seven hundred was missing.

(14) How had Sirrah managed to get the three scattered divisions together? How had he managed to drive all the frightened little animals into this place of safety?

(15) Nobody could answer these questions. But there was no shepherd in Scotland that could have done better than Sirrah did that night.

(16) Long afterward James Hogg said, "I never felt so grateful to any creature below the sun as I did to Sirrah that morning."

1. How does the setting of this passage affect the plot?

a. The country this passage takes place in is the only one in which sheep and lambs are found.
b. The lack of technology at the time caused the shepherds to rely on Sirrah while searching for the lambs.
c. The farm where the passage takes place is isolated and causes James to work alone.
d. The terrain surrounding the farm included several places where the shepherds had to look for the sheep.

2. Read this section of the passage.

He had a dog which he called Sirrah. This dog helped him watch the sheep. He would drive them from place to place as his master wished. Sometimes he would take care of the whole flock while the shepherd was resting or eating his dinner.

What do these sentences help the reader understand about Sirrah?

a. His habits kept him from eating with his owner.
b. His behavior was inconsistent throughout.
c. His commitment to his owner was unchanging.
d. His energy prevented him from resting with his owner.

3. Which line from the passage best helps the reader understand that the other shepherds care for James?

a. Morning came and still they sought. They looked, as they thought, in every place where the lambs might have taken shelter.
b. Nobody could answer these questions. But there was no shepherd in Scotland that could have done better than Sirrah did that night.
c. The shepherd soon lost sight of them in the darkness. With his lighted lantern in his hand, he went up and down the rough hills calling for his lambs.
d. At last James Hogg said, "It's of no use; all we can do is to go home and tell the master that we have lost his whole flock."

4. What is the best summary of this passage?

a. James Hogg was a poor man left alone to care for the sheep of a rich man. He was to attend to them all day and night with no breaks. One night, the flock of lambs vanished. Hogg searched for them for hours before finding they had been herded by his dog, Sirrah.
b. James Hogg and his dog, Sirrah, were responsible for caring for a rich man's sheep. One stormy night, a frightened flock of lambs scattered from a hilltop in different directions. Hogg and a group of other shepherds were unable to locate the lambs after several hours of searching and were giving up. However, they soon found that the dog had located and safely herded all the lambs.
c. James Hogg was a shepherd in Scotland. He liked to work alone to care for his flock, so he did not appreciate the appearance of a dog on his farm. A storm startled a flock of lambs and caused them to run in several different directions. Hogg searched for them and eventually discovered they had been safely rescued by the dog, leading him to appreciate the dog.
d. Sirrah was a typical dog who lived and worked on a sheep farm. He helped his owner keep the flock safe from harm. During a storm, a flock of 700 lambs managed to escape the farm. Sirrah was able to track them all down and keep them safe until his owner arrived. Ever since that night, Sirrah has been regarded as the best sheepdog in Scotland.

5. What is the most likely reason James Baldwin wrote "The Ettrick Shepherd"?

a. To give an autobiographical account of a stormy night in Scotland.
b. To describe how shepherds support one another in times of need.
c. To suggest that trained dogs can replace human farmers.
d. To share a narrative of the bond between a shepherd and his dog.

6. How does the language in paragraphs 8 and 9 affect the mood of the passage?

a. It conveys a sense of frustration.
b. It expresses a feeling of hopelessness.
c. It creates a spirit of teamwork.
d. It portrays the goal as achievable.

7. Based on paragraph 16, what can the reader predict would have happened if the lambs had not been found?

a. Their owner would have replaced the herd with new lambs.
b. The shepherd would likely have been in trouble with the owner.
c. The shepherds that helped Hogg would have been held responsible.
d. The lambs would have been found and kept by other farmers.

8. Which detail from the passage supports the key idea that loyal dogs are valuable companions?

a. They looked down, and at the bottom they saw some lambs huddled together among the rocks.
b. With his lighted lantern in his hand, he went up and down the rough hills calling for his lambs.
c. But there was no shepherd in Scotland that could have done better than Sirrah did that night.
d. He drove these to the pastures on the hills and watched them day after day while they fed on the short green grass.

Refer to the passage "The Inventions of Technology" to answer questions 9-12.

The Inventions of Technology

(1) Stories have been a part of the world since the beginning of recorded time. For centuries before the invention of the printing press, stories were passed down to generations through oral tradition. With the invention of the printing press, which made

written material available to a wider audience, books were mass-produced and introduced into greater society.

(2) For the last several centuries, books have been at the forefront of education and entertainment. With the invention of the internet, the reliance on books for information quickly faded. Suddenly, almost everything that anyone needed to know could be accessed through the internet. Large, printed volumes of encyclopedias became unnecessary, as all of the information was easily available on the internet.

(3) Despite the progression of the internet, printed media is still very popular in the forms of both fiction and non-fiction books. While waiting for an appointment, enduring a several-hour flight, or relaxing before sleep, books have been a reliable and convenient source of entertainment that society has not been willing to give up.

(4) With the progression and extreme convenience of technology, printed books are going to soon become a thing of the past. Inventions such as the iPad and the Kindle have made the need for any kind of printed media unnecessary. With a rechargeable battery, a large screen, and the ability to have several books saved on file, electronic options will soon take over and society will no longer see printed books.

(5) Although some people may say that the act of reading is not complete without turning a page, sliding a finger across the screen or pressing a button to go to the next page is just as satisfying to the reader. The iPad and Kindle are devices that have qualities similar to a computer and can be used for so much more than just reading. These devices are therefore better than books because they have multiple uses.

(6) Due to a longstanding tradition in world culture, stories will always be an important way to communicate ideas and provide information and entertainment. Centuries ago, stories could only be passed down through speech. Printed media changed the way the world communicated and was connected, and now, as we move forward with technology, it is only a matter of time before we must say goodbye to the printed past and welcome the digital and electronic future.

9. In the selection "The Inventions of Technology," what does the chronological structure help readers understand?

a. The changes to reading technology will eventually be undone and society will return to paper copies of books.
b. The invention of e-readers was a necessary part in the evolution of education in society.
c. The changes in technology over time have influenced the way stories are passed on and read.
d. The development of electronic books is more historically significant than the printing press.

10. Part A: What is the main argument of this essay?

a. iPad and Kindles are easier to read than books.
b. The printing press was a great invention.
c. The internet is how people receive information.
d. Digital text will soon replace printed text.

Part B: Which sentence from the passage most clearly supports the answer to Part A?

a. Stories have been a part of the world since the beginning of recorded time.
b. Despite the progression of the internet, printed media is still very popular in the forms of both fiction and non-fiction books.
c. With the progression and extreme convenience of technology, printed books are going to soon become a thing of the past.
d. These devices are therefore better than books because they have multiple uses.

11. How does the author's reference to examples like the iPad and the Kindle support the main idea of the passage?

a. By explaining that the internet can quickly make printed books obsolete
b. By showing how technology can change how people read over time
c. By describing how stories used to be shared
d. By creating a sense of nostalgia for the time period before electronic readers

12. How does the author's organization of this essay impact his or her purpose for writing?

a. The author compares the advantages and disadvantages of using an iPad.
b. The author tells of the events that led from reading stories to oral tradition.
c. The author lists examples of technology that remove the need for books.
d. The author gives the history of storytelling in society and shows how it has changed.

Refer to the passage "The Power of Print" to answer questions 13-16.

The Power of Print

(1) There are many ways to engage with a book. You can listen to it on audio. You can swipe through the pages on an electronic device. You can watch a video of the author reading it aloud online. However, none of these methods will ever compare to the experience of reading a physical book.

(2) The feel of printed books is one of their primary draws. Readers like to feel the weight of the book, turn the pages, and see how much they have read at a glance. There is a sense of satisfaction gained when a reader closes a book for the final time and places it on the shelf among their collection of loved titles. Even more satisfying is the feeling of gifting a treasured book to a friend who is sure to enjoy it. While a reader can see what percentage of a book they have read and loan books for limited periods through a digital library on an electronic reader, the inability to physically see or do these things makes them unfulfilling and impersonal.

(3) On the other hand, electronic reading devices function too similarly to a phone or computer. This can give reading the feeling of being a work-related task as opposed to an enriching hobby. There are also situations in which these devices are inconvenient. Electronics should be avoided around water, meaning they should not be used for poolside or beach-day reading. They can also be difficult to see in full sun. Electronic readers require access to electricity to charge, meaning there will be times when they need power and are unusable. Books are always charged and ready to read anytime, anywhere.

(4) Opinions aside, it has been scientifically proven over several studies that reading physical materials is best for learning new information. Readers retain more information when reading a printed book than they do when reading from a screen. The act of turning a page causes the brain to map information in a way that makes it easier

to remember. Similarly, it has been proven that readers recall more information when they read an article as opposed to listening to the same article in a podcast format.

(5) Overall, physical books are far superior to other methods of reading. Their physicality fulfills many needs for readers. They are always available to be pulled from a shelf and enjoyed immediately with no wait times or loading screens. Printed books are better for learning than other formats. This all goes to prove that there is nothing better than a physical book!

13. What primary claim does the author make in this selection?

a. Readers should use whatever format of book appeals to them.
b. Paper copies of books are overall the best format for all reading.
c. Electronic devices can make reading more difficult.
d. Books should be read and then shared so others can enjoy them.

14. What is the most likely reason the author cites studies in the fourth paragraph?

a. To provide scientific evidence to support his or her argument
b. To highlight the beliefs of individuals who only read physical books
c. To provide factual information on the benefits of reading
d. To eliminate any counterarguments to his or her point

15. Who is the intended audience of this essay?

a. Reading teachers
b. Authors and illustrators
c. Librarians
d. Readers

16. Read this excerpt from paragraph one.

> But none of these methods will ever compare to the experience of reading a physical book.

What is the most likely reason the author uses hyperbole in this sentence?

a. To help readers better understand the point of view
b. To provide readers with a statement of factual evidence
c. To further emphasize his or her stance on physical books
d. To appeal to the reader's sense of curiosity

Refer to the passages "The Inventions of Technology" and "The Power of Print" to answer questions 17-19.

17. In what way is the author of "The Inventions of Technology" UNLIKE the author of "The Power of Print"?

a. He or she would likely think any reading is better than no reading.
b. He or she would be more open to accepting new reading formats over time.
c. He or she would probably support increasing library funding for physical books.
d. He or she would prefer to read nonfiction articles instead of fiction novels.

18. Which topic is present in both "The Inventions of Technology" and "The Power of Print"?

a. The pitfalls of electronic readers
b. The struggle of choosing a type of book
c. The debate surrounding the best format of books
d. The impact of changes in reading on education

19. The author of "The Inventions of Technology" and the author of "The Power of Print" would both most likely agree with which statement?

a. Reading as a hobby should continue through generations.
b. Reading on devices makes it easier to read anywhere you go.
c. Reading physical books is the most rewarding hobby.
d. Reading is a pastime that should not change over time.

Refer to the passage "Ten American Girls from History: Clara Barton" to answer questions 20-28.

Ten American Girls from History: Clara Barton

by Kate Dickinson Sweetser

(1) [Clara has begun her work of ministering to soldiers on the front lines of the civil war. Her tireless efforts and care have taken her to some of the most horrific battles of the war]

(2) Clara Barton!—Only the men who lay wounded or dying on the battle-field knew the thrill and the comfort that the name carried. Again and again her life was in danger—once at Antietam, when stooping to give a drink of water to an injured boy, a bullet whizzed between them. It ended the life of the poor lad, but only tore a hole in Clara Barton's sleeve. And so, again and again, it seemed as if a special Providence protected her from death or injury. At Fredericksburg, when the dead, starving and wounded lay frozen on the ground, and there was no effective organization for proper relief, with swift, silent efficiency Clara Barton moved among them, having the snow cleared away and under the banks finding famished, frozen figures which were once men. She rushed to have an old chimney torn down and built fire-blocks, over which she soon had kettles full of coffee and gruel steaming.

(3) As she was bending over a wounded rebel, he whispered to her: "Lady, you have been kind to me ... every street of the city is covered by our cannon. When your entire army has reached the other side of the Rappahannock, they will find Fredericksburg only a slaughter-pen. Not a regiment will escape. Do not go over, for you will go to certain death."

(4) She thanked him for the kindly warning and later told of the call that came to her to go across the river, and what happened. She says:

(5) "At ten o'clock of the battle day when the rebel fire was hottest, the shells rolling down every street, and the bridge under the heavy cannonade, a courier dashed over, and, rushing up the steps of the house where I was, placed in my hand a crumpled, bloody piece of paper, a request from the lion-hearted old surgeon on the opposite shore, establishing his hospitals in the very jaws of death:

(6) "'Come to me,' he wrote. 'Your place is here.'

(7) "The faces of the rough men working at my side, which eight weeks before had flushed with indignation at the thought of being controlled by a woman, grew ashy white as they guessed the nature of the summons, ... and they begged me to send them, but save myself. I could only allow them to go with me if they chose, and in twenty minutes we were rocking across the swaying bridge, the water hissing with shot on either side.

(8) "Over into that city of death, its roofs riddled by shell, its every church a crowded hospital, every street a battle-line, every hill a rampart, every rock a fortress, and every stone wall a blazing line of forts.

(9) "Oh, what a day's work was that! How those long lines of blue, rank on rank, charged over the open acres, up to the very mouths of those blazing guns, and how like grain before the sickle they fell and melted away.

(10) "An officer stepped to my side to assist me over the débris at the end of the bridge. While our hands were raised in the act of stepping down, a piece of an exploding shell hissed through between us, just below our arms, carrying away a portion of both the skirts of his coat and my dress, rolling along the ground a few rods from us like a harmless pebble in the water. The next instant a solid shot thundered over our heads, a noble steed bounded in the air and with his gallant rider rolled in the dirt not thirty feet in the rear. Leaving the kind-hearted officer, I passed on alone to the hospital. In less than a half-hour he was brought to me—dead."

(11) She was passing along a street in the heart of the city when she had to step aside to let a regiment of infantry march by. At that moment General Patrick saw her, and, thinking she was a frightened resident of the city who had been left behind in the general exodus, leaned from his saddle and said, reassuringly:

(12) "You are alone and in great danger, madam. Do you want protection?"

(13) With a rare smile, Miss Barton said, as she looked at the ranks of soldiers, "Thank you, but I think I am the best-protected woman in the United States."

20. Which two sentences suggest that Clara Barton seems to be under the care of some form of divine guidance? Select all that apply.

a. Only the men who lay wounded or dying on the battle-field knew the thrill and the comfort that the name carried.
b. And so, again and again, it seemed as if a special Providence protected her from death or injury.
c. She thanked him for the kindly warning and later told of the call that came to her to go across the river, and what happened.
d. The faces of the rough men working at my side, which eight weeks before had flushed with indignation at the thought of being controlled by a woman, grew ashy white as they guessed the nature of the summons, ... and they begged me to send them, but save myself.
e. With a rare smile, Miss Barton said, as she looked at the ranks of soldiers, "Thank you, but I think I am the best-protected woman in the United States."

21. Read the dictionary entry (from Merriam-Webster).

Charge \ chärj \v
1. to fix or ask as fee or payment
2. to place the guilt or blame for
3. to rush against
4. to command, instruct, or exhort with authority

Which definition matches the way *charged* is used in paragraph 9?

a. Definition 1
b. Definition 2
c. Definition 3
d. Definition 4

22. Read paragraph 3.

> As she was bending over a wounded rebel, he whispered to her: "Lady, you have been kind to me ... every street of the city is covered by our cannon. When your entire army has reached the other side of the Rappahannock, they will find Fredericksburg only a slaughter-pen. Not a regiment will escape. Do not go over, for you will go to certain death."

What key idea is supported by this paragraph?

a. Clara was not always trusted by the soldiers, so her life was in danger each time she went to a new location.
b. Clara relied on the soldiers to help her understand the danger in a location so she could prepare herself.
c. Clara helped wounded soldiers in dangerous locations, which put her life in jeopardy.
d. Clara did not help every soldier that she came across when she was traveling between assignments.

23. How does the character of the officer in paragraph 10 impact the conflict in Clara's story?

a. His resourcefulness prevents Clara from getting hurt while trying to cross the bridge.
b. His dedication and sad fate emphasize the danger Clara is in and the intensity of the violence around her.
c. His rank in the army allows him to be in the same location as Clara and save her from the exploding shell.
d. The kindness and unexpected passing of the officer made Clara realize life was too precious to spend it in battle.

24. Read this information about the roots of the word Providence.

> From Latin *providentia* meaning "guidance or wisdom from a higher, spiritual force"
> *pro,* meaning "ahead or before" + *videre* meaning "to see"

Based on this meaning, what does Providence mean in paragraph 2?

a. Fragile shield of armor over one's body
b. Divine protection from an all-knowing source
c. Worldly guidance from colleagues
d. Unreliable shelter from harm during battle

25. What does the third-person point of view used in this passage help the reader understand?

a. Clara's courage and dedication to a dangerous career
b. Clara's overall opinion on the war and its purpose
c. Clara's inability to care for patients who were too hurt
d. Clara's internal motivation for continuing when warned otherwise

26. In paragraph 10, what tone does the author create?

a. A resentful tone
b. A tense tone
c. A content tone
d. A passionate tone

27. What can be inferred from the fact that the men's faces turned "white" in the following sentence?

> "The faces of the rough men working at my side, which eight weeks before had flushed with indignation at the thought of being controlled by a woman, grew ashy white as they guessed the nature of the summons, ... and they begged me to send them, but save myself."

a. The men were afraid that Clara would be seriously hurt or killed by going to help.
b. The men were glad for Clara to leave so she could no longer order them around.
c. The men were terrified of the coming war and wanted Clara to escape with them.
d. The men did not want to be moved to the hospital on the other side of the bridge.

28. What could be one reason the author wrote about Clara Barton?

a. She wanted people to understand what life on the battlefield was like during the Civil War.
b. She wanted readers to get a feeling of the conditions faced by doctors and nurses practicing medicine during the Civil War.
c. She hoped to show how great a sacrifice Clara made by becoming a nurse during the war.
d. She knew that future readers would most likely not know who had fought in the war or how Clara tended to the victims.

Refer to the passage "She Walks in Beauty" to answer questions 29-36.

She Walks in Beauty

by Lord Byron

She walks in beauty, like the night
Of cloudless climes and starry skies;
And all that's best of dark and bright
Meet in her aspect and her eyes:
Thus mellowed to that tender light
Which heaven to gaudy day denies.

One shade the more, one ray the less,
Had half impaired the nameless grace
Which waves in every raven tress,
Or softly lightens o'er her face;
Where thoughts serenely sweet express
How pure, how dear their dwelling-place.

And on that cheek, and o'er that brow,
So soft, so calm, yet eloquent,
The smiles that win, the tints that glow,
But tell of days in goodness spent,
A mind at peace with all below,
A heart whose love is innocent!

29. Read lines 10-14 from the poem.

Or softly lightens o'er her face;
Where thoughts serenely sweet express
How pure, how dear their dwelling-place.
And on that cheek, and o'er that brow,
So soft, so calm, yet eloquent,

What can the reader infer from these lines?

a. The woman is upset and expressing that in her appearance.
b. The woman tends to be carefree and clumsy.
c. The woman's face reflects pleasant inner thoughts.
d. The woman is being patient in waiting for change.

30. Which line from the poem best supports the key idea that the woman is innocent, or honorable? Select all that apply.

a. So soft, so calm, yet eloquent
b. How pure, how dear their dwelling-place.
c. She walks in beauty, like the night
d. The smiles that win, the tints that glow,
e. A heart whose love is innocent!

31. Which line from the poem best helps reader understand that the narrator believes the woman has no worries?

a. So soft, so calm, yet eloquent,
b. A heart whose love is innocent!
c. A mind at peace with all below
d. Of cloudless climes and starry skies;

32. Read the dictionary entry (from Merriam-Webster).

Raven
1. Noun: large, glossy-black bird
2. Verb: to feed greedily
3. Verb: to prowl for food
4. Adjective: shiny and black

Which definition best matches the meaning of *raven* in line 9?

a. Definition 1
b. Definition 2
c. Definition 3
d. Definition 4

33. How does the rhyming pattern of the poem "She Walks in Beauty" reflect the poem's meaning?

a. It creates a consistency that is similar to the consistency of the woman's character.
b. It makes the poem lighthearted and shows the speaker's friendship with the woman.
c. It follows a changing pattern to show how the woman's beauty has changed over time.
d. It uses an unusual scheme that highlights how unusual the woman's beauty is.

34. Read these lines from the poem.

And all that's best of dark and bright
Meet in her aspect and her eyes

What does the author use this metaphor to emphasize?

a. The woman's pure inner thoughts
b. How good the woman's vision is
c. Where dark and bright overlap in nature
d. A sense of balance in the woman's beauty

35. How can the images of darkness and light can be interpreted in this poem?

a. They show that beauty doesn't last and it should be enjoyed whenever encountered.
b. They show that people view beauty differently at different times in their lives.
c. They show that the complexities of a person be a part of their beauty.
d. They show that the speaker is devoted to the woman he is praising, no matter what happens.

36. Read lines 1-4 of this poem.

She walks in beauty, like the night
Of cloudless climes and starry skies;
And all that's best of dark and bright
Meet in her aspect and her eyes:

What do they help the reader understand?

a. The physical appearance and serenity of the woman
b. The unique way and time the woman walks
c. That the narrator is infatuated with the woman
d. The woman's innermost thoughts

Refer to the passage "Eating at the Theater" to answer questions 37-44.

Eating at the Theater

(1) Last Saturday night my family went to go see a movie, and I was introduced to an amazing movie theater, the Alamo Drafthouse Cinema. The Alamo Drafthouse Cinema is like no other movie theater experience. For one thing, no one under the age of eighteen is allowed into the theater without a parent or guardian, no matter the rating of the film. The most incredible part of the Alamo Drafthouse Cinema, and what makes it so unique, is that you get to order an entire meal, get it delivered, and eat it all while watching the movie.

(2) The Alamo Drafthouse Cinema originated in Austin, Texas, and started out as a single screen theater. The unique concept caught a lot of attention and popularity, and soon, the theater was home to film premiers, and even hosted local and visiting filmmakers. In the years since its inception, the Alamo Drafthouse Cinema has grown into a larger franchise. There are currently five locations in Austin, and the theater has expanded into Houston, San Antonio, and Winchester, Virginia.

(3) When we first walked into the lobby, I noticed the decorations on the walls. They were very intricate and three-dimensional, and made me feel like I was a part of the theater, or maybe a part of the movie. When we were able to get inside of the theater, I was surprised to see that it looked like a normal movie theater expect for a large tabletop that extended across the length of every aisle of seats.

(4) I ordered a meal of chicken tenders and French fries, and my sister ordered a hamburger. We were not surprised to find that the food was delicious. Everything about the theater was great. The members of the staff inside of the lobby were very friendly, and our waiter was very nice. Throughout the movie, he walked as quickly as he could so that he would not disrupt the movie. My entire family had a wonderful time at the movies on Saturday, and we have all decided to go back again, to the Alamo Drafthouse Cinema.

37. Which of the following statements is an opinion?

a. The Alamo Drafthouse Cinema originated in Austin, Texas, and started out as a single screen theater.
b. For one thing, no one under the age of eighteen is allowed into the theater without a parent or guardian, no matter the rating of the film.
c. Everything about the theater was great.
d. In the years since its inception, the Alamo Drafthouse Cinema has grown into a larger franchise.

38. Why does the narrator say that the Alamo Drafthouse Cinema is "like no other movie theater experience"?

a. The movies are not shown at other theaters
b. The lobby is better
c. The food tastes better
d. No one under 18 can be admitted without a parent or guardian

39. What does the word intricate mean in paragraph 3?

a. Sturdy
b. Detailed
c. Flat
d. Expensive

40. Why did the narrator say that she felt a part of the theater?

a. The lobby had three-dimensional decorations
b. The large tabletop was familiar
c. The service was excellent
d. The narrator could order a meal

41. Why was the narrator not surprised that the food was delicious?

a. Because the narrator ordered normally good tasting food
b. Because the movie was really good
c. Because food tastes better when watching a movie
d. Because everything at the theater was good

42. The narrator said that the inside of the theater looked like a normal movie theater except:

a. There were three-dimensional decorations on the wall
b. There were no lights
c. There were round tables all around
d. There was a tabletop that extended across the aisle

43. In what order is this essay organized?

a. A review of the film and experience
b. An introduction, history of the theater, and description of experience
c. An introduction, description of the physical theater, and dislikes
d. A detailed explanation of the history of the theater

44. How many cities have at least one Alamo Drafthouse Cinema?

a. Four
b. Three
c. Five
d. One

Answer Key and Explanations for Reading Test #2

1. D: The terrain surrounding the farm has hills and ravines, creating several places the shepherds must check while looking for the sheep. This causes them to search for a long time in many places without finding the sheep, which is a key event in the passages' plot. Therefore, choice D is correct. Choice A is incorrect because sheep are found in many countries, not just Scotland. The time period of the story is unclear, but no matter the time period, the lack of technology did not cause the shepherds' reliance on Sirrah. Sirrah was able to find the flock because he is a dog and has different instincts than humans. Technology would not have necessarily helped the shepherds find the flock, so choice B is incorrect. Choice C is incorrect because James was able to work with others to look for his missing flock. This shows that the farm is not isolated.

2. C: The shepherd was able to rely on Sirrah to care for the herd even when he was away. The fact that Sirrah did what the owner desired without direct supervision shows his unwavering commitment to the shepherd. Sirrah was loyal to his owner regardless of the situation, so choice C is correct. Choice A is incorrect. While the passage mentions that Sirrah cared for the flock while his owner ate dinner, caring for the flock was not just a habit of Sirrah's. It was a way he helped his owner. Choice B is incorrect because Sirrah was consistently loyal throughout the passage. Choice D is incorrect because, though Sirrah did not rest with his owner, the passage does not describe Sirrah's energy levels.

3. A: The shepherds band together and look for the missing flock throughout the night and into the morning. The author shows this by writing "morning came and still they sought," which means that they were still searching for the flock in the morning hours. This line also shows that the shepherds are going to great efforts to help James since it states that the shepherds looked in every place they could think to check. The shepherds' efforts show that they care for each other, including James, so choice A is correct. Choice B says that the shepherds could not explain or achieve what Sirrah had done. This does not show that the shepherds care for James, so choice B is incorrect. Choice C shows James's dedication to finding his own flock, not the dedication or care of others, so it is incorrect. Choice D shows that James is ready to quit the search. This does not show that the other shepherds care for James, so choice D is incorrect.

4. B: Choice B provides an accurate summary of the main events that took place in the passage. It presents the ideas in an order that makes sense and matches the order of events in the story. Choice A incorrectly states that James was not permitted to take breaks. In the passage, James was able to take breaks to eat and rest while Sirrah watched over the flock. Additionally, this summary does not include enough information about the night that the flock went missing. Choice C describes James having a change of heart toward Sirrah, but this is not shown in the passage. The passage also does not say that James likes to work alone, so choice C is incorrect. Choice D is incorrect because it includes unnecessary details. For example, the summary does not need to state that Sirrah lived and worked on a sheep farm or that he was regarded as the best sheepdog in Scotland.

5. D: The author's purpose for writing this passage was most likely to entertain readers with a story of a shepherd and his dog, so choice D is correct. Choice A is incorrect because this story is not told from James Hogg's point of view. It is also not only about the night that the flock went missing. Choice B is incorrect because, while the passage describes the support from the other shepherds, this is only a detail in the passage. Choice C is incorrect because the passage does not suggest that trained dogs can replace human farmers. Instead, it demonstrates that they can work together to support a farm.

6. B: Paragraphs 8 and 9 show that James Hogg and the other shepherds have looked everywhere for the flock. At this point, James says there is nothing more they can do other than return and tell the owner that the flock is gone. Put simply, he is giving up. Since the shepherds' efforts were not successful and James wants to quit the search, these paragraphs create a sense of hopelessness, so choice B is correct. Choice A is incorrect. Paragraphs 8 and 9 do not suggest that any of the characters are frustrated. While James says, "It's of no use," this statement could show disappointment or fear. It does not specifically show that he is frustrated. These lines do not create a spirit of teamwork, so choice C is also correct. Though the shepherds do work together, they do not succeed, and James is preparing to face the consequences of his failure. James and the other shepherds have given up hope that they will find the flock, so choice D is incorrect.

7. B: Paragraph 16 states "Long afterward James Hogg said, "I never felt so grateful to any creature below the sun as I did to Sirrah that morning." Hogg's gratitude for Sirrah's actions shows that Sirrah likely prevented a troublesome outcome for him, so choice B is correct. There is no indication that the owner would have replaced the lambs if they had not been found, so choice A is incorrect. Choice C is also incorrect. Since the shepherds who helped in the search did not work for the same farm owner, it is not likely that they would have been held responsible. The passage does not suggest that the lambs would have been kept by other farmers, so choice D is incorrect.

8. C: Sirrah's loyal behavior led him to herd the entire flock of lambs for his owner during an emergency. This feat was very difficult for the shepherds to do as a group, and it would have been even harder for them to do so individually. Failing to find the herd would likely have had negative impacts for Sirrah's owner, James. By explaining that Sirrah had done what no shepherd could do by gathering all the lambs, the author supports the key idea that loyal dogs are valuable companions. Therefore, choice C is correct. Choice A explains the setting in which the lambs were found but does not discuss the actions of the dog, so it is incorrect. Choice B is incorrect because it shows James Hogg's dedication to finding the herd, not Sirrah's. Similarly, choice D describes the responsibilities of the shepherd, not the dog.

9. C: The author of this passage uses a chronological structure to explain that the way readers consume stories has changed over time. Society has evolved from remembering and retelling stories verbally to writing and reading them in print, and now many people use electronic devices to access them. This idea is best described in choice C. The passage does not suggest that society will eventually go back to using only printed media, making choice A incorrect. It also does not state that the invention of electronic readers was necessary for education to advance, making choice B incorrect. The printing press has had a much larger impact on society and history than the invention of electronic books, so choice D is incorrect.

10. Part A: D: The author argues that digital technology will replace printed text, so choice D is correct. Choice A is incorrect because the author does not mention the ease of reading digital or printed text. The author only mentions that digital text can be more convenient than physical books and just as enjoyable to use. Choice B is incorrect because the essay is about the evolution of technology and texts. The invention of the printing press is only a detail mentioned in the essay. Similarly, the introduction of the internet is a detail mentioned in the essay, but it is not the main topic of the essay, so choice C is incorrect.

Part B: C: The sentence in choice C states that printed books will eventually no longer be used as a result of technological advancements, so choice C is correct. Choice A is incorrect because it only states that stories have stood the test of time. It does not show that the main argument of the essay is about the way that people read stories. Choice B is incorrect because it gives an example of printed materials being used despite new technology, which contradicts the main argument of the essay. Choice D is incorrect because it is only a supporting detail. It does not clearly show what the main argument of the essay is.

11. B: The main idea of the passage is that technology is continually changing the way people access information. The author suggests that the need for physical books may soon be eliminated and that readers should welcome this change. Referencing the invention of the iPad and Kindle demonstrates that technology can continually change the way people do the same activity, such as reading, so choice B is correct. The internet was referenced in the passage to give an example of how technology changes culture. The iPad and Kindle were invented long after the internet and digital text came into use, so choice A is incorrect. Choice C is incorrect because iPads and Kindles are used in modern times, so referencing them does not show how stories used to be shared. Choice D is incorrect. Because the author supports the use of electronic readers, he or she does not give the reader a reason to reflect on the time before these devices were used.

12. D: In the beginning of the essay, the author explains how stories were passed down through oral tradition. The author then states that this was changed by the printing press, which is becoming less important due to the invention of technologies like the internet, the iPad, and the Kindle. This makes choice D correct. Choice A is incorrect because the author only explains the advantages of using devices like an iPad. Choice B is incorrect because oral tradition was common before reading stories was common. Choice C is incorrect because the essay was written in a chronological structure. It does not simply list examples, and the examples of technology are supporting details, not the topic of the passage.

13. B: The author's primary claim is that paper copies of books are the best format for reading. This is supported by the author's explanation of the positive effects of reading physical books. The author also explains why other methods, like using electronic readers, are not as beneficial as reading physical books. Therefore, choice B is correct. Choice A is incorrect. The author mentions other formats of books but does not state that readers should read the format of their choice. The author wants to persuade readers to choose physical books. Choice C is also incorrect. The author mentioned the difficulties that come with using electronic readers in the third paragraph, but this is not the focus of the whole essay. Similarly, the author says that books in physical or digital formats can be shared with others, but sharing books is not the focus of the essay. This is only supporting information, so choice D is incorrect.

14. A: The author mentions scientific studies that support the argument that physical books are superior to other formats, so choice A is correct. Choice B is incorrect because the paragraph mentions and uses data that has been proven, not just beliefs. Choice C is incorrect because the passage is not focused on the benefits of reading. It focuses on the benefits of reading physical copies of books. Finally, the fourth paragraph does not include any counterarguments to the author's claim, so choice D is incorrect.

15. D: This essay is meant to persuade readers to use physical copies of books when they read. It is most likely written for people who enjoy reading and do so regularly, so choice D is correct. Choice A is incorrect because the essay does not address using reading in classroom instruction. Choice B is also incorrect. The essay does not address how writing or illustrating books is different for books of different formats. This essay is not targeted at librarians, so choice C is incorrect. The essay does not include information about choosing, lending, or caring for books.

16. C: This sentence states the author's stance on physical books. It makes it clear that the author strongly believes that physical books are the best format for reading, so choice C is correct. Choice A is incorrect. This sentence does not help the reader determine the point of view of the essay, as it contains no pronouns. Choice B is incorrect because, while the sentence is a statement, it is not factual. It is the author's opinion. Choice D is incorrect. The statement is not meant to make readers curious since it lacks qualities that would make someone wonder about the topic.

17. B: The author of "The Inventions of Technology" seems more willing to use changing and advancing technology than the author of "The Power of Print," so choice B is correct. It is likely that both authors would agree that any type of reading is better than no reading at all since both seem to believe reading is a good thing, so choice A is incorrect. The author of "The Inventions of Technology" supports the use of electronic books and would be more likely to support increased funding for them, not physical books. The author of "The Power of Print" would be more likely to support funding for physical books. This makes choice C incorrect. The preferred genre or content each author likes to read is not addressed.

While the author of "The Inventions of Technology" references a significant amount of historical information, this is not enough evidence for the reader to assume the author would prefer to read nonfiction articles. Therefore, choice D is incorrect.

18. C: Each essay focuses on its author's preferred format of books and why that format is superior, so choice C is correct. Only "The Power of Print" discusses the downsides of electronic readers, making choice A incorrect. Neither essay suggests that choosing a book format may be difficult. The authors of these essays only explain why their respective preference is best, so choice B is incorrect. The author of "The Inventions of Technology" mentions that changes in technology have impacted education. However, the author of "The Power of Print" does not, so choice D is incorrect.

19. A: Both essays focus on the best format for readers to use. This shows that, regardless of their different opinions on the format, both authors think reading as a pastime should continue, so choice A is correct. Choice B is incorrect because the author of "The Power of Print" would not agree with this statement. This author included reasons that electronic readers are inconvenient. The author of "The Inventions of Technology" would not agree with choice C. This author feels that reading on a device is just as satisfying as reading a physical book. This author would also disagree with choice D, as "The Inventions of Technology" suggests that reading should change as technology does.

20. B, E: Clara seems to be protected by some divine form of guidance that has kept her safe during many near misses and brushes with death. The sentence "And so, again and again, it seemed as if a special Providence protected her from death or injury" clearly states this. This idea is also demonstrated in the statement "Thank you, but I think I am the best-protected woman in the United States." Choice A explains how important Clara was to injured soldiers, but it does not describe Clara's own safety. Choice C explains that Clara appreciated the soldier's warning of the dangers she would face in Fredericksburg and that she later recalled the experience of receiving a request to go across the river. Choice D describes the feelings many males in Clara's position felt towards her, but it does not reveal any information about Clara's fate.

21. C: In paragraph 9, the author uses "charged" to describe the actions of the lines of soldiers advancing across the field toward the enemy. This most closely matches "to rush against," as it is used to refer to their movement. This meaning is shown by the use of the word *over* after *charged*. If something goes over something else, it has to move. Definition 3 is the only definition that involves movement. Definition 1 would be used to refer to money or payment owed in exchange for something. Definition 2 would be used if someone had committed a crime and was being formally blamed. Definition 4 would be used if an individual of higher authority were telling a lower-ranking individual what to do.

22. C: By describing Fredericksburg as a "slaughter-pen," stating that no "regiment will escape," and telling Clara that she will "go to certain death," the soldier is warning Clara that she will surely die if she attempts to go into the town. This supports the key idea that Clara Barton risked her own life by providing care for soldiers in dangerous locations, so choice C is correct. The soldier does not imply that he or other soldiers will harm Clara. In fact, he expresses his gratitude for her care and tries to warn her to protect her, so choice A is incorrect. Choice B is incorrect because the rest of the passage suggests that Clara Barton knows that each place she visits will be dangerous and horrific. She does not need the soldiers to tell her what she will see and encounter. Choice D is incorrect because this is not a key idea of the passage. Additionally, this paragraph does not suggest that Clara did not help the soldier. In fact, he states that she has been kind to him, which suggests that she helped him in some way.

23. B: Clara and the officer interacted shortly before he died and was brought to her. This demonstrated how common death was in this situation and how close Clara had been to danger, making choice B the correct answer. There is not enough information to support the idea that Clara would have died crossing the bridge without assistance. The officer only helped her to step over debris. This makes choices A and C incorrect. Additionally, the officer does not show resourcefulness in this paragraph, and there is not enough information to see that his rank influenced where he was at that time. Choice D is also incorrect. The death of the officer made Clara feel lucky, but it did not deter her from working on the battlefields. It made her feel safer doing so, as she thought it meant that she was protected from harm in some divine way.

24. B: In paragraph 2, a bullet narrowly misses Clara Barton but kills a soldier. This is followed by the statement "and so, again and again, it seemed as if a special Providence protected her from death or injury." Using both the information provided in the question and context clues in the passage, it can be determined that it seems as if Clara is being protected by some heavenly source that knows what is going to happen. As such, the best meaning for Providence is "divine protection from an all-knowing source." Therefore, choice B is correct. There is no suggestion that Clara's protection is fragile or unreliable since she is continually kept safe. This makes choices A and D incorrect. Because this protection comes from something that can "see ahead," it is not from colleagues, or the people that work with her. This makes choice C incorrect.

25. A: The passage highlights Clara's dedication to aiding the wounded during the Civil War. It makes it clear that doing so is dangerous and shows that Clara decided to continue her work anyway. This makes choice A correct. Clara's opinion of the war is not made clear in the passage, so choice B is incorrect. Choice C is incorrect because the passage does not discuss patients who were too hurt to be saved. Choice D is incorrect since the reason Clara was motivated to help is not discussed in the passage.

26. B: The author uses statements like "exploding shell hissed through between us," " a solid shot thundered over our heads," and "a noble steed bounded in the air and with his gallant rider rolled in the dirt not thirty feet in the rear" to show the danger Clara is facing. Though the author does not directly state that Clara is in danger, she creates a sense of tension for the reader. The tension continues to build until it is revealed that the officer who helped her in this paragraph has died. Therefore, choice B is correct. Choice A is incorrect because no character's feelings toward another are described, and there is no sense of resentment. Paragraph 10 does not suggest that Clara is happy or pleased with what is occurring, so choice C is incorrect. While Clara is clearly passionate about helping injured soldiers, the language in this paragraph is not used to demonstrate this, making choice D incorrect.

27. B: This sentence shows that the men had a change of heart toward Clara and that the likelihood that she would be harmed or killed deeply upset and scared them. The men understood that "the nature of the summons" was that Clara was being asked to go to a dangerous place, so choice A is correct. The men clearly cared for Clara because they were eager to take her place on a dangerous assignment to keep her safe. They were not glad to see her leave, so choice B is incorrect. Choice C is incorrect because the war had already begun and the men were willing to face danger to protect Clara. Choice D is incorrect because the men were not being asked to move to the hospital, Clara was. They were willing to go to the other hospital with Clara.

28. C: A key idea of this passage is that Clara Barton risked her life to help soldiers during the American Civil War. This is a sacrifice that she made, and it is clearly shown by the passage, so choice C is correct. Choice A is incorrect because the passage does not describe what life on the battlefield looked like. It only shows a few events and tells what Clara Barton saw and faced. This is not a picture of what life was like for soldiers or others in battle. Choice B is incorrect because this passage describes the conditions that one nurse faced during a war. It does not show what medical practices were like during the Civil War. Choice D is incorrect because it does not include many details about how Clara Barton tended to victims. It focuses on the danger that she put herself in and the fact that she was able to survive this danger.

29. C: These lines describe the woman's face and state it is where "thoughts serenely sweet express," meaning her face is expressing her serene thoughts. This is best described by choice C. The poem portrays the woman as calm. Choice A states that the woman is upset, which makes this choice incorrect.

The woman in the poem is described as eloquent, meaning she is graceful. This is the opposite of clumsy, making choice B incorrect. The poem does not suggest that the woman is waiting for something, so choice D is incorrect.

30. B, E: The line "how pure, how dear their dwelling-place" refers to where the woman's thoughts come from. This shows that her mind and thoughts are pure and good, which means that she is innocent and honorable. Likewise, the line "A heart whose love is innocent!" shows that her heart, affection, love, and kindness are innocent. She has not experienced the harsh realities of the world, and, therefore, she still is freely giving of her love. Choice A is a description of the woman that shows that she is graceful. This does not show whether or not she has an honorable character, so it is incorrect. The line in choice C is used to describe the woman's beauty, not her internal character traits, so choice C is incorrect. Similarly, the line from choice D describes her smile and appearance, making it incorrect.

31. C: The narrator uses the phrase "a mind at peace with all below," which describes a mind that is not worried about anything, so choice C is correct. Choice A is incorrect as it uses a variety of adjectives to describe the woman's behavior, not her internal thoughts. Choice B is incorrect because this line describes the woman's innocent love, not whether or not she worries. "Of cloudless climes and starry skies" is used to describe a beautiful night to which the woman's appearance compares. This makes choice D incorrect.

32. D: In line 9, the word raven is used to describe the woman's tresses, meaning her hair. This would make the adjective definition of raven, meaning "shiny and black," the correct answer. Because the word raven is used to describe something, the noun and verb forms of the term are incorrect. The poem also does not describe or mention eating, so choices B and C are incorrect. The poem also does not discuss any birds, so choice A is incorrect.

33. A: The ABABAB rhyming pattern of this poem is consistent, as each stanza clearly follows the same pattern. Likewise, the speaker describes the woman as being of strong and reliable character. The rhyme scheme highlights this by leading the reader to expect certain lines to rhyme, just as the speaker expects the woman to act a certain way. This makes choice A correct. Choice B is incorrect because it is unknown whether or not the speaker and the woman are friends. Additionally, the poem is sincere, not lighthearted. Choice C is incorrect because the rhyme scheme does not change, and the poem does not describe any changes in the woman's beauty. Choice D is incorrect because there is nothing unusual about the rhyme scheme.

34. D: The metaphor is used to describe a balance in the woman's appearance. "Dark and bright" are opposites, but they meet in the woman's eyes and create a balance that causes her beauty. This metaphor does not focus on the woman's inner thoughts, so choice A is incorrect. The mention of the woman's eyes is not related to her ability to see, so choice B is incorrect. Though the lines mention dark and bright, they are not discussing where these meet in nature. This makes choice C incorrect.

35. C: In the poem, the woman is described as having both dark and light features in her physical appearance. Additionally, in lines 3 and 4, the poet suggests that this contrast also exists in her behavior. This contrast contributes to the woman's beauty, which supports the idea in choice C. Choice A is incorrect because the poem does not discuss the passing of time or the fading or fleeting of beauty. Choice B is incorrect because the poem does not present different views of beauty. Choice D is incorrect because the speaker is merely admiring the woman. The speaker's relationship to the woman is not made clear in the poem.

36. A: Lines 1 through 4 of the poem help the reader understand that the woman is beautiful and serene, like a cloudless night. This makes choice A correct. The mention of walking is used to help describe the woman's beauty. It does not mean that she literally walks at night. This makes choice B incorrect. Choice

C is incorrect. Lines 1 through 4 describe the woman, not how the narrator feels about her. The woman's thoughts are not discussed in these lines, so choice D is incorrect.

37. C: To say, "everything about the theater was great," cannot be proven as fact. This is strictly an opinion that could differ with another person.

38. D: Paragraph 1 states, "The Alamo Drafthouse Cinema is like no other movie theater experience. For one thing, no one under the age of eighteen is allowed into the theater without a parent or guardian, no matter the rating of the film."

39. B: Intricate means extremely complicated or detailed.

40. A: In paragraph 3, the narrator states that the decorations in the lobby were "three-dimensional, and made me feel like I was a part of the theater, or maybe a part of the movie."

41. D: In paragraph 4, the narrator explains that, "Everything about the theater was great."

42. D: Paragraph 3 states, "I was surprised to see that it looked like a normal movie theater expect for a large tabletop that extended across the length of every aisle of seats."

43. B: The essay begins with an introduction as to why the narrator was at the theater, followed by a brief history of the theater to provide the reader with context, and ending with the narrator's own personal experience at the theater.

44. A: Austin, Houston, San Antonio, and Winchester all have at least one Alamo Drafthouse Cinema location.

Language Practice Test #2

Questions 1 – 6 pertain to the following story:

The Greek Festival

(1) Every October my family attends the Greek Festival at the Greek Orthodox Church close to our house. (2) We were first invited four years ago by one of my friends, Amelia. (3) Her family attends the Greek Orthodox Church and works several booths at the festival each year. (4) They telled us that everyone was welcome.

(5) When we first arrived at the festival, we could hear the music from the parking lot? (6) It was music that I had never heard before, and some of it was in another language. (7) Amelia told me later that it was traditional Greek music. (8) We also noticed the smells that seemed to come from all over the festival grounds. (9) All around us, there were signs for meat, pastry, coffee drinks, and other side dishes. (10) My mom's favorite were the grape leaves, and my dad loved the Baklava. (11) It is a dessert is made up baked thin sheets of pastry dough covered in a sweet sauce like honey. (12) Amelia suggested us eat it with ice cream and chocolate sauce. (13) As much as I liked the baklava, my favorite was the gyro pita. (14) Gyro is lamb meat in a warm pita with tomato, lettuce, onion, and a Greek sauce. (15) I ate two pitas and it was deliciously!

(16) After we had eaten, everyone gathered around the dance floor and watched as people from all different age groups danced traditional Greek dances. (17) The dancers were dressed in special clothing and black dress shoes.

(18) Amelia danced in the second group of dancers, and her mom tossed money toward her. (19) Soon, the dance floor was covered in dollar bills from all of the dancers families. (20) The food was great, the music was fun, and the dancing was even better. (21) We had a great time at the greek Festival, and now I look forward to it every year!

1. What change, if any, should be made in sentence 4?

a. Change everyone to every one
b. Change telled to told
c. Change welcome to welcomed
d. Make no change

2. What change should be made in sentence 5?

a. Change arrived to arrive
b. Change festival to Festival
c. Delete the comma after festival
d. Change the question mark to a period

3. What change, if any, should be made in sentence 10?

a. Change were to was
b. Change mom's to moms
c. Change loved to loves
d. Make no change

4. What revision, if any, is needed in sentence 11?

a. It is a dessert that is made up of baked thin sheets of pastry dough covered in a sweet sauce like honey.
b. It is a dessert, is made up baked thin sheets of pastry dough covered in a sweet sauce like honey.
c. It is a dessert. Made up baked thin sheets of pastry dough covered in a sweet sauce like honey.
d. No revision needed.

5. What is the BEST way to revise sentence 12?

a. Amelia suggested, us eat it with ice cream and chocolate sauce.
b. Amelia suggested to us eat it with ice cream and chocolate sauce.
c. Amelia suggested us eat it, with ice cream and chocolate sauce.
d. Amelia suggested that we eat it with ice cream and chocolate sauce.

6. What change, if any, should be made in sentence 15?

a. Change ate to eat
b. Change deliciously to delicious
c. Change two to too
d. Make no change

Questions 7 – 12 pertain to the following passage:

Dogs in the Park

(1) On Saturday, my mom took me to a dog show at a park by our house. (2) The sun was out, and it was a really warm day. (3) I ride my bike to the park almost every day in the summer. (4) The dogs were all lying in the grass when we arrived, and they looked warm in the sun. (5) One of my mom's friends Mary, is a dog trainer, and she invited us to watch the dog show after my mom told her how much I love dogs.

(6) Their were all kinds of dogs at the show. (7) Some were really little, some were big, and some had really long hair. (8) My favorite were the dogs in the toy category and the sporting category. (9) The dogs that were waiting to be shown were with their trainers at different areas of the park getting ready. (10) Some trainers brushed its dog's hair, and some gave treats.

(11) We sat on the grass and watched the show. (12) The trainers were all dressed up. (13) The men wore suit pants and jackets, and the women wore dress skirts, stockings, and blazers. (14) All of the dogs were lined up and stood still wile the judges walked down and looked closely at all the dogs. (15) The judges looked at the dogs' hair, paws, and teeth. (16) Then it was time for each dog to show off. (17) Each trainer ran with their dog and held the leash high in the air. (18) The judges watched as the dogs ran, and judged how good they turned corners and listened to their trainers.

(19) At the end of the show, the judges awarded prizes. (20) The dogs and their trainers gathered in a line, and the judges presented the winners with large ribbons. (21) Mary's dog won first place, and she was given a purple ribbon that was bigger than most of the small dogs in the toy category. (22) We left the park, and I told my mom that I want to learn how to train dogs.

7. What change should be made in sentence 5?

a. Change is to was
b. Delete the comma after Mary
c. Change invited to invites
d. Insert a comma after friends

8. What change, if any, should be made in sentence 6?

a. Change Their to There
b. Change dogs to dog's
c. Change were to was
d. Make no change

9. What change, if any, should be made in sentence 8?

a. Change were to was
b. Insert a comma after category
c. Change favorite to favorites
d. Make no change

10. What change should be made in sentence 10?

a. Change its to their
b. Change its to it's
c. Change brushed to brush
d. Change dog's to dogs

11. Which sentence does not belong in this essay?

a. Sentence 18
b. Sentence 11
c. Sentence 7
d. Sentence 3

12. What is the BEST transition word that could be added to the beginning of sentence 22?

a. However
b. Later
c. Otherwise
d. Consequentially

Questions 13 – 18 pertain to the following story:

First Party

(1) Today my brother turned one year old. (2) We had a big party to celebrate, and a lot of people came. (3) My ant came to the house early to help my mom hang streamers. (4) My cousin helped me make party favors for both the big kids and the babies. (5) We packed the little bags with candy, pencils, whistles, and noisemakers. (6) My parents invited a lot of people. (7) Soon the house was filled with family, friends, and even some babies for my brother to play with.

(8) My grandparents on my dad's side flew even flew in from California the day before to help. (9) My dad lighted the barbeque in the back yard and took orders from the guests. (10) He made hamburgers, turkey burgers, hot dogs, chicken wings, and sausages. (11) My aunt sliced strips of onion, tomato, pickles, and lettuce. (12) She also cuts up an

avocado because she knows that it is my favorite topping on my hamburger. (13) My cousins, friends, and I all played in the backyard after we ate.

(14) My brother slept through most of the party, he was awake by the time he had cake. (15) He don't know he was missing his party by napping. (16) My mom put him in his high chair, and we all sang "Happy birthday," to him. (17) There was one candle in the center of the large cake, and my mom blew it out since he was two little.

(18) My brother sat in his chair and ate cake. (19) Soon there was cake everywhere. (20) It was all over his hands, his face, his tabletop and chair. (21) There was blue icing everywhere. (22) He even lifted up his arms and grabbed pieces of his hair. (23) His big, blue eyes looked at everyone as they smiled and laughed. (24) He stuffed some more cake into his mouth and smiled. (25) I think he knew he had a good first birthday.

13. What change should be made in sentence 3?

a. Change hang to hanged
b. Change ant to aunt
c. Change help to helped
d. Change came to comes

14. Where is the best placement for sentence 8?

a. After sentence 2
b. After sentence 4
c. After sentence 5
d. No change is needed

15. What change, if any, should be made in sentence 9?

a. Change took to takes
b. Change barbeque to BBQ
c. Change lighted to lit
d. Make no change

16. What change, if any, should be made in sentence 12?

a. Change know to knew
b. Change cuts to cut
c. Change an to a
d. Make no change

17. What is the BEST transition word that could be added to the beginning of sentence 14?

a. Later
b. Therefore
c. Although
d. However

18. What change, if any, should be made in sentence 15?

a. Change don't to didn't
b. Change was to is
c. Change napping to nap
d. Make no change

Questions 19 – 24 pertain to the passage:

Dinner is Served

(1) Every year my friend and I celebrate each other's birthdays by going out to dinner because our birthdays are three weeks apart. (2) On my birthday, my family took us to Aribba, my favorite mexican food restaurant. (3) For Annmae's birthday, she chose a Japanese restaurant called Tomo where the food is cooked at the table.

(4) I had never eaten Japanese food before and didn't know what to expect? (5) When the hostess brought us to our table, I was surprised to see that there were four extra seats. (6) That was not the only thing that was strange. (7) The table was not a regular restaurant dinner table. (8) It was a half circle and there was a giant sheet of metal in the center. (9) The hostess came back with other people and sat them with us at our table.

(10) We filled out cards that said what kind of food we wanted. (11) We had to pick between chicken, beef, shrimp, and pork. (12) A man then came to our table and lit the metal sheet. (13) He laid out rice and vegetables, and started cutting and cooking. (14) He worked very fast it was almost hard for me to see his hands. (15) After the rice, he cooked each of the different meats and started serving plates. (16) While things were cooking he would take his spatula and fling a piece of bell pepper or carrot at someone at the table. (17) He toss the most at Annmae since it was her birthday, but they all hit her chin and slid down onto her shirt.

(18) It was really exciting watching our food cooked right in front of us. (19) The chef was nice and the food is delicious. (20) I even liked having other people sit at our table because it was like being at a party at dinner. (21) I am really glad that my friend chose Tomo and I can't wait to see where we try next year!

19. What change, if any, should be made in sentence 2?

a. Change birthday to birth day
b. Delete the comma after birthday
c. Change mexican to Mexican
d. Make no change

20. What change should be made in sentence 4?

a. Change had to have
b. Change Japanese to japanese
c. Change didn't to don't
d. Change the question mark to a period

21. What sentence could BEST follow and support sentence 9?

a. Now I understood why there were extra seats
b. The hostess smiled at us as she left
c. The woman wore a blue dress and her hair was tied back
d. I wondered how many times she was going to come back

22. What change, if any, should be made in sentence 16?

a. Change were to are
b. Insert a comma after cooking
c. Change take to took
d. Make no change

23. What change, if any, should be made in sentence 17?

a. Delete the comma after birthday
b. Change hit to hitted
c. Change toss to tossed
d. Make no change

24. What change should be made in sentence 19?

a. Change is to was
b. Change was to is
c. Change delicious to deliciously
d. Change chef to Chef

Questions 25 – 30 pertain to the following passage:

History's Unsinkable Lessons

(1) In Ruth Campbell's book Exploring the Titanic, the events of the famous ship's only journey and sinking are brought to life. (2) In 1912, Titanic was built and was the largest passenger steamship at the time. (3) On what would be its first and only journey, the ship departed from Southampton in England and was supposed to arrive in New York City. (4) The ship hit an iceberg late at night on April 14, 1912, and sunked less than three hours later.

(5) Titanic was designed by some of the best engineers and had the latest technology of the time. (6) The ship was made to carry over three and a half thousand passengers and crew members, but had only twenty lifeboats. (7) There was not enough lifeboats for all of the people onboard, and as a result, only seven hundred six people survived.

(8) One interesting thing about Titanic, is that the ship was divided into classes. (9) The most expensive tickets were first class, and first class passengers had the biggest and much luxurious rooms. (10) The first class rooms were the closest to the ship's deck. (11) Because this the majority of survivors came from first class. (12) They were able to reach the deck fastest to get a seat on a lifeboat. (13) The third class rooms were located the farthest below deck, and the majority of the third class passengers did not survive.

(14) Ruth Campbell's book was very interesting but also sad because the story of Titanic is true. (15) However, Campbell ended the book by talking about the positive things that have happened because of this tragedy. (16) Most importantly, experts now recommend that ships' carry enough lifeboats for all passengers onboard. (17) This would have saved a lot of lifes. (18) It was a good book, and it displayed a good message in history that lessons should be learned from mistakes.

25. What change should be made in sentence 1?

a. Change ship's to ships
b. Insert a comma after book
c. Change are to is
d. Change brought to bring

26. What change, if any, should be made in sentence 4?

a. Change sunked to sank
b. Delete the comma after 14
c. Change hours to hour's
d. Make no change

27. What change should be made in sentence 7?

a. Change There to They're
b. Delete the comma after onboard
c. Change lifeboats to lifeboats'
d. Change was to were

28. What change, if any, should be made in sentence 8?

a. Change was to were
b. Delete the comma after Titanic
c. Change divided into divide
d. Make no change

29. What is the BEST way to revise and combine sentence 11 and sentence 12?

a. Because, the majority of survivors came from first class as they were able to reach the deck fastest to get a seat on a lifeboat
b. Because of this, the majority of survivors came from first class, as they were able to reach the deck fastest to get a seat on a lifeboat
c. Because this, the majority of survivors came from first class, they were able to reach the deck fastest to get a seat on a lifeboat
d. Because of this, the majority of survivors came from first class as they were able to reach the deck fastest to get a seat on a lifeboat

30. What is the BEST transition that could be added to the beginning of sentence 13?

a. Lastly
b. For example
c. On the other hand
d. Therefore

Answer Key and Explanations for Language Test #2

1. B: because told is the correct past tense of the verb tell. Telled is not a word. A is not correct. When used as a noun, everyone is one word. C is not correct. Welcome is not a verb in this sentence and therefore does not need to be in the past tense like the rest of the essay.

2. D: because this sentence is a statement rather than a question. As a result, it should be punctuated with a period and not a question mark. A is not correct. Arrive is in the present tense, and the rest of the paragraph is in the past tense. B is not correct. Festival is not used in this sentence as a proper noun and therefore does not need to be capitalized. C is not correct. When we first arrived at the festival is an introductory clause, and a comma is needed after the introductory clause.

3. A: because the subject of this sentence is favorite. Favorite is singular; therefore, the verb also must be singular in order for the subject and verb to agree. Were is plural. Was is singular. B is not correct. Mom's in this sentence is possessive and an apostrophe is needed. C is not correct. Loves is in the present tense, and the rest of the essay is in the past tense.

4. A: because this is the simplest way to express the idea in a grammatically correct sentence. B is not correct, because this sentence is not grammatically correct. C is not correct, because the second sentence is a fragment.

5. D: because it is the simplest way to express the idea in a grammatically correct sentence. A, B, and C are incorrect because these sentences are not grammatically correct. This sentence is not grammatically correct.

6. B: because deliciously is an adverb rather than an adjective. It describes the noun, pitas, not the verb. A is not correct. Eat is in the present tense, and the rest of the essay is in the past tense. C is not correct. Two is spelled correctly and indicates the number. Too means "as well" or an indication of excess.

7. D: It is correct because a comma is needed to separate the interjection of the name. A is not correct. Even though is is in the present tense and the rest of the essay is in the past tense, the sentence is describing a current person and should be in the present tense. B is not correct. A comma is needed to separate the interjection of the name. C is not correct. Invites is in the present tense and the rest of the essay, as a past event, is in the past tense.

8. A: It is correct because a homonym has been misused. There is used to indicate a physical or abstract place. Their is used to indicate possession. B is not correct. In this sentence, dogs does not indicate possession and does not need an apostrophe. C is not correct. Was is in the present tense, and the rest of the essay is in the past tense.

9. C: It is correct because the verb in the sentence, were, is plural, and the subject must be plural for subject-verb agreement. A is not correct. Was is in the present tense, and the rest of the essay is in the past tense. B is not correct. A comma is not needed because and the sporting category is not an independent clause.

10. A: It is correct because there is plural and displays possession. Its is singular. The subject, trainers, is plural; therefore, the possession is plural as well. B is not correct. It's is only used as a contraction for it is, not for possession. C is not correct. Brush is in the present tense, and the rest of the essay is in the past tense. D is not correct. Dog's is possessive and needs an apostrophe.

11. D: It is correct because although this sentence provides new information, the content is not important to the rest of the essay. A, B, and C are because these sentences are important to the essay.

12. B: It is correct because the opening phrase, We left the park, indicates a time lapse from the earlier events of the essay. An appropriate transition word would indicate time. A is not correct. However is not a good transition because sentence 22 is not contradicting anything in the previous sentence. C is not correct. Otherwise is not a good transition because sentence 22 does not suggest an alternate to something that occurred previously. D is not correct. Consequentially is not a good transition because the content of the sentence is not cause and effect from the previous sentence.

13. B: It is correct because a homonym has been misused. Ant refers to an insect, and aunt refers to the sister of one's mother. A is not correct. Hang is not the verb of this sentence and does not need to be in the past tense. C is not correct. Help is not the verb of this sentence and does not need to be in the past tense. D is not correct. Came is the verb of this sentence. Comes is in the present tense and the rest of the essay is in the past tense.

14. A: It is correct because the sentence discusses the grandparents traveling from California to help with the part. Therefore, this sentence should be placed after the description of the party and that a lot of people came. B is not correct. Sentence 4 discusses the cousin helping with party favors, and therefore a sentence about the grandparents' travel would not follow well.

C is not correct. Sentence 5 discusses the party favors, and therefore a sentence about the grandparents' travel would not follow well.

15. C: It is correct because lit is the correct past tense for the verb light. A is not correct. Takes is in the present tense and the rest of the essay is in the past tense. B is not correct. Barbeque is spelled correctly. BBQ is an abbreviation, not a word.

16. B: It is correct because cuts is in the present tense, and the rest of the essay is in the past tense. Cut is in the past tense. A is not correct. Even though the essay is in the past tense, the act of the aunt knowing is a present and ongoing action and should be in the present tense. C is not correct. In this sentence, the article an is followed by a noun, avocado. Avocado begins with a vowel and a vowel sound; therefore, it needs to be introduced with the article an.

17. C: It is correct because although means "in spite of" and is appropriate within the sentence. A is not correct. Later is not an appropriate transition word because it contradicts the beginning of the sentence. B is not correct. Therefore is not an appropriate transition word because there is no cause an effect from the previous sentence. D is not correct. However is not an appropriate transition word because sentence 14 does not contradict anything from the previous sentence.

18. A: It is correct because don't is the conjunction of do not. Do not is in the present tense, and the rest of the essay is in the past tense. The past tense of do is did. B is not correct. Is is in the present tense, and the rest of the essay is in the past tense. C is not correct. Napping is a verb in this sentence, not a noun.

19. C: It is correct because Mexican is a proper noun, and proper nouns need to be capitalized. A is not correct. Birthday is one word. B is not correct. A comma is needed after an introductory clause.

20. D: It is correct because the sentence is a statement, not a question, and needs a period as punctuation. A is not correct. Have is in the present tense, and the rest of the essay is in the past tense. B is not correct. Japanese is a proper noun and needs to be capitalized. C is not correct. Didn't is a contraction of did not and is in the past tense, like the rest of the essay. Don't is a contraction of do not and is in the present tense.

21. A: It is correct because the sentence both supports the previous sentences and provides additional information. Sentence 5 states that extra seats were available at the table. This sentence provides additional information that supports sentence 5 as well as sentence 9. B, C, and D are incorrect. Although these sentences provide new information, they do not link and support the previous sentences.

22. B: It is correct because While things were cooking is an introductory clause, and a comma is needed after the clause. A is not correct. Are is in the present tense and the rest of the essay is in the past tense. C is not correct. Take is part of would take and is in the past participle, not the present tense.

23. C: It is correct because tossed is in the past tense, like the rest of the essay. Toss is in the present tense. A is not correct. A comma is needed before the conjunction when two independent clauses are joined by a conjunction. B is not correct. Hit is the correct past tense of hit. Hitted is not a word.

24. A: It is correct because was is in the past tense, like the rest of the essay. Is is in the present tense. B is not correct. Is is in the present tense and the rest of the essay is in the past tense. C is not correct. Delicious is an adjective, not an adverb. It is used in this sentence to describe the noun, not the verb. D is not correct. Chef is not a proper noun and does not need to be capitalized.

25. B: It is correct because a comma is needed to separate the interjection of the book title. A is not correct. Ship in the sentence is possessive and requires the apostrophe. C is not correct. Are is the plural of is. The subject, events, is plural and therefore the verb needs to be plural in subject-verb agreement. D is not correct. Are brought is in the past participle, and bring is in the present tense.

26. A: It is correct because sank is the correct past tense of the verb sink. Sunked is not a word. B is not correct. A comma is needed to separate dates of the month from the year. H is not correct. Hours is not possessive and does not require the apostrophe.

27. D: It is correct because were is the plural past tense of is. The subject of the sentence, lifeboats, is plural, and the verb also must be plural in subject-verb agreement. A is not correct. There is used correctly. They're is a contraction of they are. B is not correct. A comma is needed to separate the interjection, and as a result. C is not correct. Lifeboats is not possessive and does not require the apostrophe.

28. B: It is correct because there is no need for a comma. As it stands, the comma disrupts the normal flow of thought in the sentence. A is not correct. The subject, ship, is singular, and the verb also must be singular in subject-verb agreement. C is not correct. Was divided is in the past participle. Divide is in the present tense, and the rest of the essay is in the past.

29. B: It is correct because it is the simplest way to express the idea in a grammatically correct sentence. Because of this refers to the content of the previous sentence. A is not correct. This sentence is not grammatically correct. C is not correct. This sentence is not grammatically correct. D is not correct. This sentence is not grammatically correct and needs a comma after class.

30. C: Choice C shows the contrast between first-class and third-class passengers. The previous sentences explained why majority of the survivors were a part of the first class passengers. Sentence 13 shifts to explain explains why most of the third class passengers did not survive. "On the other hand" clearly signals this contrast. "Lastly" is not an appropriate transition word, as there was not a series of listed facts. "For example" is not an appropriate transition to use since it is not giving an example. "Therefore" is not an appropriate transition word because the new information does not involve cause and effect with the previous sentences.

Online Resources

Due to our efforts to try to keep this book to a manageable length, we've created a link that will give you access to all of your online resources:

mometrix.com/resources719/terranextg7rl

It's Your Moment, Let's Celebrate It!

Share your story @mometrixtestpreparation